CLUTTER'S
LAST STAND

It's time to De-Junk your life!

by Don Aslett

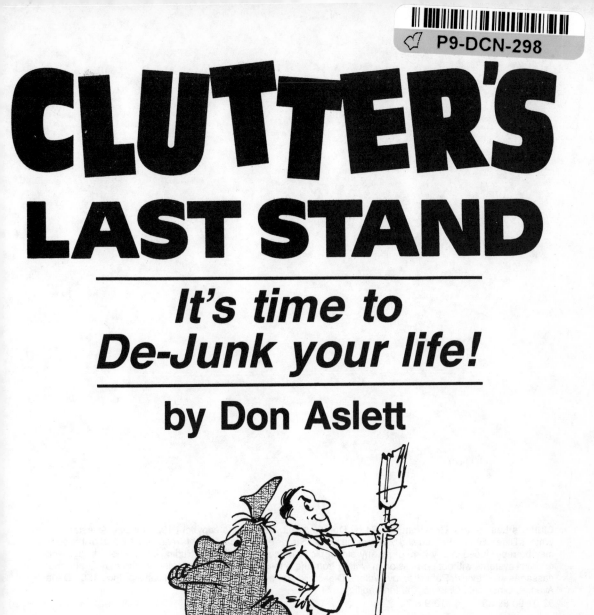

Illustrated by
Judith Holmes Clarke

Writer's
Digest
Books

Cincinnati, Ohio

Library of Congress Cataloging in Publication Data

Aslett, Don, 1935-
    Clutter's last stand.

    1. Conduct of life. I. Title.
BJ1581.2.A83   1984   158'.1   84-3683
ISBN 0-89879-137-5

Book design by Craig LaGory.

Table of Contents

The Ultimate Self-Improvement Book

This book will make you happier, freer, neater, richer, and smarter. With a little help from you, it will solve more home, family, marriage, career, and economic problems than any book you've ever read. De-junking your life will cost nothing and will pay 100 percent returns.

" You'll immediately lose 100 pounds without dieting "

OK... I'll confess first...

On a remote ranch in southern Idaho, I grew up raising those world-famous potatoes. When we sold those spuds to all of you, we'd often end up with bales of old burlap bags, or "gunny sacks," as we called them. Once used, they generally began to rot, or had rips or holes in them, but we kept them—they might someday come in handy for stuffing gopher holes, as towels for bathing pigs, as curtains (in the next depression), as lawn mulch, to flag down a rescue plane if we got

snowed in . . . and there was always the hope that someday, when Mom got all our clothes sewed, she could put a heavy-duty needle in the old Singer and patch them all. Oh yes . . . and the best reason of all to keep those useless sacks—they were perfect to store other useless things in—anything and everything that could be bagged: worn-out machine parts, old clothes, smelly coyote hides, colored popcorn, lengths of rope we might splice one day, etc.

Keeping stuff still seemed reasonable as I grew older. When my drawers,

shelves, and closets filled, I followed other people's example and got more drawers. I built more shelves—and raised my bed so there was more room under it for storage. Then I left the farm for college, and when junk crowded me out of my dorm room, I finally began to get smart. My junk took up all my living space, and if I was going to do any living, I'd have to clean it out.

Cleaning clutter and junk out of my life was so exhilarating, I began to clean other people's clutter, dirt, and junk. I organized my own cleaning company,

called Varsity Contractors, and as I finished my schooling over the next eight years, built it into a multi-state operation. I graduated from the university knowing more about coping with clutter than I did about dissecting frogs or philosophy, so I stayed on in the business and today own one of the major cleaning companies in the country.

During this time, thousands of people brought their clutter and cleaning problems to me. In an attempt to offer a solution, I wrote a book titled *Is There Life After Housework?* To my surprise, it soon became an international bestseller (on one bestseller list I was ahead of *Joy of Sex* and *30 Days to a Beautiful Bottom* for a whole week).

Because I had become aware that a good 50 percent of housework was not just cleany-clean scrubby-scrubbing, but shuffling clutter, litter, and junk from place to place, I included a chapter called "Treasure Sorting" in *Life After Housework*. Its basic message was that getting rid of junk is the easiest way to free yourself from household imprisonment.

The response to this chapter was overwhelming. In the more than 600 radio, television, and newspaper interviews I did in the next two-and-a-half years, my readers' and listeners' most intense interest was in junk. Phone calls, letters, and live audiences throughout the U.S. and England—even celebrities—willingly confessed their clutter and how it had negatively influenced their lives.

It got so that when I went to do an

interview or appearance I would end up expounding less on cleaning secrets and efficiency and more on de-junking. Everyone wanted me to tell them how to spot, sort, rid, and/or hide their junk. As I gathered and reflected on this junk wisdom, I found it shocking but stimulating. I discovered that people suffered acute guilt and actual damage from the junk that clutters their lives. I found that every one of us is a junker—and that it's the single biggest reason for personal unhappiness.

My enthusiasm to produce this book became uncontrollable; I collected so much information and so many impressive testimonials on de-junking that I had to share it with you. I *had* to write this—*everyone* is suffering from clutter.

I hope you'll find this volume inspiring and enjoyable; I hope it sheds some light on junk and its harms that you weren't aware of. Some of the information and opinions might bite a little, but please don't be offended. My only intention is to help you get more quality, love, and enjoyment in your life.

Don A. Aslett

It *is* a pretty good life, isn't it? We might have a few stresses and strains, but as a whole, we're safe and well fed and sheltered, surrounded with plenty, comfort, luxury, convenience, and freedom. We can, one way or another, attain the pleasures, places, and things we want—when and where we want them. Most of us do just that—attain, accumulate, collect—but plenty always seems to require more. Enough is never enough.

Then the big hitch comes—when we realize that all that comfort, convenience, and *stuff* really costs. We have to pay for it, keep track of it, protect it, clean it, store it, insure it, and worry about it. This takes energy and effort (in fact, a great part of your life). Later we have to move it, hide it, apologize for it, argue over it.

It stifles us and robs us of freedom because it requires so much of our time to tend. We have no time to have fun, to do the things we really want to do. Not only are our houses, drawers, closets, and vehicles so crowded we can't breathe, but our minds, emotions, and relationships, too, are crowded into dullness and immobility. We're so surrounded with stuff, we don't even have time for the people who mean the most to us.

Finally—often too late—we realize that most of that which has surrounded us, choking out good living, squeezing the physical and emotional life out of us, is just junk—*clutter*.

Millions of us are here, with feelings and sensitivity gone. Our life not only seems to be but *is* swallowed up. We don't own ourselves any more; we feel smothered and depressed.

Getting the clutter out of your life can and will rid you of more discouragement. tiredness, and boredom than anything else you can do.

There really is a solution

In this book I will try to help you:

1. Learn to identify junk and clutter, since *you* are the one who ultimately has to do it.

2. Realize what clutter is doing to you personally.

3. Give you some practical direction on de-junking.

Start now

I promise you no recipe, remedy, reorganization, or rebuilding plan will renew you like the simple, easy, inexpensive process of de-junking. I hope you'll find this book the catalyst to get the job done.

Junkee Entrance Exam

DIRECTIONS: Read the question, then rate yourself. . . .

Circle your answer and transfer the number to the "score" column.

	MORE THAN I'LL EVER ADMIT TO	MORE THAN I'D LIKE	ONLY A FEW THINGS	NONE	SCORE
1. If I had to move to Hawaii suddenly, how much stuff would end up in the alley?	1	(2)	3	5	
2. If my closets and drawers were searched right now, how much junk would be found?	(1)	(2)	3	5	
3. I have more-than-a-year-old magazines stored/lying around.	1	2	3	(5)	
4. I am carrying around excess pounds.	(1)	2	3	5	
5. I own clothes that won't fit or are ugly or hopelessly out of style.	1	(2)	3	5	
6. I have shoes I don't like or don't wear.	1	2	(3)	5	
7. I have old games/puzzles/patterns with pieces missing.	1	2	(3)	5	
8. I have photos I seldom look at because they're stashed away and hard to find.	(1)	2	3	5	
9. I watch junk shows on TV and junk movies.	1	2	3	(5)	
10. I have keepsakes that I can't remember what sake they were kept for.	1	2	3	(5)	
11. I keep toys (adult or juvenile) that are broken, outgrown, or not used.	1	2	(3)	5	
12. I save old uniforms or maternity/baby clothes I don't need any more.	1	2	(3)	5	
13. I use drugs, medicines, seltzers, salves, and treatments (prescribed and unprescribed).	1	2	(3)	5	
14. If I held a garage sale, how much stuff would my customers get to paw through?	1	(2)	3	5	

37

	MORE THAN I'LL EVER ADMIT TO	MORE THAN I'D LIKE	ONLY A FEW THINGS	NONE	SCORE
15. I have paraphernalia from hobbies, projects, and classes I started and "may someday" re-activate.	1	(2)	3	5	
16. When someone visits my home, how many excuses does my junk seem to call for?	1	2	(3)	5	
17. How many unused recipe cards/cookbooks/do-it-yourself manuals do I have?	1	(2)	(3)	5	
18. I consume colas, coffee, and other stimulants to revive me and keep me going.	1	2	3	(5)	
19. I have machinery and appliances that don't work or have parts missing.	1	2	(3)	5	
20. I store old paint (half-cans or less), stiff brushes, and matted rollers.	1	2	(3)	5	
21. I hang onto broken or never-used hair gadgets (dryers, stylers, hot combs, electric curlers, etc.).	1	2	(3)	5	
22. I have empty no-return or other honestly useless bottles inhabiting my house.	1	2	3	(5)	
23. I have old wedding announcements, greeting, or Christmas cards squirreled away from acquaintances I scarcely recall.	1	2	(3)	5	
24. I keep unread junk mail and lapsed driver's licenses and expired policies.	1	2	3	(5)	
25. My medicine chest holds bottles of ancient vitamins and antique prescriptions.	1	2	(3)	5	
26. I have furniture or other items I am going to fix, sell, or refinish some day.	1	(2)	(3)	5	
27. I have souvenirs or knickknacks that I dust, clean, store, and abhor.	1	2	(3)	5	
28. I use toppings, dressings, spices, and sauces on my food.	1	2	(3)	5	
29. I keep plain old ordinary empty boxes.	1	2	3	(5)	
30. I save leftover scraps of Christmas wrap or rumpled gift wrap that I never use.	1	2	3	(5)	
31. I have bad habits that really mess up my life.	1	2	(3)	5	
32. I've kept books and paperbacks I couldn't force myself to finish.	1	2	(3)	5	
33. I clip out coupons and special offers on products that I never buy.	1	2	(3)	5	
34. I save colognes and after-shaves I can't stand the smell of, or makeup I tried and didn't like.	1	2	3	(5)	

66

	MORE THAN I'LL EVER ADMIT TO	MORE THAN I'D LIKE	ONLY A FEW THINGS	NONE	SCORE
35. I save notes, clippings, ideas, and plans that haven't been filed or acted on.	1	(2)	(3)	5	
36. I eat sweet, salty, or greasy snacks or other junk food.	1	2	(3)	5	
37. I have old curtains or blinds stashed away that I've dragged from past residences.	1	2	3	(5)	
38. I keep old plans, patterns, and scraps of any kind that are probably destined never to be used.	1	2	(3)	5	
39. I spend time in places that I don't really enjoy.	1	2	3	(5)	
40. I save every drawing my children ever made, and all their school papers since the year one.	1	2	(3)	5	
41. I keep ballpoint pens that skip or dried-out felt-tip markers.	1	2	(3)	(5)	
42. I hoard odd socks or pantyhose with one ruined leg.	1	2	3	(5)	
43. I own costume jewelry, pins, badges, brooches that I never wear (for good reason).	1	(2)	3	5	
44. I don't throw out tools and gadgets I know are worthless.	1	2	(3)	5	
45. I have wristwatches or clocks that aren't working.	1	2	3	(5)	
46. The trunk, floor, and glove compartment of my car are filled with old torn maps, inoperative flashlights, and fast-food debris.	1	2	3	(5)	
47. I put up with people who hang on me and waste my time.	1	2	3	(5)	
48. If someone gave me $10 for every piece of junk I have, how much money would I get?	(1)	2	3	5	
				TOTAL	

0-100	100-150	150-175
A TERMINAL CASE . . . Therapy or a massive transplant might help, but maybe you should just give up.	THE END IS NEAR . . . You're in trouble. Read *Clutter's Last Stand* three times, gird your loins and start de-junking ruthlessly. You might possibly survive your junk.	YOU'RE ON THE BRINK . . . If you start to de-junk today, you can make it. Read *Clutter's Last Stand* and commit yourself to do it.

175-225	225-240	
THERE IS HOPE . . . If you can clean up/come to terms with those few problem areas, clutter won't have a chance to spread.	YOU ARE PURE. Read *Clutter's Last Stand* to perfect yourself and then pass it on to a junkee friend or relative.	

CHAPTER 2

The Genealogy of Junk

In the beginning...

there was night . . . no clutter. As soon as light was created, people could see things. Immediately they began to acquire them. They hoarded, fought for, lied for, died for substances that mostly were or became worthless junk. Junk soon became more important to mankind than clean air, beautiful land, pure love, and total freedom. Clutter indeed can be traced back to Adam, who, when his fig leaves were worn out and should have been discarded, pressed and saved them as a memory of bygone days.

For centuries people have traced their roots and ancient relatives to find out just where their names and characteristics might have originated. They are proud to find they have Indian blood, or royal blood back there somewhere—even a cat burglar or carpetbagger or two adds a bit of flavor to family history. But where did our clutter inclinations come from? Were they inherited, absorbed, evolved, hatched, home-grown? Perhaps all of these—or perhaps Adam, when commanded to multiply and replenish the earth, thought that possessions were included in the instructions. One way or another we did it. You and I are the gods of junk—we create and procreate it.

So clutter began with our uncontrollable desire to have more, better, bigger—even if it isn't good for us, even if we really don't want it, need it, or have a place for it. Enough is never enough!

Don't feel guilty—almost every single one of us, deep in our hearts, would like to be able to roam a junkyard unidentified. We want more, no matter how much we have of our own; even if ours is a better quality than our neighbor's, we want theirs. The lust to have things is a drive almost equal to hunger and sex. *Coveting thy neighbor's clutter is the seed of all junk attainment.*

Your Junk Drive Is to Blame:

Pick up a paper and drive down the street and notice how many garage sales are going on (generations of junk is finally pushing them out of the house). It isn't the money—only fifty things are sold out of two hundred displayed. Even people who need to have a garage sale drive by other garage sales casting longing lustful eyes on the beautiful junk

displayed on tables and standing up against the garage wall, watching, wondering what they could take home. The junk drive is real, in the bloodlines of all of us (yes, even the Mr. Neats and Ms. Squared-Aways of the world).

Junking:

Our genealogy shows it started with Adam saving fig leaves and apple cores . . . Ben Hur stockpiling broken chariot wheels . . . King Arthur hoarding shattered swords . . . George Washington stowing splintery old false teeth . . . Daniel Boone squirreling away frayed tails from his coonskin cap . . . to us today, keeping thirty-five years of *Good Housekeeping.*

Mankind increased by begat. The Scriptures are full of: "And Ahaz begat Jehoadah, and Jehoadah begat Alemeth and Zimri, and Zimri begat Moza. . . ."

This goes on for pages and pages and book after book and is called *genealogy*— lineage. Junk multiplication seems to follow the same pattern.

"Joseph begat a '79 Oldsmobile, the Oldsmobile begat a trailer to tow, the trailer begat a speedboat, the boat begat a set of water skis, the water skis begat a larger motor in the boat, the larger motor begat a bigger trailer, the bigger trailer begat a bigger vehicle, the bigger vehicle begat a bigger expense, the bigger expense . . . a family fight."

Yes, most psychologists and professional cleaners would agree—more junk damage is done by training and conditioning than by the junk fever in our veins. Let's see how this comes about:

1. We start early—repeating the lesson over and over—so they understand the "real value."

"Be good and Mommy will give you a nice big surprise."

2. We remind them as they grow of important lessons.

"Atta boy! Keep them picked up and Daddy will buy you a bigger box."

3. We continue to reinforce junk values as age increases.

"Be good and Daddy will bring you home a fine souvenir."

4. We continue coating clutter like sugar plums with the necessity to give and receive junk periodically.

"What do you want for Christmas?" "What are you going to get Stevie for his birthday?"

5. They learn that few occasions can pass in our lives without an exchange of something tangible—called a gift. We make it clear that any tangible gift can save face.

"Hurry up and decide— you have to take *something* to the party."

6. We carefully tell them how to save, keep, collect and store, but seldom what to do with it or why they have it.

"Let's put it up there so the kids won't take it and play with it and it'll stay nice."

7. They are then ready to be turned over to the school to be educated.

"Keep all articles, magazines, clippings, etc. You never know when you might need records."

8. As they reach teenhood, vanity and glamor are overwhelmingly established as more important than practicality or reason.

"We're going to go out tomorrow and buy your first *real* pair of high heels."

9. Good examples are set for faintheartedness in the face of a bargain, or a deal.

2 for 1

"Now we can buy the purple one, too!"

10. Jobs inject a little more clutter into their lives.

"Lead in sales for the quarter, Junior, and we'll give you a trophy and send you on a national trip with nothing to do but pig out on junk food and drink— won't that be nice!"

11. Serious clutter collecting often begins when we get married or buy a house. We're short of cash so we use our parents' or grandparents' old things, which become so dear by the time we can afford better that we keep them, too.

"But if I cook in the new pans they'll tarnish and won't look so nice on the wall."

12. The worst of it is, everybody else is doing it, everybody else has one.

13. And then, in a grim twist of genealogy, we inherit other peoples' leftovers (junk), and keep it forever—or for as long as we have a place to store it. "Inheritance" generates about 50 percent of our clutter.

"I'm the only one who knows how to sew, so I'll take the old machine and all Mama's buttons and patterns and fabric scraps."

So junk came to pass, by both *creation* (starring you as the creator) and *evolution* (from your inherited desire to acquire junk).

It's helpful to understand where clutter came from, but it's a lot more important to know where it's going. . . .

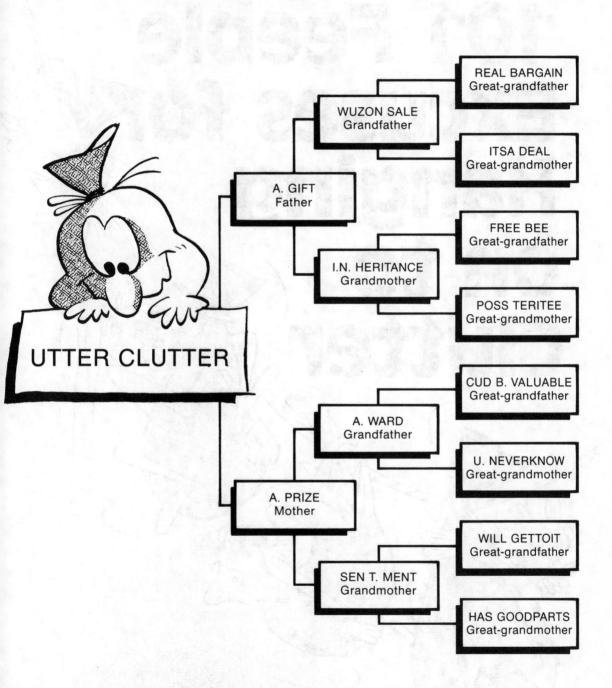

UTTER CLUTTER

		REAL BARGAIN Great-grandfather
WUZON SALE Grandfather		
		ITSA DEAL Great-grandmother
A. GIFT Father		
		FREE BEE Great-grandfather
I.N. HERITANCE Grandmother		
		POSS TERITEE Great-grandmother
		CUD B. VALUABLE Great-grandfather
A. WARD Grandfather		
		U. NEVERKNOW Great-grandmother
A. PRIZE Mother		
		WILL GETTOIT Great-grandfather
SEN T. MENT Grandmother		
		HAS GOODPARTS Great-grandmother

17

CHAPTER 3

101 Feeble Excuses for Hanging on to Clutter

The biggest reason clutter piles up on us and chokes us out of living is because we know and use all manner of excuses to justify keeping it—which, if repeated in a reverent enough tone, no one will question.

We've heard ourselves and others spout these rationalizations so long that we think they're Scripture. But they're not; this is why I've taken the time to assemble some of the most common of the thousands of excuses I've collected from junkees over the years.

Breeze through this condensed list of invalid excuses—excuses you'll not be allowed to use when you begin to de-junk your life.

Let's start with a few of the classics:

Bent rolls of leftover Christmas wrap: *"I can always iron it."*

Correspondence and birthday cards from long-ago acquaintances you scarcely knew then (they probably moved to Chugwater, Wyoming): *"I need to copy these addresses off the envelopes."*

Abandoned do-it-yourself projects you found you *couldn't* do yourself: *"I'm going to write the company and tell them their instructions are lousy."*

A broken watch: *"It may never tell time but I can use the crystal for a magnifying glass in a survival situation."*

Ugly $8.99 wind chimes: *"I only bought them to change a twenty."*

Puzzles with pieces missing: *"Oh well, we never put them completely together anyway."*

Dresses and pants you haven't been able to zip for years: *"They're a good incentive to lose weight."*

Partly used bottles of the wrong color makeup: *"Who knows, maybe I'll get a tan next summer."*

Stacks of expired coupons for products you never buy: *"These are still some really good buys."*

Three-quarters-full notebooks from past classes: *"I may want to brush up on that someday."*

Recipes that bombed: *"I ought to give them one more chance."*

Dishpans and buckets that leak: *"These might be cute outside somewhere with petunias planted in them."*

Cheap ballpoint pen that mostly skips or won't write: *"Maybe I can pick up some cheap refills."*

Bottles of expired vitamins: *"Well, we'll just have to take twice as many of them now."*

Old pilled-up blankets with frayed bindings: *"These can be used in a pinch for quilt bats."*

Faded bedspreads and curtains from former homes: *"Maybe I could dye them."*

Stacks of empty adding machine and aluminum foil and freezer paper rolls: *"I'm saving these for when I have grandchildren."*

Leftover roll-ends and scraps of wallpaper: *"Someday I'll build a doll house."*

A plumpie: *"The poor kids in India are starving; I can't let this banana split go to waste."*

A chain smoker: *"It takes a lot more guts to face up to cancer than to quit smoking."*

Never-used gadgets and fancy attachments for now-defunct equipment: *"This is still a perfectly good automatic toenail polisher."*

Long outdated packets of garden seeds: *"Those expiration dates are just gimmicks to get you to buy new seeds."*

Favorite parlor games with half the pieces missing: *"If we buy a new one, we can use these as spare parts."*

Assortment of four-inch-wide neckties: *"You never know when these will come back in style."*

Pantyhose with a two-inch runner up one leg: *"I can always wear them with slacks."*

Owner of a world-class junk collection: *"It runs in my blood—show me a Dane [Pole, Italian, Scot, German, etc.] and I'll show you a clutter collector."*

Cheap bargain-store tools you've found to be worthless: *"I'll save these to loan to the neighbors."*

The dresses you used to wear with go-go boots: *"I can always convert these to tunics."*

Tangled wads of leftover yarn and embroidery floss: *"These will give me something to do on a rainy day."*

Three extra cars: *"I'm the victim of a materialistic society."*

Hand-knitted slippers with the bottom nearly gone: *"The top is just fine; I can always wear socks with them."*

Half-read books you couldn't force yourself to finish: *"If I get jailed, snowed in, or hospitalized, these will be my salvation."*

1901-1958 sewing patterns: *"I'm waiting till I have a chance to go through them."*

The circa 1940 refrigerator: *"It doesn't work too well, but it has beautiful lines."*

Lone earring: *"I can always make it into a pendant."*

The float you made for the Fourth of July parade six years ago: *"I still have plenty of room for it."*

Old chamber pot: *"I'm saving it for a white elephant party."*

Can of apple filling that went down the Colorado River with you: *"But we went through a lot together."*

Stuck-together stamp collection: *"One man's junk is another man's treasure."*

Pots from all the plants that died: *"If I'm de-junked, I'll be too sterile a person."*

Lidless cookie jar: *"Throwing innocent objects into the garbage seems merely a step away from murder!"*

Fabric scraps your mother, sisters, cousins, and friends were delighted to get rid of: *"I'm a natural scavenger."*

The stained and sagging couch that's perfect for the family room you don't have: *"I'm saving this in case I have to furnish another house."*

The great horned owl head your Uncle Otto left you: *"It would cost too much to replace."*

"It's a conversation piece."
It gives people who come to my home something to talk about: "What's that?" "What does it do?" "How old is it?" "Amazing." (Does this mean you're too boring to get by without it?)

"Someday I intend to fix it."
See Chapter 5. *"I'll have more time later."* This is sometimes expressed as—to fix it . . . to finish it . . . start it . . . look further into it. . . . Another variation on this is *"When I retire I'm going to. . . ."*

Who would dare doubt a senior citizen's dream? I don't really need to comment on this, do I? Who ever has more time later? Have you gotten any less busy as you've grown older?

"It's been in the family for years!"
"I might want to look at it for old time's sake."
"I'm saving it for posterity."
"I'm sentimental."

See Chapter 7 for some guidance through this quagmire of guilt and good intentions.

"I paid good money for this."
See Chapter 15.

"I'm married to the head pack rat."
See Chapter 16.

*"W*hy do I keep it? Because of 'someday'. Someday I'll quit doing PTA business, diaper business, my husband's business, and I'll have time to try out 597 recipes, file a few thousand magazine articles, and leisurely reread all my old *Reader's Digest*s. Someday there'll be a bread sack shortage and I'll need 1,300 bread sacks. Someday they'll pay me for my old telephone pole insulators. But someday is like tomorrow—it never comes."*

Stacks of Christmas cards you got in years gone by: *"I'm going to take up decoupage when I retire."*

Half-finished sewing project that you ended up hating: *"Maybe when my daughter gets this size she'll finish it."*

Twenty-three-year-old shorthand book:
"I bought it to learn shorthand as a spare-time project. I know I'll never get around to it, but if I throw the book away it means I've given up. As long as I have it, there's hope."

Tons of clutter can trace its ancestry to a worthwhile enterprise. The excuse for keeping it is: I'm saving it for a (Scout, 4-H, church, school, hobby, club, class) project. This might have been true ten years or even ten months ago, but if an undertaking is dead—I mean its interest or its value lost to age, geography, or a change of friends and interests—*don't keep it*, even if it has cash value. Give it away or sell it before it drains all the energy it once gave you. *Decide!* (whether you want to learn shorthand, want to finish that dust ruffle or not). The unresolved is probably unnecessary.

Aftershave and cologne you never liked the smell of, a wallet you wouldn't be caught dead carrying, knock-'em-dead earrings that will indeed, a tie not even Dick Tracy would wear, a crewel covered bridge that does *NOT* belong in your living room: *"I hate to hurt Aunt Annie's feelings."*

Yes, it's worthless, but it was a *gift*—you'd have to be a heartless wretch to throw out any gift. You have to keep it and maybe even display it, don't you?

See Chapter 7 for some guidance on this sticky subject. And remember: Why did someone give a gift to you in the first place? As a *token* of feeling and appreciation. Love isn't a tangible thing, so whether you keep the gift or not it has no effect on that all-important relationship between you and the giver. Many of us junk gift keepers are insecure or egotistical—we have to keep and display the "evidence" to assure ourselves that we're loved.

Those Wonderful Second-Bests

Is second-best clutter or "just-in-case?" Add up all your second-bests and tell me what you're doing with them now. I'll give you a few minutes.................

Can't think of much but "spares," eh? I'll help you. You've just bought a new watch, work boots, briefcase, gloves, blender, fishing pole, tennis racket, butcher knife, tea kettle, sewing machine, bike, salad bowl. Where are the second-bests?

OK, a little more help. Why did you obtain a best? That's easy: because you were unhappy with the old one—it was worn, old, getting ugly, not working right any more, or you were simply tired of it. Why do we keep things we're not happy with? No answer, except that we're clutter collectors. It's just like an old piece of chewing gum: we hate to pitch it because it still works (has no flavor but plenty of flex!). Sure, there's some glimmer of hope for those old worn watches, stiff work boots, leaky air mattresses, the bike with the bent frame, the too-small briefcase, that battered and shabby purse, that balding dress coat, the nicked butcher knife with the cracked handle, your no-longer-favorite rifle—but once you have the new in hand, those seconds (like the gum) have lost their flavor. Once you get your ego snuggled up to the new one you'll never want to be seen with the old one again—don't keep it around to disflavor your life!

Here's an example: everyone I know has a suitcase with a broken latch. After it pops open on the airport carrousel or in the cheerleaders' bus, they're shamed into the purchase of a nice new "best." But the old one is never pitched; it's a "spare" or "extra" that to justify its retired status is filled with junk and stored.

"It may come in handy someday."
"I may need it someday."

You may be right, *if you can find it*.

"Button, button, who's got the button" isn't just a funny game for the family, but a frustrating reality for all those who strip and save old buttons. A few spares are wisdom; a few jars full are runamuck junk you'll spend hours pawing through (once you find the jars).

Most people can't find it or forget where they put something when they do "need it someday"—so they usually end up buying another one.

Another version of this old favorite is: "I'll always be ready for _____." The only thing clutter collectors are always ready for is to rummage to try and find something they think is there. People free of unnecessary "stuff" are really the only ones who are prepared for action.

"This _____ is still perfectly good."
"I'm saving it for spare parts."

Ever notice that when someone throws out an old shoe, the leather is probably still worth almost what it cost when the shoe was new? Nobody has trouble pitching the shoe, but everyone takes out the old lace and keeps it forever. I've hardly met a person who doesn't do that, and haven't met anybody who ever uses the lace!

If there's anything resembling a good part on something worn or broken, we want to strip it off and save it, whether we need it or not: buttons, buckles, belts, the feathers and bands from old hats, doorknobs, shades that will never look good on another lamp, any old wheel or tire.

Watch it, or strip or "rescue" junk will strap you. What was once an important instinct is in this modern day (when time and space are more valuable than most manufactured items or materials) a mighty questionable venture. Do you really have room to keep it, or time to inventory it *in case* you can ever use it again? If you're honest with yourself, you'll realize you probably don't.

> "*S*omeday I'm gonna need it! When the Lord comes in the Millennium, He may ask me for that ice-cream scoop with the broken handle, those boxes of baby food jars, the bottoms of all my cut-off Levis, or the pile of paper bags (all folded neatly)."

"As soon as I get rid of it, I'll need it."

This is one of the feeblest of all feeble excuses. The truth is, the day after we get rid of it (*if* we ever do) the guilt of feeling like we murdered it mounts up, so for the next two years we unconsciously search for a use and always find some weak application to feed the feeling that we prematurely disposed of it. It's like the light fixture we took out of the living room during a remodeling job six years ago. It was junk then, but keeping it made us feel better. Several months after we chuck it, one of our new ginger jars goes on the blink—and our junking soul instantly activates the old "I knew I should have kept it." If we did have it, *we wouldn't use it anyway.* Only the fact that it's gone gives us the courage to consider it.

Evidence Junk

Dumping our raw, glaring, worthless junk is easy, but on the second go-round I found, undumped:

1. Three boxes of original edited manuscript and rough art from my first published book.

2. A drawerful of worn-out work gloves.

3. My first wristwatch I bought in 1949.

4. My college textbooks.

None of this stuff was of any use to me—and certainly not to anyone else, so why did I keep it? For *evidence.* Because it seems that nothing can beat hard cold evidence as a souvenir of our maiden voyages through life.

Junk proves that I was there: that I once had a 26-inch waist, that I once did score 31 points in that game against Inkom, that I once had curly blond hair. . . .

I wanted to have my "original" manuscript to show off in writer's speeches, to show my kids or clients what I went through to write a book. I wore out all those gloves in three weeks building a large masonry shop in my spare time; I showed off the gloves and they made a striking impression, but less and less of one every year. The fact that the building stands there or that the book is still in print is surely evidence enough, far more impressive than any of this "evidence junk." Evidence junk is among the most difficult to dispose of; the best solution is probably to spread it out and photograph it—dive down in the middle of it if you must, and have someone take a snapshot of you embracing it (with a look of convincing reverence on your face). Take slides; then you can project your evidence on a wall, or get a color print made so you can flaunt it easier.

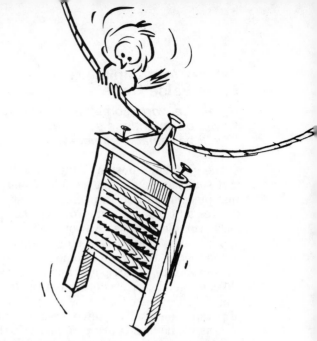

"But they aren't making it any more."
"They aren't making these the way they used to."
"Someday you won't be able to buy one of these."

Those may indeed be true statements, but why do you suppose they quit making them in the first place? Simple—there was no market, there was no longer enough demand for it to produce it. It was out of date, out of style, or something else now does what it did better or easier. You can bet that if a thing is valuable from *any* angle, someone in our competitive economy will make it available for the market.

Stored in remote corners of buildings you'll find, under the dust and cobwebs, 900-pound woodstoves, retired mangles, old treadle sewing machines, 40-pound frying pans, ghastly huge (and warped) pieces of furniture, massive electric roasters, 12-foot clocks with chimes so loud you can only turn them on for

exhibition, etc. Their era is gone; they've been replaced by lighter, quicker, safer things—but because they're thick, heavy, and have put in service time, we keep and coddle them. It's amazing the tools we keep for things we don't need to do any more—from bucksaws, cranks, and butter churns to fire bellows and buggy-whip winders. I love these old things, and marvel at the sentiment they can stir, but we can't keep the whole farm. If we keep too many of them for "atmosphere," we won't be able to breathe.

How many of us want to hunt with a 19-pound smoking flintlock shotgun when we can use a sleek 7-pound self-loading automatic? Who wants to lug a 70-pound hinged hardwood trunk through airports when a 5-pound nonsagging fiberglass suitcase will do the job better? Sturdiness alone is not a reason to keep the old; if so we would still use covered wagons, wooden shoes, and serge stockings. If you're unwilling to *use* something (do you really want to fuss with an icebox?), if you hardly ever *look* at it, if it doesn't delight your soul or stir memories every time you look at it, if it's just rotting out in the shed—do it (and yourself) justice by getting rid of it.

Selling Your Junk . . .
Some False Hope

"It may be worth something someday."
"It will be an antique someday."
"It will be valuable someday."

The glittering illusion of the possibility that someday you might be able to sell that piece of junk for a phenomenal sum creates an excuse to cling to even the most worthless items. All sorts of appetite-whetting success stories appear in the media, telling how some lucky soul wandered into his attic and found a rare old coin, kettle, or credenza that made him rich. Don't let that hope get you out of perspective—only a few pieces of junk in tens of thousands are rare and valuable, and if you averaged the value of all the hours spent to sort and clean it up to sell it, your wages would probably be about 7¢ an hour. There isn't much cash in your closet, mostly clutter. I've seen many people spend $100 on gas, signs, and advertising for a garage sale to take in $50—and that isn't profitable either in terms of the pocketbook or of your life's time taken.

If you have doubts in your bouts of deciding what to keep, don't waste time listening to friends (fellow junkers). Take a few minutes and call an expert and ask, "How much is a 1917 corn husker worth?" You'll know instantly—and can then make a decision to keep or sell. Many a clutter keeper has gone to a lot of trouble to keep worthless stuff because he "imagined" its worth. Remember, since the onset of mass production and the craze for antiques and collectibles, fewer and fewer items are scarce enough to become valuable. (Yes, that does cast suspicion on your set of commemorative moon landing glasses and Bicentennial bell jars.)

The Ubiquitous *They*

"They left it . . .," *"They* gave it . . .," *"They* bought it . . .," *"They* insisted . . . ."

This excuse was eloquently demonstrated by a fellow passenger at the airport who walked ahead of me to the baggage-claim area. It was apparent he had been gone awhile from the way his family swarmed him; after all the hugging his wife cast a quick glance at him and said in a disappointed voice, "Looks like you ate well." He patted his protruding middle: "Yes, I must have gained ten pounds—*they* fed us to death, *they* served too much, *they* should have eased up, but *they* didn't, *they* put lots of pounds on all of us." One of the kids piped up: "Those people just don't care how you look," and they all left, the blame for the weight squarely on the feeder, not the feedee.

A cruel fact of clutter is that there is no one to blame—it is mostly *our* fault. Yet we often feel abused—the "world" (our parents, our mate, the government, the company, our society) has inflicted it on us, we were innocent bystanders, seduced and left wounded.

My favorite wall motto:
"Your situation is exactly what you make it, or what you allow it to be."

No one guides your quivering hand in a junk shop but you, no one holds your face in junk reading, viewing, and listening, no one but you says yes or no, keep it or throw it. Your present clutter quotient is where *you* put it, where *you* allow it to be. None of the excuses listed in this chapter (or any new ones you might think up) can excuse clutter or the damage it will do.

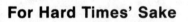

For Hard Times' Sake

"I was raised during the Depression and we were taught to save everything. . . ."

"I'm saving it for hard times." We've all heard this one, and I've saved it till now because it's a real heartbreaker. It would be downright reckless to stop saving for hard times—or would it?

Horror stories of the Great Depression have planted fear in all of us and if such a dire event should roll around again, we want to be somehow prepared. Hair-raising stories from our folks and grandfolks of no food, fuel, tools, toys, or blankets give us a compassionate view of all of the clutter they're stashing away. Believe it or not, there are lots of "depression savers," who survived the last one and are saving *everything*—rewearable, restorable, reusable, or not—to have on hand during a coming downswing.

There is good news and bad news for you depression savers.

The good news is that your junk *will* have a use during the next depression—as fuel for your fire to keep you warm. The bad news is that the last thing of value will be junk. No one will have cash to buy your clutter except the filthy rich, who will already have too much of their own junk to guard. Stash food, friends, talent—those might save you. When things get tough, the less you have to tote, store, keep warm, and watch out for, the better off you'll be.

Hard times were put well in perspective by a clutter confession I received in the mail:

All my life I've been told to save for hard times. So all my life I've saved for harder times to come. But no matter how hard times got, it has never been hard enough to use or re-use all the worn-out, broken junk I've saved. I finally realized that the hard times come when you try to clean around it, keep track of it, or move to another house. Please help me to not want to save everything that passes before me.

let go of the stuff, pull their hands out, and run away?" Well, they didn't because they are, in that respect, human. They refused to let go of something they had. To hang on meant the stewpot, but the thrill of possession overruled all risk and reason.

We could all entertain a crowd of monkeys for hours with our "junk traps"—all of us have clamped onto things and even though they have us trapped, immobilized, stripped and strapped, we hang on, refusing to release and run away to better, safer things. The monkeys at least have the excuse of being hungry; for much less good reasons we want our goodies so much that our minds, like the monkey's fist, close up and there's no giving up. Like the monkeys, we jump and scream to go and do and are denied because we refuse to turn loose our loot.

Too often we confuse ownership with companionship, not realizing that certain things, even good things, change and lose their value and we don't need them any more. We've outgrown, outlasted them, or something new and better has come along. We have to release them, but in our greed and possessiveness and "loyalty" outdo the monkey and hang on, even at the peril of our physical and spiritual lives.

I've seen fine farmers who refused to let go of horse machinery lose everything. I've seen families refuse to sell and move off a beloved but unproductive old homesite—and deteriorate in poverty. I've watched merchants who hung onto old styles and procedures be forced out of

Don't Let Clutter Make a Monkey Out of You

We've all heard the story of monkey traps. When hunters discovered how greedy and possessive monkeys are, instead of running them down with nets and spears, they took coconuts, made a hole in each of them, tied them to a tree, and went home. The next morning they'd return to find dozens of wild monkeys, unharmed, with their little hands stuck in the coconuts. How did this work? Simple: the hole in the coconut was cut just big enough for a monkey's hand to squeeze through; inside the coconut were placed some tasty goodies (maybe monkey M&Ms). The monkeys would creep up on the trap, smell the bait, reach in and grab a fistful of whatever—and when they tried to bring their hand out, the fist of course wouldn't pass through the hole. The monkeys all jumped and screamed and struggled to get free, but unwilling to release the bait, they were caught.

Now being smart humans, we instantly reason: "Why didn't the stupid monkeys

existence. I've seen companies who refuse to change communication systems and sales methods corner themselves into bankruptcy. I've seen owners of old, outgrown buildings who refuse to let go and consider new construction concepts lose their life savings. I've seen hundreds of people refuse to let go of deadly health habits suffer serious (and unnecessary) medical problems. I've watched mothers, fathers, and grandparents miss trips and other life-enhancing experiences because they wouldn't loose their death grip on their junk. I know people who hang onto old lost loves so tight that no new love can squeeze in, and they wilt and die miserably. Our refusal to surrender worthless harmful worn-out things keeps us from growing and maturing.

Odd, isn't it, that the junk itself has to initiate action. We actually have to be injured by an old quack remedy or medicine before we quit it (then after we stop using it, we store it just in case aging it a little might improve its potency).

We actually have to reach the point where our junk inflicts pain or inconvenience on our physical and emotional selves—that it interferes with our lives—before we're smart enough to think of shedding it. Most of the time it just lies there, dormant and useless and often out of sight—until one day we have to move it for the carpet layer, or move to another house, or we stumble over it, or somebody makes us account for or insure it—before we consider releasing it. It has to affect our appearance, our strength, our speed, finally offend our *vanity* enough that we realize it would have been wise to let go. *Hanging on will hang you.*

The Air Force has it in perspective: my brother-in-law, a lieutenant colonel, told me once that when his transport was delivering a $7 million piece of complicated scientific equipment they lost power in two engines and immediately dumped the equipment. I was impressed at the quick decision to release all the expensive machinery. "When we take off," my brother-in-law said, "we're told that the nine human beings in that plane are the only things that will not become obsolete, that are not expendable." *You,* your loves and life and relationships are all that count.

Face it: there is a wisdom in letting go of things that clutter and choke your life. There is nothing more stimulating and noble than change and growth. Most of us never taste the new, the fresh, the zestful because we have our heads and hearts gripped clear to the quick in clutter.

CHAPTER 4

Committing Junkicide

Junkicide is a slow, painful strangulation and dying of the senses. Although our brains are still intact, we've simply replaced *thinking* with *things*. We've crowded out creativity with accumulation. We've frozen flexibility with profusion. We've snapped up so much free stuff and bought so many things to keep, store, clean, polish, and protect that we don't have any freedom.

Junkees are destined to commit junkicide. They are the ones of us (all of us) with a tendency to load up plates, places, vaults, homes, and conversations with more than is needed.

Junkees are afflicted with the endless urge to have more. Enough is never enough. The have-notters want some, the have-enoughers want more, even the have-too-muchers want more. Ever wonder why most frauds, schemes, cons, embezzlements, etc., aren't committed by the have-nothing desperate but by the nice well-to-do citizen? People with plenty, position, and more things than they can already use are often the people who defraud to get more. Jails are filled with people who never could get enough.

Junk is insidious because it's so gradual. Like those extra pounds of flesh, it silently, sneakily mounds in and around, on top of and under us until we're surrounded. It's all so slow and subtle we don't realize how much is there.

Clutter Will Cramp Your Style

In 1979 I took ten Boy Scouts on a two-week trip to Philmont, the 30,000-acre Scout camp in the rugged New Mexico mountains. Sprinkled in the vast wilderness were twenty base camps, each designed to educate Scouts in a different subject—gold mines, archaeology, lumbering, mountain climbing, etc. We were to spend eleven days on foot with a pack, hiking from camp to camp. We were cautioned before we started out about footwear, bears and snakes, getting lost, etc. Then, sensing our junkee tendencies, the ranger put us through a pack shakedown (which would be a neat idea for all of us). We had to spread a blanket in front of our tent and dump our packs out on it, showing everything we were going to take on the eleven-day hike. (It shamefully revealed everything from toothpicks to love notes.) Then the ranger walked through and de-junked everyone's treasures, giving reasons such as, "You won't use this," "This is silly," "This is too heavy," "This attracts bears." Out went the smuggled radios, bulky binoculars, blow dryers, cast iron kettles, comic books, and all that was junk on the trail. The ranger said, "We have a tendency on our journeys to take more than we want to end up carrying." I nodded agreement and saw to it that my boys had lightened loads. Then I spotted the fold-up fishing rod and other things the ranger had booted out of *my* spill of goodies. I repacked my Jansport, and when the ranger wasn't looking threw in some books (a taboo), a couple of sharpening stones, two wood rasps, and a few other extras in case I had spare time. This made my pack a firm, compact fifty-five pounds. For ten days and nights, in 50°-to-98° weather, going up and down 10,000-foot peaks, fording slippery streams, I sagged under my pack and stumbled over my dragging feet, groaning, promising myself that never again would I take more than I could carry. My junk was such a burden I could scarcely savor the fun of the trip.

Clutter is doing the same thing to your journey through life—your job, raising your family, going to school. Junk will dilute the quality of our life, not add to it as we thought when we packed it in.

As a personal demobilizer, clutter rates right in there with crippling diseases, being bedridden, unable to drive, or trapped in a prison cell. Our junk ties us down—away from adventure, affection, and accomplishment—and we can't go when and where we want to.

I had a mild case of junkitis, as most of us do. How can *you* tell if you're a candidate for committing junkicide? Check the list on the opposite page.

Junk seldom gets the blame for life's problems, but it's one of the biggest contributors (if not *the* biggest). There is probably more violence—arguments, fights, and killings—over worthless junk than over anything else.

Marriage and family failures are often the result of selfishness—someone is spending too much time surrounding and securing him- or herself with junk. Often couples have so insulated themselves with clutter in the form of excess clothing, jewelry, hobby gear, housing, transportation, etc., that they can't get to each other to love. When we're extending our feelings to junk, we're exhausting emotions that could be generating affection. It's like our house—if we fill it with junk, clutter, and things, there's no room to keep or exercise anything of value. Junk uses *all* our space. When loving people come our way they can't find us or our feelings. And this dulling of our sensitivity and compassion by junk and clutter is so gradual that few of us realize it's happening.

If you wander through shops and garage sales when you don't need anything in particular, you're infected. Aches and pains will soon develop—the aching tendency to weigh a good thing down with too many extras, the pain of wondering why you don't have as much fun as you used to.

There's no escape from the toll clutter takes of our life. The most valuable "someday useful" junk will stymie our

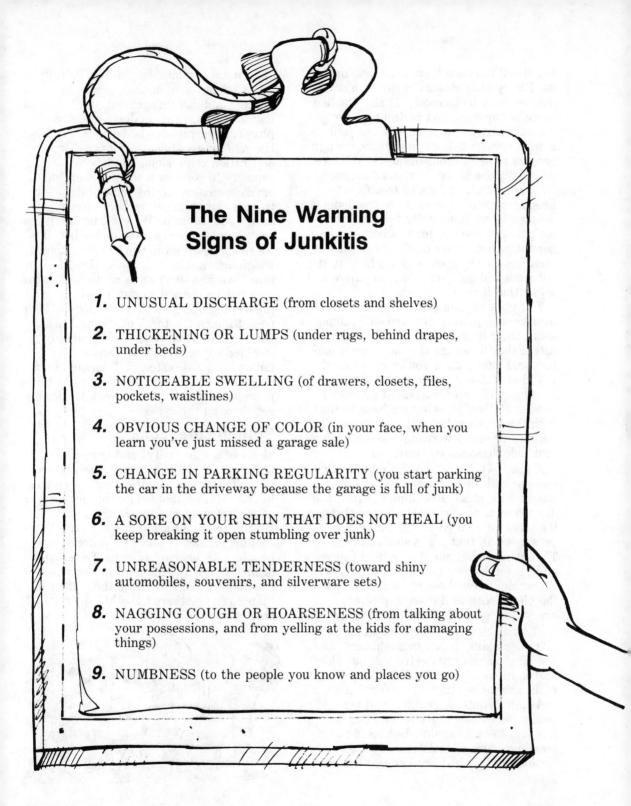

The Nine Warning Signs of Junkitis

1. UNUSUAL DISCHARGE (from closets and shelves)

2. THICKENING OR LUMPS (under rugs, behind drapes, under beds)

3. NOTICEABLE SWELLING (of drawers, closets, files, pockets, waistlines)

4. OBVIOUS CHANGE OF COLOR (in your face, when you learn you've just missed a garage sale)

5. CHANGE IN PARKING REGULARITY (you start parking the car in the driveway because the garage is full of junk)

6. A SORE ON YOUR SHIN THAT DOES NOT HEAL (you keep breaking it open stumbling over junk)

7. UNREASONABLE TENDERNESS (toward shiny automobiles, souvenirs, and silverware sets)

8. NAGGING COUGH OR HOARSENESS (from talking about your possessions, and from yelling at the kids for damaging things)

9. NUMBNESS (to the people you know and places you go)

emotional freedom if we let it pile up on us. Everything stashed away or hidden, discreetly or indiscreetly, is also stashed away in our mind and is draining our mental energy. We can't hide our junk in a deep enough hole or in obscure enough corners to keep it out of our mind. Once physically discarded, it's also discarded from our mind, and we're free from keeping mental tabs on it. But as long as we own it, we'll mentally tend it. We feel obligated to use our junk, whether we need it or not. If we don't or can't use it, then we worry about why we have it at all! Junk will get you—don't sit there and argue that it won't.

The guilt of junk possession is overwhelming. Just get someone talking about their junk and stand back and listen: they'll release the most incredible personal information you've ever heard. It's kind of like a public confession of sin. Feeling guilty and frustrated about our piles of clutter, knowing we have to deal with the problem but not knowing where—or really wanting—to start is pre-junkicide depression. Watch out!

A stately German woman who survived the war considered herself wise, but wasn't wise at all. Recalling her past the day we met, she said, "We lasted through the war, we held on to our things, preserved all that was valuable to us. Then it all ended one day, late in the war: a big bomb hit our house and we lost everything; my whole life was gone with the blast. With all I'd accomplished, everything gone, I felt it no use to go on."

She had clearly committed junkicide. Her pots, pans, sofas, mantelpieces, and dwelling place were destroyed, but all that is replaceable. She didn't stop to realize that she still had perfect health and sight, youth, ingenuity, and her family (as well as her land and the freedom to build again). But all her blessings were of little consequence, because clutter had preoccupied her for years.

Junkitis is generally the real culprit when people cave in or fall apart in despair and discouragement. Junk pushes our thoughts, time, budget, space, and physical energies to the edge. Then, when the *real* crises of death, sadness, or separation come along, we haven't the capacity to cope with them. When the big emergencies or strains come and we have to rally our total self to hold up, we just aren't able to do it. We can't handle it; we can't love and serve and endure because we're so absorbed in worrying, watching, weighing, waiting on, and wishing for junk. We just don't have anything left to give: we've burned so much fuel preserving our junk that we have little or none to burn the torch of strength when it's needed. A big strain on an already strained capacity usually results in failure, if not disaster. But demand on a person who isn't worrying about clutter just causes him or her to work harder and get through the crisis.

Bottom Line: Junk

"Loss of productivity" and unrealized ambitions, if dissected, will often be from junk. That's what inefficiency is—clutter in one form or another getting in the way of achievement and inspiration. Businesses and businesspeople can commit junkicide, and I've watched people with brilliant talents of every kind (athletic, artistic, musical) not be able to use an ounce of it because the clutter in their lives smothered and hid their ability.

Are You Indisposed?

The sure sign of evolution from a mild to a chronic junkee is when we save (or even have the *urge* to save) disposables. Many things are made just well enough to serve once, then be discarded. With great imagination or dexterity they might squeak by another trick, but all in all a disposable, for health and wealth, should be disposed of.

Before you think of pointing the finger at all your friends who are saving no-return bottles, examine your own behavior.

Are you:

- Saving lids from long-gone jars?
- And the little plastic hangers from new pairs of socks?
- Occasionally reclaiming used plastic wrap?
- Tempted to reuse a tea bag?
- Graduating "throwaway" plastic tumblers to the china closet?
- Keeping and using foil pie tins until they're wrinkled beyond recognition?
- Slow to throw away dull disposable razors?
- Salting away fast-food containers and used Styrofoam cups?

- Always fishing parts of saved plastic forks out of the base of the dishwasher?
- Hoarding those cute little film canisters?
- Saving the boxes from every piece of jewelry you've ever bought or been given?
- Keeping appliance package padding (in case you reship)?
- Stockpiling empty whiskey decanters and cologne bottles?
- Sometimes trying to straighten out old straws?

(If you checked three or more, keep reading.)

> "*I* watched her spend $95 on drawer organizers so her 2,700 used twist-ties wouldn't get mixed in with her 4,500 reusable coffee stirrers."
>
> *Cathy* comic strip

Do you want to spend your life in junk games?

J	U	S	T	I	F	I	C	A	T	I	O	N

U
N
K

Form a circle—the leader in the middle, who walks around suspiciously and suddenly stops and names a junk item (tangible or intangible) and points to a person, who says "Guilty" or "Not guilty." If not guilty, leader repeats the procedure with another item. If the person yells "Guilty," then he has to justify it to the group on the spot, in one sentence. If he fails, the group yells "Junkee" and the person is out of the game. "Save it" means he stays. Last one out is the winner.

J

J	U	M	P	I	N	G

N
K

A game of real ingenuity in using one piece of junk to vault your whole pile of junk in one leap. Can be played outside or inside, depending on how big a stack you have and your running room.

J U G G L I N G (crossword with JUNK intersecting vertically)

A game that takes all your physical and emotional concentration to keep all your junk in view/exhibited. The object of the game is to get so engrossed with keeping your clutter circulating that you completely forget the people and other things in your life.

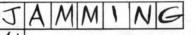

J A M M I N G (crossword with JUNK intersecting vertically)

This is seeing how much junk you can get in the smallest spaces (like seventeen sweaters in one drawer). Only fists and feet can be used for stuffing. Can be played with drawers, closets, shelves, rooms, and trunks.

J O U S T I N G (crossword with JUNK intersecting horizontally)

Consciously or unconsciously prodding each other with your clutter. This is where you choose a partner and try to cruelly knock him or her around and off balance with your junk.

Junk Shows on You

No matter how sharp you are, what you own, how famous you are—if you eat, wear, live, and love junk it will cause ugly bulges somewhere on your person or your psyche.

So many of us worry about cancer and accidents, we can't imagine how anyone could commit suicide, yet with our junk we're slowly, daily doing that very thing.

A junkee works more and more hours to get more money that is almost all spent on excess—*junk*—that he never has or takes the time to enjoy. We run in this circle of nothingness until we drop—or just wear out—watching, chasing, and weighing junk.

Junkees gain little sympathy from friends or loved ones. People feel compassion for the sick or handicapped, but where sickness is self-induced (cirrhosis of the liver, insomnia) and is essentially self-abuse, people feel that somehow we got what we deserved. Nobody these days at work or home or play has time to dig us out of a pile of junk places and nonproductive habits.

We've become so conditioned to clutter's call that we look out for "things" often *before our own lives*. Once, years ago, native American and white men were working on a big reservoir construction project. One of the levels above where they were working had a flaw in it and about mid-day, when the water pressure mounted, the levee gate broke and a flash flood descended on the workers just a short way down the valley. Although all the workers were together in the same area, when the casualty report was finished, all the twenty-five white workers had drowned—and not one Indian.

"That's incredible," said the investigator. "How could that happen?"

One of the Indians had the answer: "When the dam broke and the big water came, we Indians saw, we ran for our lives, we reached high ground. The white man ran for his money, and he drowned."

Why wait until clutter has choked you to death before thrusting it off?

YOU KNOW YOU'RE A JUNKEE WHEN . . .

- Strangers say your house is "interesting."
- You send a search party into your basement—and they never return.
- You entertain dinner guests by showing them your odd sock collection.
- You'd like to change the channel—but you can't find the pliers.
- The Welcome Wagon comes and leaves you travel brochures.
- You dust off the picture of the President proudly hanging in your library—and it's Herbert Hoover!
- You have to tear yourself away from those little piles of sample squares outside carpet shops.
- You call an accumulation a collection.
- The fortune on the scales says, "Come alone next time."
- Throwing out an empty jar takes an enormous effort of the will.
- You have stacks of plant pots in the garage with mice nesting in them.
- Only *you* know what the tangled masses of rusted iron in the shed once were.
- You win an all-expense-paid trip to Hollywood and a date with a star—and you choose Sanford and Son.
- You've still got your 1961 Student Activity card in your wallet—right behind your Howdy Doody Club membership.
- The cat has a pile of plates of his own.
- You still have the aftershave your kids gave you last Christmas. And the one before. And the one before that. And you've kept the wrapping. And the ribbon.
- You set your handbag down to write out a check and passersby chuck trash into it.

39

CHAPTER 5

The Economy of Clutter

The well-known 80/20 rule of business says: If all of a given category of items are sorted in order of value, 80 percent of the value will come from only 20 percent of the items. Think about that in terms of clutter. Eighty percent of the space on our shelves (and in our mind) is occupied by stuff we never need. Eighty percent of our beauty and hygiene routine makes use of only 20 percent of the cosmetics and potions we have stacked around. (How much of the remaining 80 percent is junk?) Eighty percent of our family fun comes from 20 percent of the games and equipment and puzzles we've got jammed into our closets. (How much of the remaining 80 percent could be junked without it ever being missed?) Eighty percent of our reading enjoyment and information comes from 20 percent of the material in our bookcases and magazine racks. (How much of the unopened 80 percent would we ever miss?) Eighty percent of our home maintenance and upkeep is done with 20 percent of the accumulated paraphernalia in our cellars and garages. (How much of the remaining 80 percent is unnecessary clutter?) Eighty percent of the outfits we wear come from 20 percent of the clothes cramming our closets and drawers. (How much of the remaining 80 percent could Goodwill get more use from than we do?) Is this all just fancy business theory? Not on your life! If you got rid of the 80 percent that's clutter you'd be more than 20 percent more efficient.

Clutter Makes Every Job Take Longer

Clutter is one of the greatest enemies of efficiency and stealers of time—and that includes yours.

For every chore he tackles, the average person spends more time getting ready—hunting for a place, the tools, a reason to do it, etc.—than actually doing it. It takes only six seconds to drive a nail, often ten minutes to find the nails and hammer. But the nailing is all that counts and brings the benefit; the fumbling and finding doesn't. If a job is buried in junk we never get started—we just thrash.

I'm often asked, "How do you get so much done?" The answer is that I (and anyone else "successful") hit the ground in the morning running and doing, and plan so I don't get hung up hunting for information, tools, and help. There is a great frustration in having to (or waiting for someone else to) sort through piles of junk to get to the *action*. We end up unfulfilled and unsatisfied, bogged in the nonrewarding junk preliminaries.

Clutter makes every job harder and makes cleaning take forever. Any project we tackle, from building to disassembling, will be slowed, dampened, and diluted if we constantly have to fight our way to it in the midst of clutter. As a professional rug cleaner, paid by the square foot, I noticed that sometimes my crew would clean a large living room in one hour; sometimes the exact same size room and type of carpet took three or four hours. First I figured some workers were just plain slower than others—but closer scrutiny proved I was wrong. In the first house, for example, it took 15 minutes to move stuff, 45 to shampoo, and 15 to move the stuff back; in the second it took 1½ hours to move stuff, 45 minutes to shampoo, and 1½ hours to move the stuff back. There was so much stuff you could barely find the floors.

If junk is taking up your good storage room it means you have to reach further and dig deeper to get the tool, book, suitcase, shirt, etc., you need. "Getting something out," instead of being a few-second job, often ends up a twenty-minute search-and-rescue mission. I've watched bedlam occur in homes when $2.50 in change is needed to pay the paperboy or a roll of tape is needed to repair something. We can't progress when we spend all our time pausing and pawing to find the "good" in among all that clutter.

Take the stuffed shelves of the average kitchen pantry. You're making soup one day and decide to toss in a can of tomatoes. You have to rummage past the celery soup bought by mistake, the canned lotus root for the Indian dinner you've never gotten around to fixing, the aged pinto beans you ought to throw away, and the rum extract you use only at Christmas. You find a can of tomatoes and pitch them into the soup—whoops, they're the elegant plum tomatoes you were saving for sauce, not the grade Bs you wanted, but they're tomatoes. Later, putting the leftover soup away, you poke through the orphaned canisters, that incredible assortment of glass jars you've saved, and all that Tupperware, and finally find a whipped topping container that's just the right size. But where's the lid? You try lid after lid from the pile. None fit. You push the containers aside on the shelf thinking the lid must have rolled to the back—and you knock over a jar, which falls to the pantry floor, shattering and spraying shrapnel over half the kitchen. You now have to sweep or vacuum the whole kitchen and empty the whole bottom of the pantry (the toolbox, the garden sprayer, those flattened slippers and bags of rags, the fan, the space heater, the cat litter) to be sure you've eliminated all those deadly shards.

The junk in your pantry has just cost you an extra half hour in one day. An unnecessary half hour of shuffling clutter around every day adds up to an entire week each year. (And how many of us repeat this sad scenario in one form or another *more* than once a day? We have to dump out and claw through a shoebox or sewing-box full of unwinding spools to find the navy blue thread we need to put the blazer button back on, run an arm up into sixty pairs of wadded (washed or unwashed?) pantyhose to find three runless pairs to throw in the suitcase.)

*T*ime is part of your LIFE

43

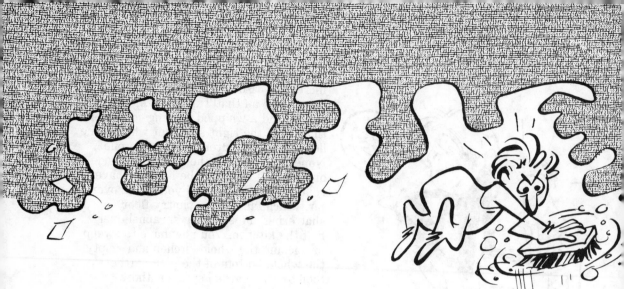

Clutter Makes Cleaning Take Longer

As a maintenance design consultant, I've become super-conscious of the tendency to clutter up even construction. We seem to take quality items (even beautiful, expensive building materials), then pile, I mean almost *cram*, them onto a structure—trying to give it life or looks or "atmosphere." While sitting in a lecture hall of a fine university, I took note of the fact that in the interior of that one room there were nine different types of material making up the walls: glass, wood, paneling, carpet, stainless steel, tile, paint, fabric wall covering, brick facing, and Formica—all fine materials. But to take care of all the variations in surface material and texture took an extra janitor and a cleaning cart the size of a foreign car (which skinned up the facilities as it moved around). Whenever we try to crowd in too much, we pay a toll in "taking care of"—and the bottom line is less time for living.

This goes back to the first value of de-junking: it creates simplicity. The amount of time saved by simplicity is phenomenal.

44

Don't Let Clutter Call the Tune

Have you noticed that as we grow older our time to do things is more condensed? At the age of ten we had all day to play, make a project, or get a chore done; at eighteen, only part of the day; at thirty, only hours; then, years later, we often have only minutes. We simply have so many more people, places, and things crowded into our lives that we *have* to condense or become more efficient if we intend to make good use of the little spare time we have.

I found this the case with my music. I get a lot of pleasure out of strumming and honking around with guitar and harmonica, so over the years, like the rest of you into any kind of music, I've collected lots of songbooks and sheet music. Like you, I often bought an entire songbook for the two or three songs I wanted inside and, of course, kept the entire score of that special once-in-a-lifetime performance. My shelves and drawers were bulging and the piano bench wouldn't close.

Recently I had fifteen minutes free to play a number or two, and attacked my music pile—it took ten minutes of sorting and digging to find "Blue Tail Fly," "Lara's Theme" from *Doctor Zhivago*, and "Aunt Rhody," so I ended up with only five minutes to play. I suddenly realized that 90 percent of my pile of music was never used—and it was actually keeping me from enjoying the 10 percent of it I loved.

The day I decided to de-junk my music was the day I began again to have time to use and enjoy it. I piled it all up in a giant heap and, in a few hours, pulled and ripped out all the music I really used and wanted and for $3 copied and bound it into a ring binder. When I went through my little mountain of music, I threw out all the ruined sheets, the songs I never liked and the ones I'd fallen out of love with, and songs like "Malaguena," which

*L*ESS IS MORE
Here's some simple math to prove it. Good Stuff + Clutter = Junk.

has chords and keys I couldn't play (and after keeping it around for twenty-nine years hoping to absorb it by osmosis, I finally was willing to admit I never would).

While I was at it, I took back the four hymnbooks I'd accidentally carried home from church, and cast off the choral music that called for 600 people to sing with me. I ended up with all my music in one neat file drawer.

Man, what a change—no more sorting and searching and thrashing—I use *all* the time now just to play.

Caring for It Costs

On a special contract assignment at a Sun Valley resort one year, my company furnished decorated Christmas trees to the guests. The company that provided this service the year before lost $5,000 on the job, because they hired carpenters and highly paid laborers to put up, adorn, and take down the trees.

Hoping to improve efficiency, we enlisted local college kids and bought the decorations and trees wholesale. When the holiday season was over, our crew picked up the trees, took off the lights and metal stands, and packed and stored them for the next year's use. When it was totaled up, we lost only $900—an improvement, but still a deficit.

Then we did some "de-junking" thinking, and the following year made over $2,000 clear profit with half the headaches. Our secret? We just followed the basic rule of de-cluttering economy: when the Christmas holiday was over, instead of picking the trees up, undecorating them, accounting for all stands, and sorting and packing, hauling the decorations to the storage warehouse, etc., we just pitched the trees—decorations and all—into the trash. The feeling of "waste" kept me awake for a while until I weighed it against the reality of the rewards. The savings on storage, light, heat, energy, fuel, and labor were far more than we paid for the decorations!

But these things are valuable, you say? What about the value of the life and time to store, to clean, to insure, to transport, to protect—what does that cost? More than money: "afford" is not simply a question of money, it's also an emotional and physical appraisal—what is the effect on your job, your physical being, your peace of mind? "Afford" is the capacity to absorb into your being, not your bank balance.

Have you ever talked to people who've lost all their physical possessions to flood or fire or hurricane? Have you noticed how rapidly they seem to adjust—and are often whistling, singing, and humming a few days later? If they lose their loved ones, their reputation, health, or position they often *never* recover. Yet the majority of their time and effort is spent acquiring, protecting, and caring for physical possessions instead of the loved ones. It doesn't make sense, does it?

The Value Is in the Using

Rich people, poor people—when it comes to junk, one is as bad as the other; one's junk may just be a little more expensive. Rich people are notorious collectors of things they always wanted when they were growing up. There are people who all their lives dream about the ranch or restaurant or yacht or whatever they want above all, and as their life nears its

No matter how you look at it, clutter takes your time.

end they finally accumulate the cash to have the big dream come true. Even if they can't use it much, they go buy it— thinking that the having is the ultimate. But it all comes to little because they can't smell and feel and share in the glory of production. The value is in the using and building and growing, not simply the *having*. They have to hire someone else to run the operation for them; they only get the woes and financial drain; maybe once a year they visit and look over their kingdom—it generally becomes just another piece of junk to them.

Deadbeat Junk: Doesn't Pay Its Way

Thinking about fire extinguishers and spare tires might cause us to ask: How often do you have to use something to justify owning it? What about those hand-thrown pottery apple bakers—is the annual meal of apples worth it? How about cherry pitters and melon ballers and butter molds, pasta machines, fondue assemblies, and cheesecake pans? That's a lot of stuff to shuffle, store, and maintain.

Don't be awed by ownership. "I own it" is a ridiculous statement to make about anything, when you think about it. *Use* is the only value a thing has. War, fire, flood, famine, robbery, or death can undo and devalue ownership instantly. Don't get too attached to "mine"—*my land, my house, my lake, my plane, my book* . . . might be my undoing.

Like you, I hate to rent, I'd rather not borrow, I like to own—but don't be too proud to change. People buy $700 worth of ski stuff to ski once a year, or a 30-foot ladder to reach the eaves of the house once every four or five years. In either case they could rent the right equipment and not only save money but the lugging, storing, selecting, insuring, and general complication of their lives. *Use* should be the deciding factor—and not just *will*, but *how often* will you use it. And do you really like (or need) what it will do for

you? Maybe you could just eliminate the activity or area it's "needed" for right out of your life.

Storing It Costs

Out of sight, out of mind might apply to lovers, but not to junk. We pay money and emotion for it, no matter where it is.

Storage—(or, more specifically, lack of it) is one of the most frequently asked questions in the "house care" world. There never seems to be enough. When you point out to the average American that they have on the average 50-75 cubic feet of storage per person they look at you perplexedly and say, "Well, then, what's wrong?" It never crosses our mind that it's what we have too much of—not too little of—that causes the problem.

*R*emember that storage costs money: Storage space rents for 10¢-13¢ a square foot (or as much as $10 a square foot, if you're using house space for storage). Clutter also serves as an enticement for burglary and fodder for accidents, *and it makes nice fuel for fires.*

Not only is up to 25 percent of our homes devoted to storage, but we have to seek ways and means beyond our own walls to store the overflow. And once we discover how easy it is to damage something by packing it too tightly or packing a heavy item atop it, we take the reverse approach and pack inefficiently, wasting the space we do have. But no matter *how* we store, we expand. We butt it under beds, under stairs, in wall units, in attics, basements, furnace

rooms, "spare" rooms, fill the garage and the garage attic with it, then migrate to the yard and get little sheds . . . they fill and then we head for the local rental unit.

I had a friend who bought a wrecked car for $25 to get $125 worth of parts, a smart move—but then he had to obtain a $30-a-month rental storage unit to stash it for a year until he got to it. And how smart would you say a person is who'll rent a $300-a-year storage unit to store $150 worth of junk? Millions do it. A "self-storage center" in a town of only 40,000 near me has 600 storage units, and there's a six-month waiting list.

Storage units are the ghost towns of clutter, a testimony of shame. Why do people store things in another place? Because *they aren't using them!*

If we could peer behind those sliding tin doors and into all those locked vaults and cubicles (and many of us junk voyeurs would like to), we'd be disappointed; we'd see all the same worn and broken-down stuff about to overflow our own home—they're simply ahead of us in the progression. Most of it is non- or never-again-used stuff. A rental unit is a kind of oversized Emotional Withdrawal box (see Chapter 16).

Storing is in most cases a hypocritical practice—when we decide to store it away in a rental unit, or Grandpa's old barn, or the extra room at home, we're usually acknowledging that we don't need it any more. It served well and enriched our life—but when that time of our life is past, we should release the old junk so we can have the freedom to greet a new season and grow again. Paying ransom in money, time, or emotion for bygone clutter is pathetic.

Most buildings and houses don't burn easily; it's the *contents*. Fire inspections always reveal burnable storage as the greatest hazard (you just can't win storing junk).

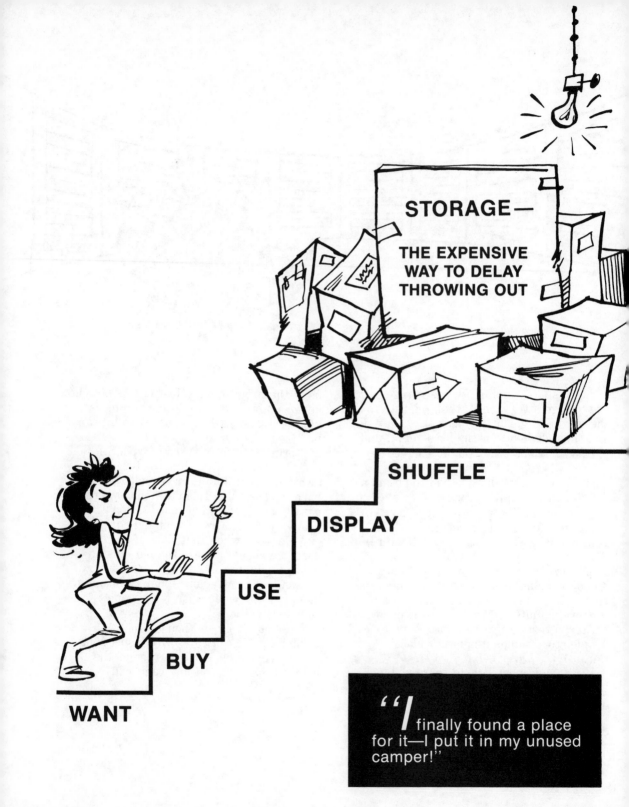

STORAGE—

THE EXPENSIVE
WAY TO DELAY
THROWING OUT

SHUFFLE

DISPLAY

USE

BUY

WANT

"I finally found a place for it—I put it in my unused camper!"

50

Guarding It Costs

If your junk is valuable enough that you're willing to take the time to move it and the money to store it, it may also be attractive to predators—both the two-legged and six-legged variety. And then you have to protect it.

You can either take the fortress approach—energy-eating floodlights, an intruder-eating Doberman, and an expensive sophisticated alarm system—or stash your smaller valuables in those costly and inconvenient little safe-deposit boxes—or cold storage. No matter how you choose to guard the mink, the emeralds, the home computer, or your super-good sound system, it takes time, money, and mental effort. And of course, it all has to be insured.

Insurance is simple, you say? Just pay the premium. However, other "premiums" are paid, in the case, for example, of elaborate alarm systems. I've been in homes where the anti-burglar devices are so complicated it's hard for the owner to get out unshackled (let's not even discuss the complexities of getting in). And every night the alarms have to be set, just before the four hours of sleep you might

get before the cops roust you out to check out the false alarm.

Only you can decide whether it's worth it to de-mothball and re-mothball your wool opera cape every time you wear it, or to remember to switch off the car's burglar alarm before the parking lot guard comes at you with handcuffs, or to pick up your great-aunt Wilma's sterling from the bank every Thanksgiving and take it back the Monday after. But you at least ought to *think* about whether it's worth it—instead of automatically going to all that trouble.

Moving It Costs

The average American moves fourteen times in a lifetime. If a third of your stuff is clutter, you could save eight moving van loads if you de-junked! People spend literally millions moving junk.

A couple of my acquaintance, promoted to a new assignment, was amazed at the boxes they had to put away after the van unloaded and pulled away. Three of the first eleven boxes were boxes of trash and garbage to be thrown in the alley, but the movers, apparently unable to see much difference, had packed and

The Evolution of Moving

B.C. (Before Clutter)   **1720s**   **1820s**

1920s   **1940s**

1960s

Today

transported them across the entire U.S.

We all haul junk around at great expense and effort—at moving time, not to mention all that moving of things from room to room, to and from all our storage areas, our briefcases, and even pockets!

It's an unnecessary load; dump it before you move on—it's a lot easier to cope with *before* than after. You'll *never* have the time to "go back through."

All our stuff-shuffling even has a (loony) life cycle of its own:

People with apartments collect and store tons of extra things they don't need in preparation for the time "when they get a house." Finally, after suffering years of crowded inconvenience, they *get* a house and spread stuff all over to fill it up—just in time to retire and move back into an apartment, and there is all that stuff that must be disposed of. Is the short span worth it? Think ahead when you're gathering (and saving) "treasures!"

Any move—to college, camp, a new job, a new home—is a trauma in itself, but add 4,000 pounds of excess to the transition and it's a nightmare. If you have any hint you're going to move, de-junk three months prior and you'll bless yourself for it.

Even Owning It Costs

If we really hated taxes, we wouldn't be junkers. All that extra that we don't really need doesn't just slip by uncounted. I had a few office machines, some scaffolding, some old worthless desks, some extra property, and old lawn equipment not being used, just sitting around, fully paid for, so it seemed to be harmless, not costing me anything. WRONG. Taxes don't retire when you retire clutter. I received my tax bill and a list of the taxable items—there was lots of junk on that list! I was shocked to discover that "extras" aren't only a pain to look at, shift around, and protect, but I have to pay for them, not once, but year after year after year, until I get rid of them. Great de-junking incentive, eh?

Tragedy . . . Clutter's Ultimate Cost

Beholding the fresh beauty of a baby or small child can affect most of us more than any other experience. And so no matter what state of exhilaration I might be in, when I read or hear of a tiny boy or girl being drowned, run over, or hurt, I'm upset for days; I find it almost unbearable when such a needless tragedy occurs to a friend or family. The hours following these happenings often kindle anger when the cause of the loss is known: hundreds of cheerful playing children smother to death each year in carelessly discarded junk appliances and containers; thousands die painfully from old poisons and cleaners piled in junk stacks: thousands die in fires from non-used flammables, carelessly stored solvents and fuels, or from negligent smoking habits. Junk!

When you hear of a death or serious injury, notice how often it results from some kind of junk we were too lazy or too sentimental to get rid of. Junk on vacant lots and in storage yards takes a heavy toll. Many an adult is laid low by clutter in the home: What did they stumble over, what was on the stairs? What did they try to lift? What did they bump into? Too many times it's clutter. Many a car accident happens because of objects in cars that impede or distract the operator—junk!

A medical lecturer told me once that over half the illnesses in the United States are mentally or emotionally induced—have nothing to do at first with physical impairment. If you were a betting person, what percentage of that half would you say was caused by worry and stress over junk—or a junk habit? If clutter doesn't inflict some physical damage on you, it'll take its toll of your psyche—you can count on it.

No Matter How You Look At It, Clutter Is A Poor Investment

It's a poor investment indeed when we put so much of our life and our money into compiling a collection of treasures that suddenly it begins to dictate our schedule and make our decisions. We can't or don't dare leave it for a trip. We yell at the kids whenever they get near it, worry about the babysitter or our mother-in-law somehow messing it up.

When we find ourselves in this situation we have two choices:

1. Spend more money and time (life!) to earn more so we can protect and keep our junk.

2. Have less junk to maintain.

A profit and loss statement is basic accounting. Figure a balance sheet before you invest in more junk.

Item: Genuine handmade Laplander doll dressed in real reindeer hide

ASSETS

1. Cute souvenir to prove we've been to Lapland.
2. People back home could see what real reindeer hide looks and feels like.
3. Has genuine hand-painted narwhal ivory eyes.
4. Grandkids would think it's cute.

LIABILITIES

1. Who needs proof we've been to Lapland?
2. I'll have to protect it from moths and silverfish.
3. Would cost me $65 plus duty.
4. Too expensive for the grandkids to play with.
5. Doesn't fit in with my decor at home.
6. Where would I put it?
7. Would be hard to keep dusted and clean.

(Conclusion: If I really think it's that cute, take a snapshot or slide of it for less than a buck, save $65 plus duty, and still have proof to show people back home, if I need it.)

Item: Red silk blouse with electric blue flowers

ASSETS

1. It's on *sale*—I'd save 30 percent.
2. Silk blouses are really in right now.
3. It's my size.
4. It's got a designer neck label.

LIABILITIES

1. I don't have anything to wear it with. It would cost me more than the 30 percent I'd save to buy something to wear with it.
2. I'll have to be super-careful washing it—or dry clean it.
3. Puffy-sleeved blouses don't do much for me.
4. Who's going to see the neck label?
5. I like red, but I don't really care that much for the electric blue flowers.
6. I've got sixteen blouses already.

(Conclusion: Take the 30 percent I would have saved, and save it until I find something I *really* like—then I'll probably be able to afford it!)

Item: Night out on the town

ASSETS

1. They have a great floor show.
2. I can mention that I went there. It will make me sound like a swinger.
3. I can drink away a few pressures.

LIABILITIES

1. The whole thing cost me $131.50.
2. I can't remember how much fun they told me I had.
3. I've got a terrible hangover.
4. I lost my leather gloves.
5. I don't remember having that scrape on the right front fender.
6. I insulted my friend.
7. I have to apologize to the boss for a bad joke.

TOTAL...................... ———   TOTAL .... ———

Make a ledger sheet on some of your junk. If the liabilities outweigh the assets (be honest), it's time to de-junk.

Age—Don't Fight It

If old Ponce de Leon had truly found a fountain of youth, many of us would enthusiastically immerse some of our clutter before ourselves. Aging is a natural life process in ourselves *and* in the things we use—accept it! We junk up our quality of living by trying to retard aging, cosmetically or otherwise. When an era, an item, a vehicle, a system grows old, let it go. We can't stop aging, but we can start new things and grow and enjoy again instead of letting dying junk take some of our strength with it.

Time after time I've watched an ancient backyard tree start to wither away. The owner goes crazy vaccinating it, wiring it, propping it, performing limb surgery on it. The twisted stump still sprouts a single leaf-yielding limb, so restorative repairs are continued. All for what? It's unsightly, costs a terrible amount of time and money, and gives no benefit in looks or shade.

Had the owner dug it up, used it for a cheerful Christmas fire, and planted a new tree, he would have been stirring some new growth in his own life, too. Metal, mortar, wood, glass, places all get old in time and change is needed. Don't cling—you'll be cluttered if you do!

We've been taught we're bad if we waste—"waste not, want not." But we waste more valuable time and energy working over and trying to save worthless junk than many an object was ever worth originally.

Why spend (waste) an afternoon (or a week) restoring and finishing a slivering old wicker chair that you never *have* used and never will? Or get a hernia moving a 250-pound roll of worn-out carpet we're saving for some place that hasn't popped into our mind yet? Why spend three hours every couple of months reapplying naval jelly and porcelain patch to an ancient sink that's going to keep rusting no matter what?

Like you, I'd never think of throwing away anything I like that's still good. But why not be a little more realistic about the almost-gone gizmos? We often foolishly risk our financial (and physical) necks trying to squeeze 5 percent more use out of an item that has served its honorable time.

One summer a surge to save $5 cost me over $400. There was a worn tire on the back of our Trans Van: it had served long and well, but on examining it before a trip to San Francisco, I had to see if I could squeeze 2,000 more miles out of it. In the middle of the loneliest stretch of Nevada desert it gave up its life, causing the other (good) dual to go. Then there was the $175 tow to the Desert Automotive Service and the cost of two tires at premium price, not to mention the six hours lost and the accident involving my family that I had risked.

"I'll Fix It!"

About 2 percent of broken junk is ever fixed. Mass-produced molded or stamped objects of this era are difficult to repair. (Forget the miracle glue ads, because few things will stick together as permanently as your fingers.) Few people have the time or facilities to fix things, and most of us don't like to use or display patched stuff anyway. Do you or your kids wear fixed clothes? Rarely! Do you know how many heels broken off high-heeled shoes are waiting somewhere to be fixed? Well, they can't, and won't be.

Most things wear out first, then break or cease to operate—but a few things *do* break while they are in the prime of life, and it's uneconomical to "bury" them. They can and should be fixed, and the act of fixing them can contribute triumphantly to your emotional well-being. But don't try to get this elative creative charge tinkering on undeserving gizmos.

While in New York once my wife and I were roving downtown streets when a

"Fix-It" Tally Sheet

Answer honestly—how many of these broken items have you fixed lately?

- [ ] shredded cassette tapes
- [ ] hair dryers/hot combs
- [ ] pot or pan handles
- [ ] broken chains
- [ ] torn upholstery
- [ ] toasters or waffle irons that burn
- [ ] leaky teapots
- [ ] Christmas tree lights that don't
- [ ] chaise longues with rotted webbing
- [ ] dead flashlights
- [ ] loose-headed hammers
- [ ] defective clocks/watches
- [ ] inaccurate thermometers
- [ ] broken strollers
- [ ] socks or sweaters with a hole in them
- [ ] umbrellas with one cracked rib

- [ ] sprung scissors
- [ ] sagging screens
- [ ] shaky card tables
- [ ] ruined electrical cords
- [ ] frozen lawn mowers
- [ ] TV with a bad tube
- [ ] eyeglasses with broken frames
- [ ] broken mobiles
- [ ] dismantled lamps
- [ ] chipped teacups
- [ ] broken antennas
- [ ] broken zippers
- [ ] dismembered dolls
- [ ] injured musical instruments
- [ ] cracked dishes
- [ ] unstrung rackets
- [ ] suitcases that won't latch
- [ ] wobbly chair legs/arms

IF YOUR SCORE WAS:

15-34 You must own a repair shop.
10-15 You must be part Scottish.
5-10   Your TV must be broken.
2-5   You deserve applause.
0-1   You're normal (and honest).

Now de-junk the other items and sigh a great sigh of relief.

guy jumped out of an alley, flipped open his coat, and gave us a "want to buy a (hot) digital watch" pitch. Wanting a real "con" experience, we bought two, mainly as conversation pieces. They were cheapos, but what the heck, a bargain! We gave one to our son and one to our son-in-law. In a few months, my son's flickered into timelessness and with no regrets he chucked it. But our son-in-law's was a brute— he managed a concrete/brick plant, worked as a mechanic, welder, loader, and that watch ran and ran. It told better time than my or my wife's expensive quartz models. He beat it, jarred it, drowned it, but it ran and ran, keeping absolutely perfect time. We all began building a certain loyalty and respect for that watch—it's still running today, two years later. But I know someday soon it will twitch and quit. And when it does, do you think we're going to chuck it? Not on your life. Amazing how we forge a relationship to a thing; we actually think we owe it something— surgery, even a life-support system if necessary.

We don't owe it and you don't owe it anything. It isn't worth fixing; don't let love affairs with things junk up your life. They have a way of ticking their way into your heart, but be objective: if fixing isn't worth it, dump it (without a wake or mourning).

Give Broken Things a Break—Make Fixing Easy (Accessible!)

The biggest reason fixable things never get fixed isn't lack of mechanical ability, time, or even industriousness. It's lack of *availability*. For example, I find a split in the seam inside my suit jacket. I know my wife can fix it in seconds, but it never gets fixed, and every time I wear it I get irritated because she hasn't performed her seamstress act on it. Of course, each time I wear the jacket I hang it in the closet; how could she know the bad seam is there? She can't— she's no mind reader!

The kitchen towel drawer sticks and is miserable to open and close—the rollers need adjusting. Every time my wife opens the drawer she's irritated with me for not doing my mechanical fixing number. I never use the drawer, I never know—so I never fix it! My coat gradually rips and ruins (it's her neglectful fault, of course). The drawer deteriorates from kicking, beating, and prying—that's my fault!

Nonfixing is generally caused by such lack of awareness and refusal to surrender the item in question out of activity. So set up a Fix-It box—

throw your genuinely fixable items in, and you'll be amazed how sensitive everyone at home, work, etc., will become. The box will be the perfect cure for "broken communication." Things *will* get fixed, and the backlog of repairables will be a great "what-to-do-in-spare-time" provider and inducement to industry for everyone. Try it—you'll fix it!

Twelve Hands Are Better Than Two

When I was on the "People Are Talking" show in Philadelphia last spring, to demonstrate the cost of clutter/litter I handed six members of the audience each a slice of bread, and had them tear the bread in pieces and throw it on the floor in front of them. Then, with one TV camera on the clock and one on the host, I had him pick up everyone's discarded bread as fast as he could. It took 25 seconds. I then gave each of the same people another slice and had them tear up and throw down the bread again. But this time I had each one who threw the bread pick up his own mess—or in essence, take care of his own clutter. It took *less than 5 seconds*.

But the art of comparison is often our enemy—just because 5 seconds is less than 25 doesn't mean it's smart to handle junk at all. Less clutter-handling is better but *no* clutter-handling is best. No junk is efficient or economical to care for, because it uses up time, energy, and emotion—in other words, *life*.

The picking up of *other* people's junk (as in the example above) is the most inefficient and expensive clutter cost of all—like the mother who spends all her time picking up after a cluttering husband and careless kids. Women all over the world are wasting their youth and high spirits and creativity playing janitor to their families. If your family habitually leaves clutter around they're going to keep doing it—are you going to keep picking up? Do you think tolerating that kind of thoughtlessness in them is really doing them a favor? Have a house meeting and put everyone over two years old on notice—hubby included—that mess is picked up/cleaned up by whoever makes it. They'll be better people for it!

Littering

At 7:00 one fresh spring morning I was standing in front of one of America's most stately hotels. The place was immaculate—the brass outside polished, the flower beds manicured, the mats "living room" clean. Then the litterer arrived. He walked through the door and stood waiting to be picked up. After he flipped his mangled toothpick in the flowers, he ripped open a pack of cigarettes—dropping the cellophane at his feet and following it with one, two, three cigarette butts. He blew tar stains on the glass, dropped ashes and gum wrappers in the flower bed, and clipped his fingernails on the carpet before someone finally hauled him away.

You might try to classify litterers as mild, medium, or chronic, but maybe they should fall under one classification—*slob*. Harsh, perhaps, but litter results are harsh, too. The litterer is an inconsiderate clutter strewer who thinks nothing of harming his fellow humans or the environment.

In many buildings more is spent to clean and police the cigarette butts, bottle caps, gum, etc., out of the entranceway and exterior than to maintain all of the landscaping outside. *Clutter—our own or others'—doesn't come cheap in our lives; we pay for it.* I don't want to be guilty of foisting my junk on others, do you?

Any residue we leave in life should be contained. If we are old enough to mess up, we are old enough to pick up after ourselves.

Nothing exists in and of itself. Everything has a cost to acquire and to maintain. And *all* the costs of clutter add up to one mighty bad investment.

CHAPTER 6

Home Sweet Home . . .

(Full of Junk!)

Do you need a double garage . . . maybe a triple? . . . or a commitment to de-clutter?

While cleaning a large, plush home during my junior year in college, I managed to wade through and clean a luxurious, treasure-laden bedroom and embarked on cleaning the closet. In addition to the expected arsenal of pricey wearing apparel, I had to move five exquisite cigarette lighters, forty-seven pairs of women's shoes (I kid you not), a case of 1920s *National Geographics*, several tennis racquets, fourteen boxes of Christmas cards, a side-saddle, six poodle collars, and numerous other items. It was a neat but completely stuffed closet, in harmony with the style of the woman who lived there. She was fifty-five years old, and possessed a handsome home filled with elaborate art and delicate tapestries, carved furniture and exotic lamps that she had spent part of her life collecting and the rest of her life cleaning and dusting and keeping track of. This project of shuffling treasures around had taken

her over half a lifetime; she had been committing junkicide for thirty-five years.

Sound a little like someone you know? Well, I can beat that. Some friends of mine helped a family move into a new home. They piled all their stuff in several downstairs rooms, lived there a while, and like most of us, never got through all the junk they dragged with them. They decided to have a fireplace put in the family room downstairs and called a local mason. When they gave him the address he thought a minute and said, "I put a fireplace in there two years ago." They ran downstairs, moved the junk, and there it was—a fireplace!

Another friend told me his mother was a "collector." Since her health was no longer robust, she had to move from her home of fifty years to an apartment. When her son and a helper went to move her belongings (she'd told them to only bother with the good stuff), they backed a 16-foot-long, 4-foot deep, 2½-ton grain truck up to the side of the house and started in the attic. They filled the truck to level, then heaping—and were still on the upstairs. The son, an avid junk collector himself, only managed to salvage a couple of boxes of "good stuff" for his mom and one small box for himself; the rest was pure, unadulterated clutter. The woman never missed the three truckloads her son took to the dump, and found her de-junked life a happy one.

I'm sure we could fill several books with this kind of junk story, and that you could add a few fascinating chapters of your own (about your friends and relatives and they about you).

Most of us are in the same (junked) condition as the owner of forty-seven pairs of shoes. We can find our fireplace, but not our matches, and our junk could strain a semi instead of a grain truck. Our house treasures may not be as expensive, but we have as many cubbyholes for them—that we shuffle through, sort and re-sort, climb over, worry about, and maintain for hours on end.

Not only can we not take it with us when that final departure date arrives, but keeping it with us under the same roof is creating more conflict than we imagine. We really can't win with clutter. Sooner or later we're sick of it, tired of being a slave to it. It doesn't matter if it's valuable or not: if it's unused, in the way, and takes emotional and mental energy away from us, we feel guilty about it—in fact, deep in our heart, we hate it. Every time we come home from the shopping mall with more pictures, trinkets, and goodies for the walls, shelves, drawers, and sideboards, we're more frustrated

*T*he difference between man's junk and woman's junk: he builds a $3,000 shop around his and calls it "tools."

because there's no place to put anything. We're tormented by the thought that we may have to throw out some old junk so there will be room for the new—in a house that already looks like a department store or a rummage sale. There are rarities hanging all over, we want to show everything off—but are, as of late, having difficulty getting through the house, not only to check on things and clean but just to stroll. We hesitate to de-junk that house; we want to be able to wander through to show off our treasures—maybe even build a museum and charge for it. But sad to say, few people are interested in our holdings. We toil to accumulate things that will impress others, but when it comes to house junk, nice or elaborate, little kids don't care, teenagers think our obsession with inanimate objects is obscene, rich friends hate us for our cheap junk, poor friends hate us for rich junk, medium friends think we're showing off because our junk matches theirs. The truth is all of these—plus the fact that the house is using *us* instead of our using and enjoying *it*.

Clutter Is Alarming, Not Charming

Most junk is overkill; that's exactly what makes it junk. I read in the *Wall Street Journal* about some people outfitting their bathrooms to "flush plush," spending millions of dollars on gold-plated faucets and other elaborate accessories:

mother-of-pearl sink stoppers, heated towel racks, and mink toilet seats. Around the same time, I saw an article in a family home magazine, titled "Put Charm in Your Bathroom." It took a nice functional easy-to-clean bathroom and added ungodly apparatus to every surface and fixture—wall hangings, inlaid shelves, decorative cabinets, elaborate lights and accessories that made it a grotesque spectacle as well as a nightmare to clean.

It's hard to do much living in a living room these days. There's so much stuff on the end tables, coffee tables, bookcases, and magazine racks that a rail has to be installed so none of it will fall off. Lamps are lucky to find a place to roost these days and even spots to *sit* are at a premium. The floor, too, is taken up with ceramic wolfhounds, ivy-planted spittoons, and colonial cat doorstops tailor-made for tripping over. Aside from it being difficult to move around in, it's tough to dust and vacuum and straighten up a cluttered living room—and that's the room we always want to look nice for company.

We do much the same thing with clothes, jewelry, food, automobiles—often until the clutter almost totally obscures function, i.e., the doorlatch to the bathroom is so fancy, we can't figure out how to get in.

A workshop is a place to work, relax, create, and fix. A kitchen is a place to conveniently cook. Look at what we have done and are doing to both these areas. Kitchens are getting so overdesigned with accessories, decorations, gadgets, and "storage" that we're afraid to cook in them because we'll mess them up, or they'll take too long to clean afterward.

Every other issue of the home

magazines has an article on "beautifying your kitchen": the pictures show a room rife with aspic molds and giant stirring spoons, and so many colors and textures it looks like the inside of an Easter basket. There are enough ovens and cooking apparatus to feed a whole barracks of soldiers. There are racks, holders, clamps, and even art objects so thick on the walls and shelves that the average person would do $50 worth of damage just trying to have a bowl of cornflakes. Too much is junk. Don't let those who don't *use* kitchens talk you into one of these gorgeous galleys of gimmicks and gadgets. It will only clutter and complicate your life.

A hammer, saw, and bench was a workshop when we started out and we actually produced. Now we spend most of our time mounting and storing all our new progressive tools and producing nothing. Did you know the average guy with a workshop buys his shelves premade?

There's a Little Pack Rat in All of Us

As a little fellow, I remember helping install a freezer on the back porch of our farmhouse. A floorboard was lifted up— and Mom uttered a shriek and took to higher ground, mumbling something about a "rat's nest." I peered into the gap where the floorboard had been and there was an intriguing sight—a total inventory of all the items we'd lost, cushioned in cotton, rags, and a little straw. To me it looked just like my hobby drawer (or one of my aunts' sewing boxes). "Stay away from there," my mom yelled, "it's a pack rat's den!" She then explained that the "no-good rat" scurries around and picks up things and takes them to his home and stuffs them in every available spot, then curls up in the middle and lives there. He has no reason to take the stuff—doesn't use it or even know what it is—but just

can't stand not to have it. That didn't sound too strange to me. I'd watched my parents, uncles, aunts, friends, and teachers doing the very same thing for a long time.

Every one of us has pack rat inclinations and expresses them by stashing clutter in unviewable areas (attics, cellars, closets, under the beds, under the eaves and rafters, by the footings, under the steps). Look in, around, and under your house and in your private nesting areas. I'll bet if you sprinkled a little cotton, rags, and grass on it, pack rats would want to hold a convention there. Get rid of the junk and clutter before someone lifts *your* board and shrieks.

It's not enough to de-junk the visible eyesores—"out of sight, out of mind" doesn't apply here. Your hidden "rat's nest" will clutter your mind as well as your premises. A life spent collecting and storing debris you don't need (regardless of its value) is a waste of time. *Only a rat would do it!*

Room Spells Doom

Too often we judge our capacity to own by the room we have available, not our actual need. Did you know that the average American dwelling has at least forty drawers, twenty-four cupboards, six closets, three bookshelves, two medicine cabinets, and one file cabinet? Some homes have more than a hundred places deliberately designed to harbor junk (mine has over three hundred!). Now add to that the additional possibilities of a pantry, assorted knickknack and curio shelves, various nooks and crannies, an attic and/or basement (with all the attendant boxes and trunks), a garage, a rental unit, a friend's (or relative's) spare room, and you're looking at well over 150 places!

With over a hundred junk hangouts, is it any wonder we get migraines just finding something or when we think about cupboard-cleaning day, or getting ready to invite guests?

The amount of room or places available in your home for "stuff" can have either a disciplinary or a devastating effect on you. If you start thinking it's wasteful to leave space unfilled, you're dead. Wide open spaces are American! Walls don't have to be peppered with pictures, attics don't have to be insulated with magazines and old clothes. Basements don't have to resemble clutter-aging cellars. Just because a shelf exists doesn't mean that it has to be filled; ripping it down or leaving it stark and simple are choices, too. Drawers are for the convenience of keeping active everyday usables out of sight and unsoiled by dust—they aren't archival vaults for junk. Room is reasonable and relaxing. When you clutter your closets and drawers with things, you're cluttering your feelings and thinking—freedom in your dwelling allows freedom to dwell in *you*.

*T*he "junk room" is an accepted, even honorable, convention in our society— like the fruit cellar, the guest room, or the recreation room. Are you surrendering a full quarter, fifth, or even tenth of your hard-won home space to an idle collection of clutter? The true name for your junk room or area is "The Indecision Room."

You Can't Stow Home Again

Many of us not only have our homes and bins and carports filled but have junk out to pasture yet farther afield. We have a boat in our brother-in-law's yard, a snowmobile in the shed out at Grandpa's. And the most convenient place of all (once the junk stashes under our own roof are exhausted) is the parents' house! I've had many a conversation with people who, when their possessions are being reviewed, will say enthusiastically, "Boy,

you haven't seen anything yet. I have more stored at my parents'!"

Only a low-down cur would inflict clutter on his or her parents. When you leave home it's only moral, decent, and merciful to extract your junk. Parents have enough of their own; how can you put them in a position of gate-keeping— guarding yours too? You may choose to inflict clutter on yourself for various reasons, but forcing, because of bloodlines, your trash on someone else (who feels *obliged* to store it) is unforgivable. Go get it *right now*—they need the room!

De-Junk or Perish

With all that we have to worry about in our busy lives, it's not necessarily our fault that things accumulate so fast (and in so many places!). But rationalizing worthlessness after we discover it *is* our fault. Most of us will go to all kinds of creative measures in order to avoid that inevitable showdown with our home junk.

We'll go so far as to:
- buy and build accessory storage sheds
- claim that "We're just getting that room ready to repaint"
- wait till after dark to put the car in the garage
- train our children to decoy company away from the entry closet while we hang up their coats
- threaten bodily harm to anyone who opens a drawer in front of company
- hang an "Out of Order" sign on the bathroom whenever the Avon lady comes
- claim that our basement is the drop-off point for the local charity drive
- and so on, and so on

But, as you know, this mad deception can go on only so long (maybe five or ten years). Eventually we all must come to the same point—de-junk or perish!

Free Yourself from Household Imprisonment

One woman, never able to get all her cleaning done, had to move—but not to a permanent place at first, so she packed all the family's belongings in boxes and sealed them, holding out just what they needed to use. They stayed at different spots from month to month, leaving the sealed boxes in the basement, and strangely enough, the packed-up belongings never were missed. And the woman noticed that by some miracle she had a clean house. At last! It had been the clutter that broke her back. Her case of junkitis was dormant in the basement; she was temporarily cured.

Think about the storage problem in your home: a lot of the stuff you're storing is useless; it's a constant source of worry. Much of it is unsafe, outdated, and ugly, so why keep it? Why spend a valuable part of yourself polishing, washing, dusting, and thinking about it? *You can't afford clutter.* It will rob you physically, emotionally, and spiritually. Freeing yourself from junk will automatically free you from housework (and it won't take any soap and water either). If you'll just de-junk your home, you'll have the time to take that course, write that book, run that marathon, or make that visit.

It's unbelievable the effort some people go to to have an immaculate germ-free house when even platoons of germs and layers of dirt can't hurt the quality of our life like clutter can. A germ might give us a sniffle or two, but junk around the house can create a monster in our basement that will dissipate our energy, thwart our values, misdirect our emotions, and steal our money.

"Well, you've got to be able to live," claim most junkees whenever their beloved clutter is questioned or threatened by a mate, a friend (or this book). But *live*—in the sense of the things that you most enjoy, that most turn you on—is exactly what junk prevents you from doing.

The big question is whether it is *active* or *inactive*. Even an unsightly pile of stuff is not junk if it's stimulating some personal or group improvement. I've seen fathers who never teach their sons to build anything because they don't want any sawdust around the house or to dull up any of the tools. I've seen mothers who wouldn't teach their daughters to sew because the patterns and the snippings would be clutter. Not so! It's not making a mess—but leaving one and living with it forever that is harmful. "Growth projects," such as finishing a room or remodeling, create temporary junk or mess, but it's going to a good end.

The unfinished house is exciting: it's a living lesson and visual aid. The family learns to do without, build, appreciate— which they never would in a fully finished house and grounds. The clutter of construction is something positive and is not junk.

Too Much Is Junk . . . So Is Too Nice

Something that is "too nice to use" is undoubtedly about the most ridiculous kind of junk one can own. Yet our homes in America are crammed with "too good to use" things, or things put up until later because they are too nice to use at this time in our lives or in *this* house. I knew a woman who had a living room she was saving for the Queen's or President's visit; her kids were only allowed in there if their shoes were off and their Sunday clothes on. It held an array of beautiful furnishings, of which the crowning feature was the plush velvet chairs and couch. The problem was, every time someone visited and sat in those chairs or on the couch, a big fat imprint would be left, so vivid one could tell exactly where Uncle Jim, little Heidi, or cousin Donna had sat. The minute the company left, the woman had to get a pan of water and a little brush and brush all of these prints out and stand the nap up so her room would look good again. Can you imagine spending your valuable time and life getting out *rump prints?*

You can't? Well, before any of us get too self-righteous on this matter, let's sit down and take a little inventory of the things we have now that are put up, hidden, stored, still in the box, etc.— because they're "too good to use." Austere as I like to think of myself, I notice I have a couple of expensive (gift) wallets stored in my drawer that I push aside every day to get to my socks and hankies. I've had them for years: my old calfskin wallet seems to last forever, and besides, if I did use them, I'd get paint on them, get them wet, or nick them with my putty chisel. I've also got a sweater I'm hoarding to wear when I'm an old retired author. I'll probably end up retiring to Tahiti; meanwhile, it's in the way every day of present living.

You'll be surprised how many "too good to use" things you have—lots of it is clutter! Use it or lose it.

Racked, Stacked, Packed Away

On a beautiful fall afternoon, a fourteen-year-old neighbor boy spotted me home from a European trip and walked half a mile across the meadow to visit. We worked together a while, and since the last of my six children had recently left the nest, he was a welcome and refreshing experience (plus I was getting some great project help out of him). "I can stay until Grandma comes," he told

me. "Do you have a pair of binoculars I could use to watch for her?" I have two pair but . . . you guessed it, they were so well packed and hidden away I didn't use them—and in fact, until he reminded me, I'd forgotten I had them. I dug them out and they made a much longer visit possible.

After he left, I stood with the binoculars looking out over the beautiful valley and marsh dotted with cattle and migratory geese, muskrats scurrying down the creek banks. I took the first real look in a long time at the craggy snow-capped peaks fingering down into rugged ravines, the ancient eroded lava flow bristling with stubby junipers, the old abandoned narrow-gauge railbed and the overgrown traces of the storied Oregon trail. . . . I'd been missing lots. One very good reason to de-clutter is to allow you to find and use all that "good stuff" you've almost forgotten you have.

I Know I Have It Here . . . Somewhere

You know you have it: Is it in the pantry cupboard, or the hall closet, or . . .? How embarrassing to have so much clutter you don't even remember where it all is! Having extra vacuum cleaner bags, spare fuses, candles, a cake decorating set, a chimney cleaner, a hiking compass has no merit when you can't find them. When you don't know where something is, you'll dig like a hungry dog for a bone trying to unearth it and tear up every storage area in the whole house.

Having useful or even valuable things and not being able to find them is no better than not having them! Basically, de-cluttering your home involves getting rid of the things you don't use, that you don't enjoy, that aren't necessary. This leaves plenty of room for the things you really need, because *where* you put the things that will be used is important.

Make sure you have a place to put everything you really do use that's close to where you use it. That's why most of us keep toothpaste in the bathroom or the spice rack over the kitchen counter. But we don't always carry out this principle in the way we arrange our drawers, closets, and other storage areas.

Think about the way you live and the things you use most often; this is the stuff that should go at the front of drawers or on the most accessible shelves. (You can also use this principle to encourage good habits—maybe the dental floss should go right out on the vanity.)

Refills should be stored as near as possible to where you'll run out. Remember not to pack objects in so tightly that you can't shut the drawer again unless everything is just so; you should be able to reach into a cupboard or drawer and grab a commonly used item without disarranging everything else. And while you're at it, set up a loose classification system to help you remember where things are—medicines at the top of the bathroom cabinet, for instance, toiletries at the bottom.

Converting Clutter by Relocating It

Some things we like and use are clutter only because of where they're located. We had some of the best fruits and fresh potatoes and carrots and all sorts of good things from our farm. However, they were in the root cellar, fifty yards across the snow and ice from our kitchen. That fifty yards caused lots of good food to rot, because when we wanted something it meant coats, hats, boots, and shoveling the snow off the cellar door. Most of the time we decided we didn't want it that bad and so didn't go. Had they been in the next room, we would have consumed and enjoyed them all.

Another such case for me was my safety goggles. I kept them in my briefcase (to be ready for consulting jobs) or in my toolbox. Trouble was, whenever I worked with metal or my big electrical grinders, the goggles weren't there. They were junk to me simply because I wasn't using them. A piece of steel finally got me in the eye, and so I hung the goggles right on the side of the grinder—so simple but I hadn't thought of it before.

We all have lots of good things that are junk simply because we haven't located them for easy use. What good is a pocket knife in the top dresser drawer? Why do we put towels in the hall closet—why not in the bathroom? Most of us end up using one towel to death while a dozen sit unused in the hall closet . . . why? . . . location. Where is your flashlight right now? I bet if the main breaker blew in the basement, a real search would begin in the dark. The flashlight (at least one) should be by the breaker box. Your umbrella: how many of the people you see wilting in the rain have umbrellas at home—almost all of them! Why are those people getting wet? They couldn't find an umbrella, or it was on a top shelf in an upstairs room—not worth the effort to retrieve. Fly swatters, too, are a piece of junk if they aren't handy when the pesky fly appears. Garbage cans are worthless if they're too far from the source of the garbage. When you can't find, can't reach, or it's too unhandy to use, what good is it? And much clutter comes from things that are too inconvenient to return or replace.

Do me and yourself a favor. When going through your junk and all that good stuff you buy and never use, ask the big question about location. You'll be surprised at what you can activate and not have to store or throw away. I don't need to outline the exact process for you because your places and purposes are different from mine. It will be easy.

Do You Really Need More Than One?

Of some items it seems logical to own more than one: these are usually little things that contribute to big important end results, like a measuring tape. I own at least eight of these wonderful tools, but never have one in hand when I start a construction job. Light jackets, scissors, address books, screwdrivers, sponges, can openers, and rolls of tape are also charter members of the "got-more-than-one-but-I-can't-find-any" club. And these are high-use items. Knowing you have more than one of something around has a way of making you more careless ("I'm bound to stumble across one of them")— and all that extra clutter compounds your problems.

I struggled with this for twenty-nine years, and finally figured it out. One is easier to keep track of than eight. Then I did three things that helped:

1. Put my name on it (big!).

2. Decided on an exact place to put it.

3. Always *returned* it to that spot the minute I was done with it.

Knowing where everything is is important, but I'm the last to direct anyone to a tidy/perfect/set way to put, hang, or box everything. More and more bags, hangers, racks, and trunks aren't an asset; they just help turn de-junking into re-junking—just help you compact and hide a little more clutter for a little longer. They're *junk bunkers!*

Junk Bunkers

We finally reach the day when our clutter is so overwhelming that there's not a single place left to put anything: even the walls are full. It is then that we're most vulnerable to the hidden persuasion of a *junk bunker.* That, simply, is an item we

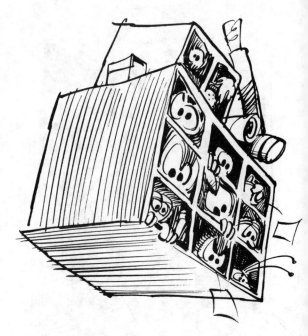

can use to store more junk, stacked higher and packed tighter. Junk bunkers come in various models, called desk organizers, closet racks, shadow boxes, shoe organizers, gun racks, pen-pencil holders, trophy cases, entertainment centers, china cabinets, jewelry boxes and ring holders, pegboard organizers— and magnets (so what you can't hang on walls, you can stick on your refrigerator).

Once we get that handy-dandy "holder," we're psychologically primed for paraphernalia. It irresistibly beckons us to fill it up:

- There's that **seven-story tool box** that encourages us to buy piles of handsome exotic hardware to fill it.
- The **solid oak knife block** with four empty slots—which leaves us no choice but to buy four more knives we don't need.
- The **utensil holder** that beckons us to buy more utensils to balance the set.

- The **new shelves** we feel compelled to fill with vases and other bric-a-brac.
- Those **two extra rooms** we built for just-in-case have to be filled with furniture.

Have you ever noticed that most of the books and articles on how to more efficiently organize a house really show how to hang up, hide, file, tolerate, and make decorative use of junk? I paged through a pile of top-selling books, magazines, and catalogs that had one page after another of slick hangers you can buy (or make) to hang up coats you never use (coats that should be given or thrown away), racks for hats you never wear, see-through boxes for sweaters you've outgrown, drawer organizers that take up a good 10 percent of the drawer's total space, and tiny trinket shelves with which you can clutter your walls with utter abandon.

Consider those vegetable bins to handle refrigerator greenery; they end up taking twice the space and only provide a place for vegetables to rot organized and unseen.

Then there is the big pouch shoe holder that attaches to the back of our closet door: the perfect place to put all the shoes we were going to have to throw out. Now and forever they can swing and bounce on the door, nestled down like baby kangaroos. And let's not forget the one- or two-story desk-top organizer that stacks and divides and stands up all the papers that were all over our desk. Our desk will be just as messy as ever—but the clutter will be vertical instead of horizontal. (And probably forgotten—because having put it in the organizer, we feel something's been done about it.)

Some of the sneakiest junk bunkers are the vinyl slipcovers or handsome leather binders for magazines. Timed almost perfectly to the moment our stack of magazines has left us no alternative but to throw the ugly old things out, the publisher will offer an impressive slipcase or "volume binder." Wherein those outdated, stained, dog-eared periodicals can be clasped together in a coat that makes them blend right in with the classics on our shelf. What an excuse to keep a bunch of stuff that we'll never look

at again. (The cardboard coffins available at stationery stores for old letters fall right in here, too.)

For floors, walls, and furniture saturated with clutter the junk bunker tycoons sell devices to hang clutter from the walls or ceiling. There are even instant junk bunkers everywhere in kits, just snap them together and presto—a clever rack for the back of the toilet, the top of the TV, or under the sink—you can stash three times the junk.

Junk bunkers are like a shot of morphine: they ease the pain, take care of the problem for a short time—and then back it comes. Most of them can accommodate only a *little* junk, and as they become overstuffed, they also become saggy and ugly and dangerous. They don't sort our stuff in quite the way that would be most useful, or they have too many or too few drawers for what we have/need. Or they tempt us to over-organize things in a way that isn't really functional or realistic—so we don't keep it up. And they collect dust and are hard to clean.

There is no redeeming way to better organize and store clutter! Throw it out or give it to someone for whom it won't be junk. The Lord will bless you for giving, and you'll bless yourself for getting rid of it.

If you've stooped to buying organizers for junk, you're swinging on rusty hinges. Once you get all that junk neatly placed in or on the organizer, pick it up and heave it, bunker and all!

Where did all that junk in the bunkers come from? Well, a lot of it is home gadgets.

Gadgets . . . Make Life Easier?

Americans are bombarded with clever, handy gadgets that are not really needed but are too tempting to turn down. Going for a gadget, depending on artifice or automation instead of our own ingenuity, is an accelerated way to collect and own clutter. Just because something works faster and neater than we might doesn't necessarily mean it saves time or makes life easier. It all depends on when and how often we use it, how much time and effort it takes to care for it, and how well it really does the job at hand.

Take corn-on-the-cob holders, for example: those couth little pins with handles you stick on an ear of corn so you can eat more graciously. But you only eat corn on the cob a few times a year—and then you can't find the gadgets. Unless company is there, you never do use them (you forget); and even if you do, they're hard to stick in the cob, and hard to hold onto. Your company has never used them either, and feel as stupid as you do when all of you try to use them. To top it off, they're hard and dangerous to clean, and they have to be stored. You have corn on the cob three weeks of the year and have to shuffle those sharp piles of holders around for the other forty-nine. Are they worth it?

High on the list of useless gadgets/tools is the TV or bargain store do-it-yourself spray gun. The sucker bait on this gadget is, "Just press a button (or pull a trigger) and presto, the work is done." But they don't work half the time (they clog so easily), they're tricky to adjust, they aren't fast (if you count all the times you have to start over and redo), they're messy, and unless you've had a lot of practice you'll end up with a terrible job (you should have stuck with the brush or aerosol). You can't get a good spray gun for $19.95, $49.95, or $99.95—and even the $3,000 ones I've used professionally are a headache; without great skill you'll get misses and runs and bubbles (and ants and bugs stuck in the three square inches of the job that did come out right). Plus the overspray will texturize your

neighbor's picture window. Anything sold with promises to rid your life of all work is a strong hint that you're getting some junk.

Then we have special nozzles for the garden hose (that we'd use once or twice a year, and a thumb over the end of the hose would probably work as well—then the nozzle becomes junk to store). Pipe holders for the workshop, so we don't have to set our new briar down on the sawhorse, gads! Special spears and grips to get olives out of the bottle without using our fingers (just how often do we have to get olives out of a bottle?). Hamburger patty molders, spatula resters (while the hamburger cooks), special shish kebab grills, grape draining dishes, taco holding racks, radish rose cutters, garden seed spacers—and on and on and on. Junk gadgets may provide us with the glory of the moment, the convenience of the hour, but can end up being the plague of the day. Bigger—fancier—flashier is not always better.

Most of the miracle gadgets we end up hating because we got taken—but we refuse to get rid of them because we paid good cash for them. We've been duped into believing that *convenience* is invariably desirable, even if it clutters

our lives. Convenience is often junk hypnosis: if it's a gadget, shiny, attractive, easy to reach for, easy to pay for, we buy, accumulate, and then shuffle it from cupboard to cupboard.

I'll bet every family has one or more exercise gizmos—springy exercisers, collapsible bikes, rowers, pulley ropes, gadgets that work in motels, in doorways, on fire escapes, in prison cells, boats, trains, and compact cars. Exercise equipment for the most part—for old and young, flab and fat—is found in a drawer or on a closet shelf. The most exercise anyone ends up getting from it is moving it from one junk storage area to the next.

Shocking Junk

The word "electric" offers security and sanctification to many clutter accumulators. We presume that if anything is electric it must automatically be better and faster than manual. Don't you believe it! In the time we take to find and plug in the electric charcoal lighter (bun warmer, single hamburger maker, hot dog roaster) we could have done it easier and faster by hand—even the mosquitoes have given up. A lot of these things are a waste of good electric cords and not worth owning for their infrequent use. How many people actually use their electric scissors, electric card shufflers, electric sifters, electric carving knives, electric bottle warmers, or electric toothbrushes? Ninety-five percent of fishermen never catch enough fish to need an electric fish scaler; the other five percent use an old pocket knife. At every garage sale you find an electric warming tray—why? It didn't justify the bother and space. Why was it bought in the first place? Because it had an electric cord sticking out of it. I'll bet if you stuck an electric cord on a pair of chopsticks or knitting needles, there'd be a stampede for them.

"Electronic," and "solar," too, share the same mystique. Suddenly stores announce: "This is going to be an electronic Christmas." Suddenly everything—scales, temperature gauges, light switches, doorbells, dog whistles—

has to be electronic or it's passé. Electronics are superb to have and have made life much easier, but electronic isn't automatically better. High tech is a degree of technology—not an assurance of efficient function. How comfortable you feel with things also has something to do with how useful they are to you. I still use an old manual typewriter. Beating hard on the keys releases my tensions and I can roll out reams of writing (more than many of my colleagues who insist I'm an idiot for not using an electronic processor). Of the thirty friends and associates I've questioned closely about their high-tech home computers, I've found most of them just have an expensive way to play Pac-Man.

One hour of power junk Snow blowers are an extremely useful tool, when there's enough snow to justify them. In many areas of the northern U.S., the home use for a snowblower is about one major snow every three years, or a couple of hours' work for the blower. The other 1,000 days it sits in the way of other things. It's far from being a piece of junk, yet owning one to only be used in the occasional heavy storm clutters your life (besides, a couple of hours on the old shovel, provided we go about it sensibly, wouldn't hurt most of us out-of-condition folks)— and a shovel is cheaper and stores a lot easier.

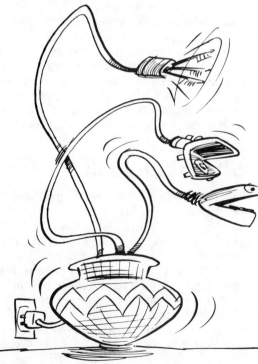

Have You Got Money to Burn?

The argument we hear for some of our latest and proudest junk is that it's "a vast saving on energy"—and who in this energy-tense day would dare question any installation or acquisition that has the potential to save energy? Take the national rage (in any place in this country even remotely northern) for the good old wood stove. Holes have been ripped in many a house and thousands of rock wall protectors installed so those "money-saving" wood stoves can be installed, and once in, it's easy to identify the owner: "I haven't turned my furnace on yet this year." Yes, wood stoves are efficient in a well-insulated home, but so is an electric or gas furnace (and the fuel for them is usually more accessible—and often cheaper). I saw the following in a newspaper; it beautifully (and quite accurately) sums up the economics of some money-saving items.

Remember, it's not just "Is it faster or neater?" but "How often will I use it?" (vs. having to buy it, store it, remember to bring it out and use it, service it) that's the issue: you might want to think twice about that automatic stamp licker, hydraulic pillow fluffer-upper, self-starting orange peeler, or electric ice cream scoop.

How You Can Save with a Wood Stove

Stove and pipe installation	$ 458.00
Chainsaw	149.95
Gas and maintenance of chainsaw	44.60
4-wheel-drive pickup (used)	8,297.04
4-wheel-drive pickup (maintenance)	538.00
Replace window of pickup (twice)	310.00
Fine for cutting unmarked tree in state forest	500.00
14 cases beer	126.00
Littering fine	50.00
Tow charge from creek	50.00
Fee for removing splinter from eye	45.00
Safety glasses	29.50
Chimney brush and rods	45.00
Log splitter	150.00
Emergency room treatment (broken toe from dropped log)	125.00
Safety shoes	49.95
New living room carpet	800.00
Paint walls and ceiling	110.00
15-acre woodlot	9,000.00
Taxes on woodlot	310.00
Divorce settlement	33,678.22
Total first-year costs	$54,941.26
Savings in fuel: first year	62.37
Cost of year's wood burning	$54,878.89

—author unknown

Junk Multiplies Junk

Bear in mind too that clutter amazingly multiplies itself. I once leafed through a pre-Christmas gift newspaper and a full 50 percent of the things in it weren't needed, but luxury, "convenience" items that when brought into your life would draw other junk items. Among other gems, there was a cookbook holder, a giant ugly thing of wood and clear plastic, maybe useful—if you'd remember to use it—but it would be hard to clean and take a place to store (and your favorite cookbook probably wouldn't fit in it).

Junk multiplication is so subtle, and so easily justified: as you get something, you need a rack for it, a place for it, and then some more junk so you can use it better—and so on.

Accessories to the Crime

I think the original intent of most accessories was to make a thing neater and easier to handle—is it working? Look at asparagus; it grew wild on the ditch banks and a few people picked it and ate it, no big deal. Then someone started inventing things to properly handle asparagus . . . like special asparagus steamers, asparagus knives, asparagus ladles, asparagus racks, special string to tie up the stalks, special dishes to serve it in. The more gizmos to handle the wild weed of the ditch bank, the more prestige it gained—and the more expensive it got (up to $5 a pound, when you can get it). Now did you know the accessory entrepreneurs are trying this same approach on the good old egg: we have egg prickers, egg peelers, egg slicers, egg poachers, egg timers, egg turners, egg tongs, egg cozies, egg holders, egg slicers, egg separators, egg platters, and deviled egg rests. They're trying with accessories to do the same thing they did to asparagus: take it out of the hand of the common man by creating a whole special set of equipment for it.

Just about any food or beverage these days sprouts accessories like fungus on a fallen log. Look at all the special coffee brewers, bean grinders, milk heaters, mugs, cups, and freezer jars to keep the beans fresh (how did people drink coffee all those centuries before freezers?). It's much the same way with wine—there are clay coolers for white wine, cooling buckets for sparkling wine, dozens of corkscrew designs—and woe to the host gauche enough to serve sherry in the wrong kind of glass. . . .

Whether we're hooking a fish or making a waffle, popping a bit of popcorn or trying our hand at homemade bread—there's a sea of gadgetry and special equipment we can easily sink in.

Unreasonable Attachments

As foods and gadgets sprout accessories, so do appliances. Most of us, for instance, have a love/hate relationship with our vacuum cleaners. Mostly, we love the cleaner, we hate the attachments. The cleaner does 98 percent of the work; the miracle attachments (which we fell for after a salesman's fast talking) we seldom need or use—so they're shuffled around from closet to closet in their clever display box until the bottom rots out—then the attachments are thrown in a drawer, never to emerge again (except maybe as "guess-whats" in a parlor game).

Nothing is more of a disgrace than owning attachments with nothing to attach them to. I'm sure *you* wouldn't be so stupid, so let's point out a few things for your attachment-laden friends. In the backs of closets you find table leaves—the table they fit was worn, warped, and whisked away to the junkyard five or ten years ago. Because the leaves were seldom used they remained like new—and who could throw out beautiful new solid wood or shiny Formica leaves? Maybe we figured we'd buy or build a table to fit, so we kept them. That's almost as bad as

keeping someone's new false teeth when he's died—you'll never find a fit! Same with the old 16-inch tires, the sheaths of those knives you've lost, those brand-new special bulbs for a light fixture you pitched years ago, the saddle and tack you've had since the horse keeled over and you moved to the city seventeen years ago.

The attachment problem is compounded by the fact that machines today have so *many* attachments available. Besides a menacing array of shiny attachments for vacuums, there is a galaxy of glamorous sewing machine attachments—little bobbin adjusters, ruffle grabbers, seam stretchers, needle straighteners. My wife, who is an excellent seamstress, has often commented that it's the accessories to a sewing machine that make everyone want one. Yet in producing the average dress or shirt or bathrobe, hardly a one of these accessories is brought into play. (By the time we find and hook one into the machine, we could have done it faster and better with a needle and thimble.)

Remember when the can opener was a handy little thing—inexpensive, easy to tuck away with the knives and forks. Of course with electricity, we did improve it and make it faster, but now just opening cans isn't enough. Hung on that once-simple opener is a knife sharpener, scissors sharpener, bottle opener, magnet, light, and top cupboard or bottom counter mounts (to make it as difficult to clean as it now is to use). Then of course we have beauty kits with motorized callous sanders, elbow creamers, eyebrow stencils, pore massagers, wrinkle relaxers. Even the kitchen mixer has all sorts of squeezers, slicers, kneaders, manglers, and juicers—next thing you know, they'll launder pantyhose. (After twenty-eight years my aunt's old mixer finally gave up the ghost; it went, but not the juicer. After all, it was brand new, had never been used—she still has it in the top cupboard today!)

House Junk Hall of Fame

PATHETIC PLASTIC

There is no "plastic surgery" for junk, yet kitchens and cupboards and cellars are full of plastics bent and bowed by heat or weight or both—plastic containers, lids, utensils. Even records get warped and are generally worthless, but notice they don't go. We have secret thoughts of restoring them to functionability—but there's no hope, and even if there were, it'd be cheaper to buy a new one. You haven't used that half-melted plastic container, that fried plastic spatula, or warped plastic lid for years and you *won't*—dump it!

BROWN PAPER BAGS

Are the mice in your home starving to death because those extra paper bags are compressed so thick and tight between the fridge and the counter that they can't get through, let alone eat anything? We save bags because we do use them occasionally—but for most of us the rate at which they accumulate far outstrips the rate at which we can use them up. There aren't enough turkeys to be baked or Sunday school projects to be made to ever exhaust your supply. De-junk before bugs breed in them or your compressor overheats and sets them on fire. And do you have sixty crumpled shopping bags stashed, though when you need one, you'll spring for a fresh crisp new one at the store, as usual? And what about bread wrappers and the little plastic bags that come on the newspaper . . .?

SCENIC SOAPS

SOAP
IS
FOREVER

We're really hard up for clutter when we buy and display handcarved decorative soap. I never found any thrill rubbing Donald Ducks over my back, and less interest in showing my soap off to a friend: "Look, after four baths, it still has the head on it." Everyone's afraid to actually use the things, so they stay around forever, turning floury in their plastic wrappers. And even if some brave soul *did* use them, a plain old bar of soap would have worked much better anyway.

FRESH FROZEN JUNK

Some of us stoop to taking something we don't want and no one will eat and putting it into indefinite suspension in the freezer, so it won't ruin while we're dodging the question of what to do with it. Eventually it gets freezer burn, or becomes so unrecognizable in its frost coating that we have to thaw it out to identify it. And then, at last, the showdown—we can't freeze it again so we have to throw it out (we should have just chucked it in the first place).

Leftovers can be junk, too, if we never did want to eat them and are just refrigerating them as a way of delaying throwing them out. Keep a sharp eye out, too, for aging refrigerator odds and ends: just because it's full of preservatives doesn't mean it'll last forever. De-junk those year-old dregs of salad dressing, that ancient bottle of seafood sauce, those maraschino cherries that are a fixture in the door shelf, the six containers of rock cornish hen giblets you keep meaning to make gravy with. . . . Patrol your refrigerator regularly for condiments and relishes moving past their prime and eat 'em or throw them out.

UNIDENTIFIED KEYS

I'll wager you have at least twenty old worthless keys, between your house and workplace. Identify (some hard thinking and detective work may be called for here) and mark every key in your possession or throw it away. Keys are clutter, if you don't know what they're to!

SEEDY SAMPLES

What is it about free samples given to us or left on our doorstep? I've watched cleaning samples sit for years and years in houses. They won't be used, but won't be thrown out, because they were free. Even after they get mashed and beat up and dented and weevily and the labels are gone we cling to them tenaciously.

If no one in the household is enthusiastic enough about a packet of shampoo/cream rinse or hand lotion to use it within a couple of weeks of its appearance at the door, chances are no one will use it ever. But do we throw the packet away? No—it sits in the bathroom drawer with seventeen other shriveling packets, awaiting the fateful day when you might run out of the stuff you usually use.

Lots of gifts and free samples arrive over the holidays to litter our homes—like calendars too big or too small, those terrible telephone chin holders with someone's company name printed all over them, skimpy wall notepads with a skipping ball point pen that won't write uphill—junk!

FAKE FRUIT

Won't rot when it gets old and will sit around in that display dish forever. Not only do you feel obligated to keep it once you put it out, because it psychologically suggests that it's *food* you won't ever pitch it (who could bring himself to waste good food?). Truthfully now, have you ever seen artificial fruit you could generate any real enthusiasm for? So why buy it and let it hang around catching dust while the *real* fruit is in the fridge, where you won't think to eat it? Melt those ugly apples, pears, and bananas down, or throw them at a junk performer.

YOU MAY HAVE A SERIOUS JUNK PROBLEM IF YOU:

- hide when the doorbell rings
- wear your coat when you answer the door so your caller will think you were just leaving
- wait till after dark to pull the car into the garage
- live in fear that someone you respect may someday open one of your closets
- have to think about how to cross a room
- finally find the Christmas tree lights while hunting for the Easter baskets
- finally replace a badly worn or broken part—then keep that broken part

- fear lifting the lid on some of the Tupperware in your refrigerator
- hide the tangled contents of a messy drawer by laying a couple of neatly folded things over the top
- drag a 22-cubic-foot chest freezer into the yard to keep the repairman from coming into the house
- have an unquenchable desire to paw through a moving neighbor's garbage before the trash truck comes

Knickknacks

Humankind, deep in its secret heart, has always wanted to create and control its own world. To do so on a big scale like the Lord did is a little out of reach, so we mortals settled on a lesser but representative approach. We created little wood, plastic, china, metal, and paper models, miniatures, and duplicates of every creature and structure ever devised, rounded them up, and put them on a shelf so we could rule over them. And we named our scaled-down universe *knickknacks*.

Creation was easy, and surprisingly enough, so was reproduction. Once they were in our possession, they multiplied and peopled the shelves many times over. Do those little suckers breed at night? No—they don't need to, with us around. As soon as we get an object, no one in the house or family rests until it has a match, mate, or companion. A pair is nice, but not as nice as a trio, because you can place three of anything in an interesting arrangement—though four would be more symmetrical—and five can be lined up in some kind of order and a set would be more impressive. . . . So

grows our world of knickknacks. A few are true treasures; the rest of those hundreds of others, those tiny porcelain people, fanciful fowls, and morose mammals just sit there with insipid looks on their faces. Some of those little Alpine yodelers we've had so long we don't remember whether they're Bavarian Burghermeisters or extras out of *The Sound of Music*.

Many of us don't look at, use, or even like our knickknacks. Then why do we keep them? Because when visitors come, that's the only thing they know how to comment on; they will always gaze intently and finally say, "Cute." That benediction, sincere or not, is sanction to save—and so lives on that shelf full, wall full, cabinet full, room full of dust and grease collectors. The only time our interest is aroused much is when one of them gets knocked off and broken; then we wail and sob like a wounded pack rat (we'd glue it back together but can't remember if it was a Mayan warrior or Pluto the dog).

Although life was never officially breathed into our knickknacks, nor did we teach them, they themselves became clutter collectors, demanding more and

more shelves, stands, racks, and cases to migrate to.

Knickknacks may be smaller than Frankenstein's monster, but they have a much better chance of doing us in. Save your "sacred" figurines or knickknacks and somewhere, somehow, someplace— dump the rest! One fell swoop of arm isn't hard to do, but plucking the marked ones singly is awfully painful. Donate them en masse to a museum so the whole county can admire them; besides, in a museum they'll be class ("culture," not "cute").

Before you throw one of your copper horses or ceramic chickens at me for suggesting genocide of your knickknack kingdom, I realize there might be some emotional value to your collection. Do you think I'd pitch my bust of Beethoven, or even my Bell System fishing lure? No way. Some knickknacks, as worthless as they might be, have real ritual value. One of our most fulfilling and relaxing pastimes is dusting, washing, and caring for them every so often. If they soothe you, regenerate you, quicken your heartbeat at every touch, keep them. (But pitch the other 182 that don't.)

Behind Closed Doors (Closets!)

The old "skeleton in the closet" didn't originate in fiction. Closets hide more ugly, embarrassing, frightening "dead" junk than any other home environment. If your closet were three times the size it is now, it would still be full, and most of us would have to rummage and burrow to retrieve the object we know "is in there somewhere." My descriptions of closet chaos in *Is There Life After Housework?* and *Do I Dust or Vacuum First?* triggered thousands of letters and comments (most of them apologies for cluttered closets).

A closet is really the most logical place in the house to put the things we need to have handy. Closets are our most functional and critical storage area, but they are also the perfect convenient place to stash useless unneeded items out of sight. Closet junk is the most emotionally devastating because we see it many times a day. I wouldn't want to go picking through your closet—it's none of my business—but if I could get you to make it one of the main events of your de-

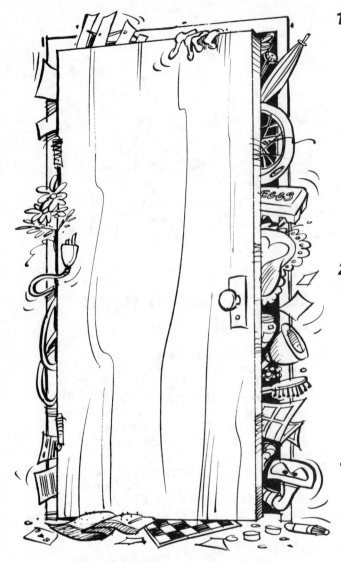

1. You start in a closet by de-cluttering it. That is the simple (and often heart-rending) process of getting rid of everything you don't use or need. We all know what is junk and what isn't. Dresses, pants, shirts, and shoes that haven't fit or pleased you for the last twelve years won't ever—pitch them! Those hand-painted ties and leopardskin clutch bags aren't coming back in style; pitch them. Those boxes of Christmas cards from 1978, 1979, 1980, 1981, complete with address list: face the fact that you'll never write them. Give them away or dump them.

2. Move the useful but used-once-or-twice-a-year (or every two to five years) stuff to a less critical (inactive) storage area. Remember, closets are your most accessible (active) storage area. Attics, under the basement steps, or basement storage rooms are not, so transfer the worthwhile but not-frequently-used stuff (like camping gear, out-of-season clothes, scuba-diving masks, suitcases, etc.) to other areas.

3. Get stuff off the floor. Floor mess is about the most psychologically devastating of all messes. Most closets have a lot of unused upper room—a few dollars worth of material and a spare hour or two and you can install (or barter with a friend to install) a second or third shelf above the one over the hanger rod. This makes more room for worthwhile keepables.

4. Wall-hang everything you can. Remember, nothing—absolutely nothing—goes on the floor. If you are a person who rotates shoes or clothes, there are wall and other organizers you may find useful. Just use your

junking marathon, it would delight me!

How can you shape yours up? If the situation is really bad you could buy an insert closet liner (like a garbage can liner) and yank the entire insert out every year and drag it to the junk pile. Seriously, though, I'd like to suggest here some junk-inhibiting practices from the Clean Closet Set:

head in choosing—and installing—storage accessories or "closet organizers." Some are real helps; others, just another kind of clutter.

5. Remember, *before* you stash is the best time to exercise control. (You'll never have the time to "go back through it.") Do you really *want* it? Do you *need* it? Does it have to go *there?* I realize most of us don't have enough closet space—but try, really try, not to pack too much into your closets. You'll defeat the purpose. No matter how cleverly you pack it all in and organize it—if a system won't stand up to quick, convenient use, it's ultimately doomed and will aggravate the mess. Overcrowding makes it a lot tougher both to get things out and to put them away. And you'll end up with a lot of re-ironing and re-pressing that shouldn't have been necessary.

6. Use hard-finish, light-colored enamel or gloss latex when you paint the closet interior, and hanger marks can be cleaned off easily.

Be careful of those clever holders and organizers that drape on the backsides of doors and doorknobs. Most of them are only places to store junk you should have tossed. And those glue-on, snap-on, stick-on "space expanders" can ruin good functional structures. The classic one of these is the over-door hanger for the extra unworn clothes you should have thrown out. Many a door, handsomely designed and carefully stained and finished (to open and close—not be a mobile mannequin) is mutilated by these poorly thought-out things. Inside most of today's (hollow-core) doors are cardboard reinforcing strips; hanging forty pounds of shabby sheepskin vests and velour outfits on the door will crush them and buckle

the door. The average new door, hung in place, costs as much as $250. Think of that when you see one of those nifty $2.49 accessories.

Spin the Bottle/Jar/Box/Tube

The perfect miniature of the clutter-filled closet is the bathroom medicine cabinet . . . such a simple, innocent, and shining thing on the outside. The medicine cabinet was placed above the sink so it would be easy to reach . . . it's easy to stash things in also. Let's just open the door and look in. . . .

Who convinced you to buy all this, anyway? It's unsafe, unsightly, and uneconomical—and most of it is just dead weight; it doesn't really do anything for you. The real name for this is "clutter chest."

Life isn't that complicated. Some of the healthiest, happiest, handsomest people in the world survive without any of this. Starting and ending every day looking into this collection of clutter has to affect your daily outlook, your dreams.

Coping with Kiddie Clutter

Most kids, if given a chance, will de-clutter themselves. Little kids, in particular, are great de-junkers; they play with or wear something until it falls apart or they lose interest (then they wisely break it, lose it, or give it to a friend). But if we really work at it, we can teach our kids to be clutter collectors too. All it takes is intense examples from us grown-ups, constantly bombarding them with junk gifts and junkee ideas.

For instance, we come unglued when we find out that our kid did away with his old plastic tricycle with the wobbly back wheels. It's gone, no good—but that night the junk-prone parents have him under the light: "Think now, Junior, where did you leave it? Did the neighbor boy touch it?" The kid wouldn't have received half the attention if he'd broken an arm or burned down the local school.

We owe kids better than this. If we let junk, litter, and clutter become a constant condition in their lives, they'll get accustomed to it, feel comfortable around it—and later will duplicate the situation in their own cluttered lives and homes.

Here are some kiddie clutter cutters:

1. Much of kids' clutter is excess we've given them—get rid of (or store and rotate) those excess toys, clothes, games, scooters; they won't miss them!

2. Give kids a place for their stuff. Growing people have their own inventory, but most of the storage space in the home is taken by adult junk. If there's a place to put it, the chances are 60 percent better that it will get put away.

3. Lower dresser and closet hanger rods so kids can hang things up easily.

4. Put casters on the toy box so the kids can pull it around to their disaster areas—it makes a pickup a lot easier and more likely.

The Nerve of Some Junkees (Exterior Junk)

Hoarding, hiding, and shifting your junk in private is at least good manners. There are those among us, however, who are natural exhibitionists. When not busy adorning their bodies, decorating their cars, or showing off their offices, they impose their clutter on others on the outside of their houses and in their yards. We all hate junky yards—even someone whose yard looks like the city dump will, when viewing another sloppy junk-plastered yard, squint his eyes and say, "What a disgrace, just look at all that trash, they must be real slobs."

You feel the same way, don't you? But how is *your* yard? Is it an All-American avalanche of "antiques"?

Right out the back door junk starts with rusted or broken wind chimes, deceased weather instruments, bent-back awnings covered with sagging lattice, a slum birdhouse or two in condemned condition, a lean-to shed bulging with sun-cracked hoses, handleless tools, and rotting stakes and bushel baskets.

YOU ARE NOW ENTERING THE COMBAT ZONE

Against the fence is an abandoned rabbit cage, car parts, decaying barrels. Then there is a coy cherub fountain, unhung hanging baskets, some broken aluminum lounge chairs, a mound of salvaged bricks and blocks, a peeling Paul Revere lamppost and a couple of faded plastic squirrels. And oh, yes—that pile of boards scrounged out of a junk pile, worn not from age, but from ten years of being moved around to more inconspicuous places. Let's not overlook those twirling plastic sunflowers, tire tulip beds, miniature white plastic picket fences, rusted swingsets, chipped and yellowed drinking fountains, abandoned outgrown swimming pools, rusted grills from the past three seasons, and the TV antenna that toppled during the worst storm of the '70s. Not to mention last year's Christmas tree saved for kindling, outdoor Christmas lights standing fast in July, and overgrown and untrimmed, dying, dead shrubbery.

Dangerous When Junked

The first time I saw an Army obstacle course I was impressed, because it took real eptness and agility to complete it—not to mention the ingenuity and planning that must have gone into its construction. But it's a shame so much time and money is wasted by those obstacle course designers and constructors when in our very own town, our very own neighborhood (maybe even our very own little acre), we have back yards that without design or intention could beat anything those colonels could ever dream up. Moving through some people's yards, dodging all the junk piles, traps, castellations, blockades just to get from the back door to the garage, is a maneuver to match topping the highest battlement. If a sharp rake or slung hose doesn't get you, you can count on being garrotted by a low antenna or clothesline wire, or stepping into a barbecue burial pit. The injuries possible from a junky

yard are scary, but still not as pitiful as the fact so much of your fine expensive green yard is so covered with junk that it can't be *used*. Imagine that cruddy clutter cheating you out of a fast cartwheel on the grass or even forbidding you to invite the Henrys into the yard for a look at your lilacs.

Seedy junky yards truly do lose us respect and friends (as well as property value). Exterior junk costs us a lot of lawsuits and injuries to children and adults as well as sheer shame.

Scout your yard, and surprise the worms, bugs, and beetles building colonies under your exterior inventory.

De-Garbage Your Garage

Once we can make our way through the yard in a straight line, it's time to stride over to the garage and take a hard de-junking look at it. The garage to most of us is our enclosed junkyard—kind of a giant seasoning cellar for our debatable belongings. Yet believe it or not, the garage is the first, most, and last used location in a home. We leave from it to work or town or the yard, and return through it from work or town or the yard, often with arms full of stuff, both coming and going. A garage is a very logical place to be kept in clean and useful condition.

It doesn't cost much (in fact *less*) to be de-cluttered. For example—three 8-foot 2x12s and a few cinder blocks can offer order, safety, and convenience in the form of instant garage storage shelves for items that get a lot of use. But that's only the beginning. Here are a few ideas that will help:

1. Store anything light by hanging it as high as reachably possible. This keeps it out of the stumbling-over path, yet readily accessible.

2. Find, buy, or make a wall-hung cabinet (six feet tall if possible) to store small hand tools, paint, lawn chemicals, etc. Concealing stuff that must be stored in the garage has emotional as well as physical advantages.

3. If you wish to mount or hang frequently used hand tools (or display them for friends who borrow) the smart, practical, and economical way is to install a 4x8-foot piece of quarter-inch pegboard on the wall (just like you see in store displays)—you can do it easily and a variety of peg hardware is available.

4. Make sure you can see! Most garages are inadequately lighted, which makes them feel like a mine shaft instead of part of a home. The wiring is usually adequate; just convert the incandescent fixtures to fluorescent tube lights. It will make the garage look better and will be safer and cheaper.

5. Paint the garage walls—90 percent of garages are unfinished, and thus look naked and shabby. Two coats of a good enamel (new or left over from another job) can be applied for a few dollars and reward you for years. (If the walls are bare studs, put up sheet rock first.)

6. Prepare and seal the floor, if it's concrete, and has been down for at least thirty days. This will make it fast and easy to maintain and improve the looks and feel of the garage.

Here's how:
Remove all possible furniture, tools, etc., from the floor; sweep up all the surface dirt. Mop on a solution of strong alkaline cleaner (TSP), or better yet, etching acid diluted in water. (Your janitorial supply house or paint store has these—be sure to follow the specific instructions on the label.) Let it soak in awhile; if the floor is old and marked, you might want to scrub it with a floor scrubbing maching. Flush the solution off, preferably using a floor squeegee, and rinse with a hose. Allow the floor to dry for at least five hours, then apply transparent concrete seal or an all-purpose seal, either of which can be obtained at a paint or janitorial supply store. Apply the seal, according to directions, with any applicator that will distribute it in a nice even coat, and let it dry. I'd advise a second coat to ensure good coverage.

Blue Ribbon Junkees

I don't like to single out any specific class or social order of junkee for dishonorable mention, but you farmers deserve it (men and women both, so don't any of you try to sneak off). Everything written in this book about clutter can be applied "double strength" to most farm people. Few city or suburban junkees can touch your bumper crop of good old clutter. Don't think I'm judging you harshly or unfairly—you know you're guilty. As I write this, I look out the window at my 100-foot-long, 30-foot-deep farm shop that contained not some, not a lot, but *tons* of junk.

Farmers have one distinct advantage over town junkers: they have more room to spread it out. They can distribute it eloquently from the north forty to "out behind the barn." They have silos, barns, sheds, cellars, extra houses, feeders, and granaries all available to store junk—and they do.

Farm men are almost twice as bad as farm women (who are twice as bad as a normal uptowner); they can blame everything on making a living and throw in a couple of big words they learned from the Extension Service agent and nothing will be questioned! Farmers keep *everything* because room is no problem— old tractors, machines, and vehicles they just park farther out in the field each time. They keep them for parts, of course, and the ancient 1880 junk they keep to snare a dumb city slicker who'll come along and pay $500 for a rusty milk can or a warped wagon wheel. Most farmers keep their old work boots so long that they can walk off by themselves— and the old gloves, hats, jackets, and coveralls they keep, alone, could stuff a silo. They have enough bolts buried somewhere to bolt the cover down on an MX missile, and as for tools, most have a $70,000 inventory. Yet they keep the wire and string from every bale of hay, and every bucket, can, barrel, sack, and container that ever ambled onto the place. (We'd *all* like to do that so we all envy them.) They never throw away a worn or broken part, because if the new one breaks, they can recycle the old one even twenty rusting years later. But the absolute clincher is: once a farmer owns a welder and a blowtorch (which most do) *nothing* is junk. Everything—even a license plate frame broken in four places—is kept because with a torch and welder you can make or repair anything and must have scrap metal around. I've seen hundreds of farmers cut some good metal off an old truck bed and then keep the old flaking skeleton for years, secure in the thought that they'd be able to pry a 10¢ lock washer off someday . . . if they need it. . . .

Brethren of the soil, I've struggled with this myself through two generations of farms and ranches and most of it is clutter! Haul it off and plant something—you'll reduce the rattlesnake breeding grounds and help prevent injuries and divorces, as well as the profanities you utter every time you're looking through it for a part.

I love farm women—they're the real class and beauty of the world's womanhood, so I won't mention the fact that they are also the champion bottle collectors of the world, the garden junk accumulators of all time, the sewing scrap savers supreme, queens of the recipe collectors, and of course the cellar shelf fillers without equal. Farm folk, de-junk—and the junkyard won't know what hit it!

By Their Junk Shall Ye Know Them

All the rest of you now chuckling at those junk-collecting farmers, don't feel too smug (or slighted that you aren't in first place) because there are other groups that are right in there. If we had a "Profession Possession Printout," you'd probably find *artists* crowding the top. They can and do keep anything and everything, even old stiff and battered brushes, because after all, everything has art form. Some of their old paints are harder than a new cook's pie crust; their half-finished canvases could ruin your appetite. They have drawers full of rusted lettering pens, colored pencil stubs, grubby bits of crayon, globs of kneaded eraser, petrified poster paint, solid oils, cracked linoleum, scratched scraper board, tea-stained drawing board, powdered charcoal, empty glue tubes, and a secret horde of half-joined-up dot-to-dot books. Their "To Do Someday" file fills two portfolios—and they keep it all, in the name of art!

Schoolteachers, too, are right in the running for the Junk World Series. Teachers have to contend with sample books, programs, and a half-century of yearbooks—not to mention the inevitable gifts from students. They pick up information (and things) enthusiastically and have the perfect excuse . . . they always need background material and visual aids.

For geologists anything on or in the earth's crust is fair game for keeping—the result often being a fine collection of fossil junk. Engineers save every broken machine and appliance and length of pipe in hope of rebuilding or salvaging or devising something useful. And book editors save every snippet.

At least professional junkees have the excuse of making a living. Junking hobbyists clutter for the sheer fun of it—and once they've filled their own homes to bursting with ceramic owls, macramé plant hangers, paint-by-number portraits, sequined light switches, and decoupaged desk accessories, they start in on their friends' and relatives' houses and fill those. By the time they've saturated their entire acquaintance list, they've become not only proficient, but *fast*—so they have no alternative but to move on to church and school craft bazaars, hobby fairs, and flea markets. They are then classifiable as professional craftspeople, and their garages and basements and spare rooms swell with stock, supplies, display materials, and equipment to match—not to mention a conglomeration of clutter in various stages of completion, because they've moved on to assembly-line production!

CHAPTER 7

Those Personal Treasures

. . . Might Some Be Clutter?

Don't think you're the only one who has a heart wrapped around treasures you'll never use, that are doing no good, but are unique, valuable, and impress others with your good judgment for possessing them. As I write this, I only have to look about to spot four of my favorites. One is a perfect replica of the first Bell telephone, handmade, only ten like it in the world, a fine and beautiful thing worthy of any Bell System consultant like myself. There's not really any place to put it, so I use it for a bookend so I can rationalize keeping it. (The books it tries to hold tumble it over easily.) Next I have a pair of genuine Mexican mariachis; they won't stand up, and roll off any flat surface I set them on. I did put them in the speaker of the genuine 1876 Bell phone for weight, and of course then when I got out a book, both the phone and the mariachis toppled over. Then there is my brass bugle, my finest treasure—I can't play a lick on it, but I've wanted a bugle since I was eight years old. One of my managers gave me one for Christmas when I was forty-five, gads, I love it, it just hangs there waiting for a battle or revival. I put it in the telephone speaker in another attempt to improve my "bookend," but it looked bad so I rehung it.

Then there is my beloved collection of toilet miniatures, including toilet pencil sharpeners, toilet erasers, toilet soup mugs, toilet squirt guns, toilet salt and pepper shakers, toilet keychains, toilet clocks, toilet charms, toilet pendants, toilet neckerchief slides, etc. Although I am a professional toilet cleaner, these beauties have cost me numerous hours of dusting, cleaning, arranging, and protecting. I can't bring myself to de-junk them, so I made a $180 recessed glass display case and now they rest safely in undisturbed beauty. That's what I did in one attempt to contain the "personal treasures" problem.

Can Jewels Become Junk?

In Hawaii at age twenty-one, I was fascinated by a little ship made out of seashells with thread rigging. I bought it because to me at the time it was a masterpiece to behold. I brought it home and moved it, dusted it, cleaned it, repaired it; it sat on my shelf for twenty-seven years and had without doubt the finest physique to capture cobwebs of any object ever invented. As the years went on, I said, "Boy, that's ugly, but I've had it twenty years, it would be a shame to break the record," so I kept it another five. It looked more hideous every day and finally became so barnacled with grime and flyspecks that a self-respecting fly wouldn't even land on it, so I pitched it. The first five years I owned the thing I enjoyed it. The last twenty years were misery—it took something from me. Clutter of many kinds evolves in our life: without changing appearance it can quietly shift from a plus to a minus.

We are free agents unto ourselves

when it comes to junking up our lives—we investigate, accumulate, and then suddenly discover much of our lives is spent regulating the clutter we have accumulated. It grows old fast, and our junk around us, on us, in us begins to irritate. Most people, when they reach the state of irritation, do the wrong things, go the wrong way; they accumulate more gadgets to help organize the junk and that only leads to more junk and more irritation.

Highbrow Junk

Cost and *class* are not always partners. The word "expensive" has whitewashed junk for far too long. We snigger aloofly at the ugly dimestore vase, while an elaborate engraved urn that does the very same thing (stands a flower up so we can smell it) gets the stamp of approval. The difference between porcelain and plaster of Paris here is piddly; both are often obnoxious, seldom

used, and not as attractive as a clean simple container would be. Highbrow junk, we can call it. Those elegant gifts or purchases of lion claw candlesticks, silver cigarette lighters, unspeakable opera glasses, chic little bowls, exotic lamps, $200 beer steins, and copper or brass kitchen extras cost a lot more but are still right in there with the five-and-dime stuff.

Many of these inexpressibly elegant things don't actually *do* anything—they are pure decoration, exquisite objects that just *sit* in a house. They don't perform any function—which is fine if you really enjoy them, take real *pleasure* in looking at them and rearranging their display. But junk is junk if you don't take much notice of it, and it has no real useful purpose.

Sold as Brass

"Brass" and "copper" are important words in the highbrow junk vocabulary. A woman I overheard commented that every time her husband came back from a foreign country, he brought her something—it didn't really matter what, as long as it was *brass*. She complained, said that she could start a metal recycling foundry in her living room, but he continued bringing things home because they were not only a bargain, they were *brass!*

Brass and copper *are* durable, but not necessarily better for every purpose and they are high-maintenance materials. They cost a small fortune to buy and a bigger fortune in time to keep looking good. (The owners of brass beds often complain they spend more time polishing than using them.) I helped clean King Charles II's 350-year-old brass candleholders in England's Winchester Cathedral—those massive, elegant things are worn thin and frail from being polished once a week for all those years. Even the solder is wearing out from cleaning. How many lifetimes have been polished away in that time? Do any personal treasures take precedence over human life—especially yours?

Elaborate, overdone furniture is a must in the highbrow clutter collector's inventory. These things are designed, built, and sold to be looked at. I can enjoy the love and association of eating at a nice big handsome table—but I have a hard time understanding how and why people will stand in line and pay to look at a table. "It's a Chippendale," someone gasps. I'll wager you nine out of ten of us would enjoy the other Chip & Dale (those two cartoon chipmunks) more.

Another fixture of highbrow junk is the twinkling crystal chandelier. As a professional cleaner, I hate those things. Light is light, and rarely can a person tell the difference between polished plastic and crystal in a light fixture, yet there the crystal must hang to hang you and your pocketbook—and impress other neck-craning clutter collectors. Crystal, like china, seems to be bought mainly to lend an elegance to the household that the dwellers seem to lack.

You could easily argue that highbrow junk is *more* immoral than lowbrow junk

because it's more expensive both to buy and own. It's more squandrous of our life's substance—or the lives of others. We could have spent that money to feed a starving child or help a struggling student, to fund a cause, friend, family— something alive! We can saturate our junking impulse in a big spree at Woolworth's and not feel too bad—we may have a pile of awful things but we're only out fifty bucks or less. Highbrow junk is hundreds or thousands of dollars and we can *still* have a pile of awful stuff.

Highbrow junk consumes a lot of our life force, especially when we have to part with it. That's the reason many people dread dying so much—they have to leave all their junk. If it were worth nothing, they'd feel they had nothing to lose and leave this planet more peacefully.

Our walls and yards sport some grotesque images we call art. But because it was expensive, original, highbrow merchandise we grin and bear it.

How many of us, deep in our hearts, would like to tear down and shred to bits some "artistic" monstrosity we've had to courteously acknowledge for years? Cheap junk is easier to chuck. Highbrow is sacred? Don't you believe it.

China and Silverware Displays

Some clutter seems to be used to resolve a family identity hangup. The classic is china and silverware. To accumulate that one special set of china and sterling (right down to the embossed liver ladle) is a lifetime dream of many. When they finally get it all, there's no way they'll risk breaking, scratching, or losing any of it. So a nightmare of a china closet is secured and therein—behind glass—is the treasure. The silver is velvet-draped in an oak casket, double-locked in the bottom drawer of the same cabinet.

Who in the right mind would really take all this space, time, trouble, and insurance money to display a bunch of *dishes?* Think about it—a bunch of eating tools—so people can gaze and say, "Oh, your saucer is so captivating. Is it Haviland or Royal Doulton?" If we're going to mount some house tool we use this much, why not something with more character—like the can opener, potato masher, even the garden spray nozzle? Most "good" china is used once or twice a

year; silverware less. It takes tons of energy to keep it. After you die someone will probably end up feeding their mangy hound dog out of it anyway. Those place settings would pay for a trip or an education that would nourish you much more than any food eaten off them ever will!

Hobbies and Collections

Some of the most worthwhile and inspiring achievements in the world come from people who gathered, preserved, restored, and displayed things and appreciated their greatness. But the value of this whole undertaking is in *sharing* it—displayed (or otherwise used) hobbies and collections stimulate our fellow humans and prod them to accomplishment.

As long as a collection produces those effects, it's probably a plus, but think of how many "collections" end up out of bounds and perspective. The model train that took a space on the floor . . . then the room . . . then the adjoining room . . . then a choo-choo rolls out of every cupboard and the dog and the kids get kicked for fiddling or playing with it. Our stained glass or jewel collection often gets too valuable to be used or left in sight and we wouldn't think of selling it—then what value is it? A time, space, and energy robber!

Locked or hidden away, collections can be a mental drain to their owner, because they generate no love and appreciation, yet the owner has to store, insure, clean, and protect them. But it can't be denied that some of us get a (perhaps not admirable) thrill out of simply acquiring, hoarding, counting, running our fingers over, polishing—all by our own personal selves—our *collections*. If it really adds to our life, then it is of unquestionable value; this again is why "junk or not" is a judgment only you can make.

Hobbies and collections can help us develop great discipline and organization, but too often, as time passes we've outgrown them—yet the skeleton remains to haunt us in the form of clutter. Use it (to show, etc.) or lose it. Make sure it rewards you and others.

Antiques

We all cherish the history, character, and spirit that antiques convey. They are great on display in museums or mounted in galleries or put to use in homes, but when our whole house becomes a "no touch" antique asylum, we may want to reassess our "valuable" merchandise. Is it just for show, status, an "I got it first" ego object? If so, it will junk your life—donate it and have them engrave your name on a plate and fasten it to the case. That way you'll get full credit, thousands will see it, and it will last many of your lifetimes (that's more than you were accomplishing with it around the house).

One of the biggest problems with antiques is that we all have a friend or have read an article that tells us we have a fortune under those cobwebs; we are often naive enough to elevate that careless inexpert opinion to a bona fide art appraisal, an endorsement to save clutter, if not an agony of unfulfilled expectations. When I worked with teams of horses as a youth, old worn-out horse collars were of zero value, and we junked them. So when in Jackson Hole, Wyoming, I saw a collar with a mirror mounted in it, price-tagged at $200—gads, I was sick; I'd thrown away at least $2,000 worth of horse collars! I resolved henceforth to save all old farm stuff in case another such opportunity arose. After six sheds filled up and seventeen dealers were craftily detoured through them and still no one was knocking at my door, I realized I was deceiving myself. Don't horse around with imagined antiques—and as for the real ones, use them or lose them.

It's amazing how an aged, broken, chipped, scarred, worn-out object dug out of storage or the trash becomes valuable—what is it that accounts for this sudden worth?

Why do people have a fascination and longing for the old, the quaint, the antique? They want to retreat to, be reminded of, be projected back to a simpler day of greater freedom and integrity—they secretly want to be *de-junked!*

Junk Doesn't Generate Self-Esteem

During an evening discussion of clutter (which one often has when writing a book about it), three sharp professional home consultants brought up an interesting concept. They visit many homes helping people straighten up their lives (and dwellings), and had observed that people (rich and poor) who have themselves and their homes overloaded with things often have extremely low self-esteem. After that conversation I began to pay close attention to those who should be de-junking. Many are professional people, astute community leaders, etc., but they don't seem to measure up to what they're trying to be. They have tons of "in" or "proper" things but seldom ever *use* them—the stuff is just displayed like banners or flags, a kind of testament of intention. These people have jogging suits but they don't jog, exercise bikes that are rusting out, how-to-discipline-children books but unruly kids, and tons of hunting or fishing or camping gear but they never hunt or fish or camp. They buy cookbooks to assuage their guilt for never cooking. By owning and surrounding themselves with the trappings, they somehow satisfy the need to be what people expect them to be.

Often the best-equipped, best-prepared person is the one who does the least—he'll buy a Whole Hog Industrial Power Pack III when a nice home-model Black & Decker would do just fine. A friend of mine once bought a 790-piece tool set from Sears in a rolling tool chest; he never turned a bolt, but it made him feel he was *equipped* to do anything that might come up.

Junk doesn't generate self-esteem or fulfill our ambitions—only *we* can do that. "Owning" is like theory, totally worthless if not put to use. Sitting there in idle beauty, clutter can in fact *undermine* our self-esteem—all those "I ought, but I don'ts" will get you every time they're brought to sight or mind.

No Strings Attached

Why do we keep old musical instruments (Grandma's organ) indefinitely?

Anything that has strummed our heartstrings like an old guitar (even two of them) is difficult to pitch. I never could part with the first guitar I had, an old flatbox folk guitar. It wouldn't stay in tune and finally was impossible to play, but I'd learned a lot of chords on it, and it was so "purty" I couldn't throw it away. I hung it on our western-styled kitchen wall for decoration, and there it stayed, collecting grease, for five years, until one day our house was robbed and the guitar went with the burglar (I'll bet he cusses me every time he tries to tune it).

My second guitar was a cutway electric I'd had since 1953 (through high school, college, and many performances), a premium model—but the treble switch was staticky and the strings finally shorted out—even people who borrowed it for free, never did so again. But yesterday, when I came home with a brand new electric guitar, throwing that old one out seemed like cutting off an arm—it was all those memories. I finally gathered up my resolve and in last ceremony played "The Cowboy's Lament," took it to the valley, laid the sod o'er it and amazingly, it didn't hurt a bit!

When four reeds are plugged on the old harmonica, when the piano ivories are headed for the elephant's graveyard, all the knobs are gone on the radio, and the stereo speakers are cracked and rattley—when you're shuffling through those warped and skipping records and the tapes you never play—do like the song says, "Please release them."

While we're tuned to the channel of freeing ourselves, let's not forget those delightful and intriguing music boxes. Though they rarely are used as the jewelry box or beer mug they pretended to be, their sound justifies their possession—and so our dresser tops boast them over time until the love theme from *Rocky XII* or "A Tisket a Tasket" no longer tinkles forth. The twirling ballerinas lapse into spasms and the latches are sagged or broken from showing it off. It's now mute and ugly but we'd sooner part with our season symphony tickets than discard that broken music box. De-junk it at its demise—thank it and cast it forth!

Lettered Litter

Anyone who thinks of starting his own business or ranch will, even before important financial and logistical considerations are weighed, immediately determine how his name or brand will appear. There is some understandable ambition in wanting to see our name in lights, and since there's no way we can drag a 3,000-watt marquee or a 12-pound branding iron around with us, having our name on smaller things—well, it hypnotizes us. If someone engraved our name on a steel manhole cover, we'd find a way to roll it home and store it. If we could, we'd carry home *all* the stuff we've ever name-branded—every beech tree, cliff, school desk, and restroom wall. Our name, even our initials, emblazoned on anything seems to be the official stamp of

discard immunity. A 35¢ hanky, once stained and stinky, can be junked easily; a 35¢ monogrammed hanky in similar condition merits full-scale restoration. People keep nonfunctional suitcases with their initials on them far longer than they keep the same non-initialed type. Same with belts, shirts, shorts, bracelets, and tools. The mystique of a monogram protects tons of junk—silly, and impractical, too. Many such things are designed more to show off a monogram than for function, and you can't even loan things!

The only thing sillier than being obsessed with wearing your own initials is being obsessed with wearing someone else's. Celebrity monograms (about ½¢ worth of thread) have about a 10,000 percent markup. I bought a suit in Miami, and because my color-matching leaves a lot to be desired, I had the salesman pick a tie out for me. A few days later when I was wearing it in Chicago on business, a man said to me, "Anyone who wears a _____ can pay the price." It turned out my tie had a designer monogram on it, which no doubt was why it cost $32.50. Why should I pay extra to flaunt someone else's advertising around? I gave the tie away! Don't waste good money and good taste flexing your monograms.

Is Nothing Sacred?

Because many people are interested in but few understand religion, with its many confusing denominations and approaches, they want to make sure they are spiritually secure. So they think owning something "religious" or "God-related" will help—the more they have, the thicker the spirit will be. And it's hard to get rid of religious junk because we're afraid dumping it might be an unholy action.

I know I'm treading on hallowed ground now, so I'll only suggest you cast an eye over all the stuff you've saved to "save" you and handle it appropriately (pamphlets, replicas, wall hangings, plaques, bottled Holy Land dust, even the magnetic cross for your refrigerator door that glows in the dark). Let me just point out something to get you going. I'm not without religious conviction—I served two years in the mission field teaching Scriptures, I speak regularly at religious events and gatherings, and try to enact Christian principles in my life and business—but haven't you noticed our hangup with *owning* Bibles instead of reading them? In the course of an average life you could accumulate, without ever buying one, a whole library of Bibles. Dusting the Bible is no joke—it could be a three-acre undertaking.

I've seen all of these Bibles in one person's possession. Check the list—how many do *you* have?

- family Bible
- his-and-her Bibles
- storybook Bible (for the kids)
- large print Bible
- red letter Bible
- Grandpa's old Bible
- school Bible
- Army Bible
- Bible you won
- pocket travel Bible
- Bible on tape
- computer chip Bible
- postage stamp Bible
- leather-bound Bible
- Gideon Bible (swiped from the motel, just in case)

Thirty-three Bibles crammed in drawers and glove compartments won't impress anyone—surely not the Lord, who said:

Not everyone who sayest "Lord, Lord," shall enter the Kingdom, but he that doth the will of my Father in Heaven. . . .

Conduct is the only criterion for blessing. Holiness is in the application of the message—not ownership of it. "God Bless Our Home"—no matter how charmingly cast in plaster or stitched on linen—won't do the trick. Wandering through a perplex of pious paraphernalia is a waste of time. Leave some space for Him in your life, the space all that junk is taking up. . . . Amen, brother.

HOW DO YOU JUDGE VALUE?

Judgments on the worth or worthlessness of things are, in the end, your business, not mine as a writer or celebrated toilet cleaner. I'll be satisfied if I manage to make you stop and think about, weigh the worth of some of the "valuables" you hoard, guard, polish, worship, and display.

Don't be like the father who had four antique guns—not one-of-a-kind collector's items, but respectable pieces worth about $5,000 each. When his daughter reached college age, the family was pinched for cash and could see no way to pay $5,000 per year to see their vibrant and musically talented daughter fulfill her education and her dream. She never did, and the father kept those old guns around in a rack until he died. Then the kids divided them up, sold them, bought cars and couches, and partied. His daughter could have been a living inspiration for all his posterity; his guns ended up valueless. I know people who buy silver saddles and snowmobiles before putting braces on their children's crooked teeth. Fascination with trinkets passes, but a self-conscious child is cheated for fifty years.

Capital Clutter

Money was once a medium of exchange; somehow it has gotten to be a measure of personal value. Of course money is needed for sustenance and some convenience, but the time and energy we spend on its handling and possession can easily be the most catastrophic clutter in our life. Let me share some things I did at home and in my business that freed me to find the time and life and production I lost when buried in "finances."

Watching the financial "geniuses," reading the financial books and papers, and paying close attention to the classy ads and articles, I spread my money around, dealt with several banks, and had a dab of money in this investment and a dab in that investment and some in different savings accounts. Really a meager amount, but it felt so up-to-the-moment and impressive (like reading the whole stock page because you own three shares of stock in some firm).

I had three drawers full of checkbooks and deposit slips and six separate files for different statements and transactions. Some accounts only had $35 in them, but took as much room and mail as if it were $35,000. For fifteen years I kept a separate savings account for some leftover escrow money—less than a hundred dollars—yet every time a statement came (expensive for me and the bank) I had to file it, and every time tax time rolled around all those times, places, and amounts—no matter how paltry—had to be added in and around. When my accounting bill got to $3,000 I realized how stupid all these little things were—some $25 insurance dividend funds cost over $45 in legal and accounting fees yearly (not counting my own time and effort).

The balancing and paperwork to keep up these financial appearances ("image") wasn't worth it. All those accounts and investments junked my life; it was a total waste of time and space. *All* financial institutions offer the same product—*money*. Who you deal with and how they deal with you is the only important variable. I finally found one banker I liked and got rid of my numerous accounts. At tax time or any other time I need anything there is only one summary sheet, one person to deal with.

Like magic, my mail and accounting costs and "personal finance time" shrank when I consolidated things and got rid of all the twinky and squirrelly financial involvements. Every day I get calls for "deals" where I only have to put in a little each day or week or month and. . . . The trouble with these, no matter how legitimate they may be, is that you forget how much of yourself will also be invested there.

People who make percentages off you are experts—when they know you can't afford something, financially or emotionally, they work out a payment deal so you can get it. Fifteen percent return on something that strains a relationship, a marriage, or your health is a poor investment.

My life blossomed when I de-junked my financial clutter. The week I used to spend rounding up all the deals, the week of the accountant's time to check and calculate, I now use for a week in Hawaii or with my grandkids. The fewer window envelopes that arrive at the first of the month, the more I can see and feel the refinements of living.

The Polite Man's Burden: Gifts

Most of us manage to obtain ample (excessive) junk through our own efforts; we don't really need the help of friends contributing to our stack, but they do. Christmas, Hanukkah, birthdays, Valentine's Day, goodbyes, hellos always inspire a gift, of cash or sentimental value. It's the thought that counts, of course, but once the thought is registered, we still have the item hanging around. We all get gifts that are junk, but it isn't couth to throw out a gift. "What if I throw it out and they find it in the trash," or "What if they come to my home and don't see it in use, won't their feelings be hurt?" Well, they probably will be, but getting rid of the stuff would help eliminate daily irritation in *your* life.

Someone gave my mother-in-law a beautiful thick hand-knitted wool Kleenex box cover, the sole purpose of which was to make a Kleenex box pleasing to look at. It also made the box bulky and hard to carry around, and pulling tissue through the slit in the top was not undifficult by any means. Her husband became a raging bull each time the knitted cover was reinstalled, but my

mother-in-law refused to part with this hard-to-clean, non-matching, totally unuseful piece of clutter—because it was a *gift*.

It is "ill-mannered" to give or throw a gift away—no matter how worthless it may be—so we keep it. Most of this is or becomes junk. (Have you ever noticed how just about everything in a "gift shop" you could get along very well without?) So those dreadful bookends and fancy pen sets, overdone ashtrays, busts, plaques, and plates accumulate, collect dust, and in general complicate life. Who needs them? Paperweights, for instance—has anyone ever established what, when, and why paper has to be weighed down? Any paper on a desk long enough to be weighed down should have been acted on or thrown out. Give a paperweight long enough and it will get scratched or stolen, broken or back-drawered, all testifying it is junk. But again, it's a "gift"—which seems to sanctify it and earn it a right to plague us the rest of our lives. The Board, the kids, the Scouts, the team gave it to us, or our sweet caring mother (and in this case, it's probably a hand-hooked rug with a decided resemblance to the Washington Monument). We'll drag it around from house to house like an old buffalo hide, never used—but *Mother* gave it to us. Or it's a razor-sharp seashell-encrusted purse that matches nothing, and holds less—but our son brought it back from the South Pacific. So our lives are "gifted" to the point of strangulation; this is when people plan fires, escape to Tahiti, or contemplate suicide. They can't face the junk any more, but can't face the donor if they dump it.

What Is the Value of a Gift?

A gift, regardless of its value, if given sincerely has a certain sacredness. It is a concise message of love and appreciation, a nod of acknowledgment for something felt. But we should always remember not to confuse the *meaning* of a gift with the gift itself. The actual gift is only a vessel to express; once it does that, it generally has fulfilled its function. Its message will live with us, be part of us—forever, possibly—but should we drag around the vessel after it has served its purpose? That's like leaving the scaffolding up after a building is finished—take it down!

An incident that sheds some light on the question of gift values occurred on the way home from a two-week consulting job. I bought my wife a dozen long-stemmed red roses and presented them to her as I stepped off the plane. She was thrilled. The roses said I was thinking of her, the velvety petals were a delight to look at and touch, the scent stimulated old memories and some reflection on our future—all in all, it showed that I cared, that she was important to me. After she displayed them for a few days and basked a little in the jealousy of her friends, the roses withered and drooped and were thrown out with no regrets. They had accomplished their job; it was $27.50 well spent.

En route to the airport in Atlanta on Valentine's Day a couple of months later, I spotted a tailgate sale on the side of the road. There was a gigantic display of oversized stuffed animals—I mean some

were five feet high—tigers, skunks, pandas, bears, deer, etc. I stopped and selected a big yellow dog with a bright red tongue; it was impressive if I say so myself. Wanting to get rid of every toy, the guy sold it to me for $27.50. It was a bear to get home on the plane, but I managed and presented it to my wife at the airport. As before, she was thrilled, the giant fuzzy doggie with the big eyes said I was thinking of her, its enthusiastic expression caused some old memories to come back and some reflection on our future—all in all, exactly like the roses, it showed that I cared, that she was important. After she displayed it a few days, stroked and cuddled it, and her friends saw it, the doggie drooped a little, one eye loosened and fell off, but no way was she going to throw the ailing animal out. It stayed around, fell over, got torn and dirty, the stuffing straggled out. It was a real pain, but it was *tangible*. The minute I gave it to her we got our $27.50 out of it, just like the roses—them you can pitch, but the mutt stayed to make life miserable.

One day we finally decided that dingy dog went or else—we'd enjoyed it, why not let it work again for someone else? A little neighbor got more mileage out of it, and again it thrilled someone (almost as much as me).

Think of the things you have received or given that cost even less than meals, roses, perfumes, etc., that are long gone, but that you got your money's worth and more out of even though you have nothing physical left to show for it. Many of the things that bring fun or enjoyment to our lives, promote good will, give us a good thrill, or carry a caring message are not *objects*. So why keep every trinket? You don't have to keep them to prove anything. The memories and feelings don't reside in the gift, but in *you*, and a tangible gift can actually become a junk millstone around your neck.

Give gifts that dissipate—like perfume! But clutter collectors could foul that up, they'd keep the bottle. . . . Give a basketful of fruit, they'd love it, eat it, and it would be gone—except they'll keep the basket!

A $5 ticket—a smile/a message—*gone*
A $5 trinket—a smile/a message—*keep*

Dare to Be Really Different

We all like to be unique in our personality and possessions, and this "individualism" contributes mightily to clutter accumulation. We'll search unrelentingly for something "different"—for us, or for a gift. Giving the unusual is the highest standard of gift giving. The harder to find, the rarer, the odder, the greater the mystique, the greater our point score and (regardless of its worth) the more greatly it is valued. An object's actual use or contribution is no consideration here—only the fact that "no one else has one." This is why those catalogs crammed with monogrammed toilet paper, electric bookmarks, talking lamps, and walking false teeth are so compelling.

What happens to such things after the giddy moment of presentation is generally ignored. The "different" thing is among the most eligible to become junk. To really be different, let's not waste each other's time and money on them. I won't dump any on you if you won't on me, because we'll both have trouble discarding them.

Can Charity Be Uncharitable?

We've all fallen once or twice for the tempestuous acquisition of a gift for no one in particular. We spot something we want, we don't really *need* it, we can't really afford it, it doesn't 100 percent suit us—but it's lovely: we want it. Our conscience sides with dejunking and tells us no!—but it's so *nice* (it could be a simple clay pot or a slab of salmon). We finally resort to Scripture, which tells us charity is the most honorable of human acts, so we get it "to give, to someone." Now that we have bought it without guilt, one of three things will happen:

1. We will never give it to anyone.

2. If we *do* give it to someone we hold dear, we'll have to give them another gift on top of it (because we know *they* don't really want it).

3. We'll end up giving it to someone we had no intention of giving anything to. We really aren't being kind—we're making *ourselves* feel better.

Listen to your conscience—IT KNOWS!

When giving gifts, don't saddle your giftee with junk. Ralph Waldo Emerson gave some good guidelines for a gift:

The only gift is a portion of thyself. Thou must bleed for me. Therefore the poet brings his poem; the shepherd, his lamb; the farmer, corn; the miner, a gem; the sailor, coral and shells; the painter, his picture; the girl, a handkerchief of her own sewing. This is right and pleasing, for it restores society in so far to its primary basis, when a man's biography is conveyed in his gift, and every man's wealth is an index of his merit. But it is a cold, lifeless business when you go to the shops to buy me something which does not represent your life and talent, but a goldsmith's.

How to Dispose of Junk Gifts

You are not obligated to prolong the misery of a possession someone (however sincerely) had the poor judgment to lay on you. We love people for the *thought* of the gift, not the gift. Once they present it and we've accepted it, the relationship is strengthened and made richer (which is the value of any gift). If the item happens to be a loser, make it a winner by chucking it.

But as sure as we finally take it to the thrift or secondhand shop, the owner will wander in the establishment the next day and weep over our heartless gesture. If we store it, it won't be visible when they visit, and they will quiver and pout. My wife always sicced the kids on unwanted gifts and they got broken and thrown out pronto. But the kids had a way of blabbing to the donor in detail how their mama begged them to play hockey with it. And the time-honored tactic of re-wrapping and re-giving (preferably to someone you don't care all that much about) is risky business in this small world of ours.

If a Gift Is Good or Valuable

Give it to someone else down the line in the family who might actually need it. "Passed for posterity" is usually accepted *within* a family.

You can take a color picture of the gift—then forget where you put it. The picture is evidence that you must have appreciated it—after all, who would photograph junk?

You can leave it in your car, on the back seat (gift-wrapped if necessary), and park your car, unlocked, in a rough section of town. If it doesn't disappear quickly, leave the window down a little. When you tell the giver the gift was literally swiped from your car, they will be flattered that (1) you were carrying it around, and (2) someone wanted it enough to steal it. That's double value—triple if you count your relief.

My brother pulled off a useful variation on this approach. He had two unwanted bucket seats so he left them on the front lawn while the family went on a trip. Sure enough, upon their return, the seats were gone. Before their next move they did it even more easily: "We just left the garage door open, old sofa in front, and as the song goes, 'Phtt—she was gone.' "

You can put your name on a gift and donate it to a museum—that really turns the giver on: they'll love you as much as you love getting rid of the junk. Or if you can, donate it to an auction (just make sure it's in another town).

If you let the word out that you don't like expensive gifts, or that it is against company or personal policy to accept gifts, it's amazing how quickly gifts stop.

As a last resort, go join a religious order, make a pilgrimage, take on a mission! Anything you rid yourself of in the name of the Lord will never be questioned.

Or you can write a book on clutter—it's amazing how fast people quit giving you trinkets. My last birthday found me in the middle of editing this book; at supper my two daughters and wife confessed they had no present for me; they'd looked for four hours and found nothing I hadn't attacked in this volume. The fact that they had spent four hours flattered me—what a gift—I loved it! We all came out ahead! My mother sent me a cassette on which she'd taped my favorite violin music, another daughter called from Ottawa, my son-in-law baked a mess of trout he'd caught, my granddaughter gave me a card she'd crayolaed on construction paper, and my oldest daughter canned me fourteen quarts of fresh raspberries. I've treasured that birthday as my all-time best!

Homemade . . . Makes It Hard

Homemade, with their own hands, from the heart—even the most heartless de-junker flinches when trying to dispose of that 400-pound solid chipboard bedstand or that pink and purple Mother's Day apron the kids made in camp or at the school shop. Show me a daddy, mommy, grandpa, or grandma who can easily part with even the most obnoxiously misspelled handicraft. Besides being hard to lift, those precious handmade shoeshine boxes, plaster hand casts, end tables, and jewelry boxes are durable as granite and will survive six generations. Once made, you're stuck: since you usually don't want to be seen with them, they don't have a chance to wear out or get broken. Deep in my heart I have a solid respect for what those schools and camps produce through a bunch of kids. They embalm a pile of popsicle sticks with white glue and those babies are indestructible. Earthquake, flood, or fire—they will survive it all, so don't consider any arsonistic approaches. And of course, no one in the right mind would steal them.

What's the solution? I'm stumped, and I have a two-pound tooled leather keychain, a three-inch-thick wooden soap holder, a painted rock, and a pine-cone panther mounted on a slab of barnwood staring me in the face right now. If there are unusually tender feelings involved, it's probably worth the sacrifice to use it—it's no worse than telling someone how great his or her cooking is when it really requires a Rolaid encore. If not, try to have it disappear on a transfer from home to office (everyone will understand).

Sneakiest of all is feigning a real act of love—give it back to them as a cherished memento of *you* to appreciate (they'll trash it, instantly, without a qualm).

What about Trophies and Awards?

Helping others, winning, succeeding, participating, playing, working, attending, or entering just about anything is likely to earn you a trophy or award. These come in the form of certificates, cards, pins, badges, plates, plaques, figurines, bookends, and desk sets.

Trophies and awards, like gifts, are basically a "thank you," a tangible affirmation of success or excellence. It's a thrill to get one, no doubt about it. But if you are really good and get better, you'll get more and more and more—and evolve from an end table to a mantel, to a shelf, to a wall, to an entire room to hold and display them all.

Every year I donate to the Scouts they give me an oak wall plaque. Every time I raise the ante they enlarge the plaque; I'll have to quit donating now after fifteen years because my wall is full.

At a seminar in Bridgeport they gave us the board that came under the eight-inch sandwich we had for lunch. Because I shared the forest on my ranch with a church group, they presented me with a plowshare on which was engraved their thank-you. At my numerous "Life After Housework" seminars I receive all kinds of gifts, from groups and individuals, ranging from miniature flowers to bronzed toilet brushes. Like all of you I appreciate these things, but at some point what do you do with all this? Too many awards can bother rather than build your life. Besides, I'm a little leery of people who have to line their walls with certificates and awards. If you've got it or had it, it should show in your personality and production. Glory is air—but the strength of character and body you developed on your way to earning the award is yours. It's not junk, but a life-giving resource.

Don't take old trophies and awards too seriously. Most of them look like they were carved or cast out of one of the same three molds anyway, and they tarnish, tear, tip over, and provide a landing strip for flies; you end up spending most of the athletic or creative skill you earned them with now manipulating them.

Cull out the dead ones and keep the living; when the living ones are no longer giving, dump them! Build a trophy room or case if you must, but if you don't get them out from underfoot, they'll become snares instead of signatures of accomplishment.

Consider *giving* them away—let your kids, grandchildren, and your neighbors' children thrill again to them as toys or rewards for chores or heroics. Kids are smart enough to wear it out or lose it. This is also a good place to make use of the photograph technique: take a good sharp photo of it for your album or scrapbook, and you may be able to part with it at last. You can even group all your trophies in one picture. The memory won't go—only the memorabilia.

And if you're *giving* an award, try to remember that trophies are basically useless. An ax can chop and serve; a trophy with a golden ax on top is good for nothing. Give a living award—films, tapes, equipment, clothing, cash, trips—not a shrine that must be tended.

What to Keep
of the Keepsakes

Memories are our most valuable possessions, and collected tokens of them can stimulate those memories to be relived again and again. Some tokens and keepsakes are valuable: they enrich life, and we should keep and take care of those. But in the lives of even the most sentimental of us a time arrives, often during a basement- or attic-sorting surge, when memories and junk have to be separated. On a thing as personal as a keepsake, that can only be *your* decision. I offer just one guideline before you start:

Don't love what can't love you back

"I am so sentimental"—aren't we all! But you don't have to *own* something to experience it. A memory, a look, a word,

a touch can generate greater good feelings than a box of "stuff."

We all want to cherish a good memory or experience forever, but preoccupation with physical reminders can lead us to live in the past. One of the toughest and most necessary things in the world for growth and happiness is to release our hold on things, places, and people we've outgrown. Too many people never grow and gain expanding new experiences because they can't see the wisdom of releasing old ones. Junk squeezes out new life. It's more fun being a present or future hero or heroine than a past one.

Consider my high school graduation tassel, a nylon witness of four long and eventful years. It was blue and white, but age turned it yellow and black (our competitor school's colors); it began to fray and shrink, and even the " '53" rusted.

Everyone knew I had graduated, and now all my kids were graduating from college. I lived those days, it fulfilled its purpose, and after twenty-five years, I finally pitched it, wondering why I untangled and worried about it for all those years.

Aftermath junk Be sure you distinguish keepsakes from aftermath junk—which has got to be about the sickest junk of all. This consists of keeping something to remind you of a terrible experience, like the knife that cut the tendon in your hand, that old cast, your kidney stones, your ex-boyfriend's insulting letter and even his frayed jacket, the tennis shoes you were wearing when you scored the goal for the other team and lost the national tournament. Some people can't stand a mate—so they de-junk, get rid of him or her—but then they keep all the little things that remind them of that person. With all the new life and love out there, constantly resurrecting old suffering memories is really straining for something to do in our spare time.

What we hold dear we become Should we choose to spend our lives collecting, preserving, and storing artifacts and inactive possessions we will find ourselves, as we wander through them taking inventory, wandering past the precious moment of life at hand. Holding fast to the unneeded and unused—no matter how valuable it once was—will crowd out the capacity for new and greater honors and accomplishments. As a reminder, record, or instructor, our "past things" have value, but the secret is to not let charm turn into chains, sentiment become a sentence.

This is one of the most important judgments you'll ever make—only *you* know the moment when collectibles have become clutter in your life, and only you have the responsibility to put it right. De-junking will fertilize the soil of your future and make room for more living.

When you stop dragging the skeletons of the past, the once-was or once-did with you, you'll have more freedom to love and be loved. Free yourself from clutter at the critical moment when what you are giving *to* it outweighs what you are gaining *from* it. De-junking is the easiest and most rewarding way to change a plain life to a plus life.

When it comes to keepsakes, ask only one question: *For whom are you keeping it?* Who is the documentation for—you? *You* don't need proof—you *experienced* it. Meaning isn't kept in things, but in memory.

There is no possession finer than a good memory of something. You can use it over and over again, it can make your pulse quicken, your heart sigh, bring tears of joy to your eyes or a laugh to your day—and a good memory of something costs nothing to keep.

Keep It in Your Heart, Not Your Closet

Two weeks after my father's death, Mother brought me his hunting boots (we wore the same size). As I went to place my foot in one, I hit an obstruction—and pulled out a piece of 2x4 carved into a crude but effective block to keep the shape. Those blocks were Dad all over—his ability to get a job done well and inexpensively. I could have cast them away there and then, but I kept them a day or two to absorb their image and feeling—and then was able to pitch them and still feel good about it.

We can't hang onto everything our loved ones ever owned or gave to us, or even to all the things of theirs we find meaningful. But don't hurry to dispose of their belongings; keep them awhile, meditate on them, store up the memories—then save a few most-cherished items and give or throw away the rest.

MINIATURIZE

Miniaturize It

It's perhaps a compromise, but miniaturizing is a solution especially suited to keepsakes and sentimental items—sort of a "reduce-it-if-you-*must*-keep-it" strategy. You might call it "tons to tokens!"

Miniaturizing is the art of taking a big piece of junk that has to go and reducing it to a little piece of junk that can discreetly stay around. It takes little skill and even less imagination to pluck just a button off that shaggy dog sweater, snip a swatch of the wedding dress, press a rosebud instead of the bouquet, salvage the hood ornament instead of the whole car, save the emblem instead of the entire jersey, keep the elk's tooth instead of the elk's head. When the pangs of reluctance tug at you to keep what must go, sit back a second, look at it, and find a way to reduce it to miniature. For stirring memories a piece, symbol, or sample is as effective as the whole.

A woman in Texas was de-junking her house, and had a special problem. Her nineteen-year-old son had died a year earlier; disposing of his belongings was difficult. She had faced the fact that he was gone, but wanted his memory to stay alive and active. He had been a pencil collector, and had accumulated a fine array of them—of no real use to anyone in the family, but a precious reminder of their son's interest. "Should I let them go, or what?" the mother asked me. I agreed that the memory of the pencil collection was important, but to cart a roomful around for the next forty years would benefit no one. I suggested that she select seven or eight that represented the collection and mount them handsomely with a picture of the boy. As for the rest, I suggested taking a couple of nice photographs of them and putting the photos in an album where others could admire and remember, then giving the remaining pencils to a special boy who might have an interest in continuing the collection.

Miniaturizing works on many kinds of clutter, and not just physical objects. If you must use abusive language, for instance, instead of two sentences of ranting and raving uncouthness—reduce it all to one little snarl or arf. It's really the most effective, impressive, and efficient way to swear.

Those headhunters had the right idea for their trophies—*shrink those babies!* Still clutter but less cumbersome.

Consider a Scrapbook—the De-Junker's Bible

I love scrapbooks! They are one of the finest ways of de-junking life and abode. A good scrapbook is interesting and inspiring even to a stranger. Experiences, awards, friends, and accomplishments can all be dramatized and summarized in the pages, where they can be easily shared or enjoyed to our secret heart's content. Well-put-together scrapbooks and photo albums have warmed more hearts, aroused more loyalty, and advanced more personal relationships than any bound book because it's *your* life and feelings between those covers. The secret is to assemble the most meaningful documents and materials, prune them down to the important parts, and display them attractively in a sequence that's logical and easy to follow. Without a good scrapbook much that's memorable in life is forgotten or damaged or lost. If you don't have one, start one today—whether you're nine or ninety—and watch the responses of others. They can now enjoy what you enjoy, feel what you feel—and what could be greater than that!

Can Posterity . . .
Be Preposterous?

Preserve for posterity, but don't become a posterity pervert. Too often our efforts to record an event for posterity end up reducing its significance. Preservation should be a by-product of an event, not dominate it. Take weddings, for example—a serious spiritual time of commitment between two people. We can't simply and quietly allow the couple to have full feeling for the occasion; too often, the whole ceremony has to be scheduled and conducted around the formalities of pictures, flower girls, souvenir-saving, and speeches. The photographers seldom stand aside and take a real action photo of the occasion; they halt the ceremony and move people around according to height, relationship, seniority, and what-have-you. They make the bride and groom stand, sit, kneel, calf-eye with every (even distant) member of the family. No one can gather around the cake at its cutting because the photographer has to be in front to get a clear shot for posterity. The rings have to be placed on the fingers two or three or four times, the cake cut and re-cut to get

the "right" things for posterity—everyone is so bent on preserving they never savor the actual rapture of the moment. Sports events, graduations, showers, baptisms, too, are often so shaped around formality and documentation that the participants are too preoccupied and harassed to feel much going through the motions—they have to look at the pictures to actually experience the event.

At a Scout Jamboree we had 3,000 youngsters to a church service, a great speaker, a great morning to remember—but the media and the posterity perverts ruined it all by trying to preserve it. My most vivid memories are of whirring tape recorders, camera/video technicians crowding their rumps in our faces, and then a helicopter (large Army model) hovering and passing over us ("whop, whop, whop")—such that we all missed most of the service.

Experiences are meant to be just that—an actual live experience. They shouldn't be prerecorded to be "aired" later in life. I've watched people at Yellowstone so bent on collecting "records" to enjoy later, they missed the beauty of the park. They were so buried in junk food, so busy shooting pictures, buying souvenirs, T-shirts, and maps to the next sight that they never took a minute to stand and soak in the actual experience of that spectacular place. We can't prerecord our life for replay, because at the replay we're only spectators. The joy comes from the participation. Laying up treasures of the event to enjoy or for posterity to enjoy is not even in the same league with experiencing the event itself, letting all preservation be an optional by-product. Preoccupation with preservation doesn't heighten an experience; it diminishes it.

Your Last Gift: Don't Junk from the Grave

We all die, but life is eternal; our spirit, legacy, legend, and influence live on! So leaving and giving junk to your family is not only unnecessary but unkind. The "gift" obligation is a hundred times stronger when the giver is deceased— they'll never be able to dump your junk or rid themselves of guilt if they do. Get rid of your clutter and collections before you cash in—don't give junk a chance to be resurrected in someone else's life.

Everyone over fifty spends too much time and emotion worrying about what they'll leave to their family; everyone under fifty spends too much time and emotion worrying about what they're going to inherit. It's downright dumb. Leaving junk to a family is often more an act of revenge than of love. It's pathetic how families are broken apart, divided into a mass of quarreling maniacs squabbling and suing over dead people's junk. Oddly enough, it's usually not the normal inheritances of land or money that everyone gets most uptight about—it's the junk, the stuff only valuable to the person who previously owned and treasured it. After deaths and divorces I've seen families split apart, people quit speaking and do ugly, ugly acts trying to get their fair share of somebody else's

junk—a $3.95 pocket knife, a monogrammed hanky, a broken arrowhead collection, a rifle that hasn't fired straight in thirty years, an old ax, a worthless sewing machine, Grandma's rhinestone brooch, a disintegrating quilt.

Inheriting the Hoard

Think a minute—what will happen to all of *your* belongings, those stashed sentimental personal items, when you pass away? Someone, someday, will have to come and unappreciatively wade through it. To you, most of it is treasure; to them, it's trash—except the particular items they most associate with you. Unfortunately, it's trash they'll feel guilty disposing of because it's *yours*—the dear departed one's. Who were you saving all this for? For *you*. That's pretty ironic, because you never seem to use it or even take the time to look at it. I know we all imagine a miniature elf version of ourselves reverently handling all our leftovers. Not so—only *you* hold reverence for your own junk. So *use* it or, if others would, give it to them now, or sell it, so you can have the living thrill of benefit, instead of nagging regrets.

Don't burden someone else with your junk. Spend it, give it away, sell it—don't leave for heaven without it. Cash in your clutter before *you* cash in—start at age forty-five just to be safe.

How would you like your obituary to read like this:

She is survived by: a ceramic Elvis decanter; six bags of lint from the dryer; a corset puller; a purple fur-flower arrangement; three pairs of bronze booties; seven hundred copies of *Good Housekeeping*; an assortment of old campaign buttons; fifty-six lid-less cottage cheese cartons; fourteen half-finished needlepoint projects; eleven matted teddy bears; two cartons of unfiled recipes; a dried-up china-painting kit; seventy-three empty cigar boxes; a jug of pennies; a Ping-Pong paddle; a box of fortune cookie fortunes; and every birthday card she ever got.

CHAPTER 8

Taming the Paper Tiger

and Other De-Junking Adventures

Touring the impressive S. Rosenthal printing plant in Cincinnati one evening, we saw massive 23-foot high machines and other astounding production mechanisms that would rattle anyone's imagination—but the grandest daddy of all, the sight that awed us out by the railroad dock, was a 1,000-pound bale of paper. Why was that colossal bale so captivating? Because both my editor and I were thinking the same thing (as you would be also)—"I wonder, if all my paper junk at home were baled, I could match this massive bundle!"

Sad to say, most of us *could* match the print shop's impressive packet if we baled up all our worthless paper.

We are inundated daily with displays of reading matter—signs, menus, magazines, maps, papers, programs, brochures, labels, newsletters, books. We don't have to ask for it or buy it—it comes spontaneously, generously, regularly, much of it free. Seventy-five percent of it is or will quickly become clutter, and will smother the life out of us if we don't exercise some kind of control over it.

Go ahead and blush over your dead magazines and newspapers, but there's plenty of other incidental papery you need to start feeding the baler. Ever notice how most people keep expired life-insurance policies? Just in case reincarnation might occur in reverse, we'd better keep it. It looks so "legal." We paid so much for it.

The other faithful piece of paper junk never thrown out is the old raffle ticket; the fact that we keep it, though the drawing date was 1965, indicates that human hope truly never dies (as long as we keep junk around to remind us of it). Deep in our heart, we feel there may yet be a telegram from heaven telling us that we won after all. It'll never come; throw the ticket out. If you can't pass up the hope for a delayed win, microfilm the stub.

How much unopened junk mail, how many outdated brochures and newsletters, obsolete schedules, old lists, worn slogan stickers, wrinkled posters and old greeting cards and calendars, half-filled-out questionnaires, old contest entry blanks and magazine subscription offers, outdated résumés, box tops, expired coupons, and unidentifiable envelopes of stuff do you have stashed somewhere? (Probably under all your old hunting, fishing, and driver's licenses, or those eighteen never-used datebooks and diaries.) What about ancient books of addresses and names of associates—met once, long ago? Will you ever use them, or will they pile up and crowd out new friends and opportunities? All those handwritten notes awaiting translation might be memoir-excusables—but not the mounds of catalogs bulging out of every nook. (I know a well-educated woman who has over 600 assorted catalogs.)

The "paper weight" on our lives from keeping all this undiscarded print is a psychological ton. We can't shake the conviction that we are morally obligated to read, or at least scan, it before the trash truck totes it away forever. But remember, 75 percent of it is obsolete hours after it's printed, and after ten years under your wing of "gonnas," I think the other 25 percent has given up the ghost. Dump it! Don't give the old "I'm waiting for the Boy Scout drive" alibi—rip into that paper. If you get over a thousand pounds, call me—I've got to see it!

What Percentage of Mail and Magazines Is Junk?

When living on a remote farm in the '40s, my dream was to have a full mailbox— that was about the only outside contact besides radio that we had. I would send for Henry Field seeds, Lone Ranger bullets, Jack Armstrong treasure maps— anything to get mail. Today my dreams, like yours, have been fulfilled beyond my

wildest imagining. My personal, company, and post office mailboxes are stuffed with tons of junk mail in the course of a year— contests, real estate offers and condo deals, catalogs, sale brochures and flyers, box holder's notices, solicitations, address stickers, name-imprinted pens and pencils—plus, of course, my regular mail. I often have to pick up my mail in crates. This happens daily (except Sunday), so unless it is processed promptly, a pyramid of junk will form that I have to fight through to get to the serious business.

How many of you have old magazines or unprocessed mail lying around?

When I ask this question of my seminar or TV audiences, I get downcast eyes and a deep moan of guilt. Junk mail—or even "good mail" that ends up junk—is one of the most universal junk problems. It is stuffed, hidden, spread, stacked, piled, stored, filed, boxed, and even carried around in such abundance in most homes and offices (dorm rooms, cars, school lockers, too) that it's actually physical labor to handle, as well as an emotional drain to keep track of. Desk tops can't be found, bulging boxes are piled in closets, drawers are so clogged with junk mail they can't be opened. Most of this aged mail is worthless and is silently destroying some of your finest nerve fiber, and taking up some of your most valuable home space.

The "ostrich approach" to the mailstream can and does hurt employment, relationships, and the pocketbook. It can represent you as a trasher and thrasher, unable to handle your personal responsibilities. Dealing with mail and magazines is one of the most shamefully procrastinated acts of all. Instead of feeling bad or casting down your eyes any longer, take care of it.

You Can Handle Junk Mail in Minutes

Let me help you sort. You don't have to do it like I do—you can adjust the process to suit yourself—but here are some guidelines to expedite the task:

First, I never throw anything away before I look at it. It is only American to advertise, sell, and offer, and you should give *some* consideration—however brief—to what is sent or said to you. I once ripped up and threw away an envelope that appeared to be an insurance advertisement, only to find out later that it was a $1,300 check I'd been waiting for. Some "junk" mail is legitimate, so give it a look.

Magazines are fun to read and the stories and ads keep you aware of what's new, but remember a couple of things. Number 1: In most magazines, nothing is printed that is too profound or controversial or they would lose advertisers; most magazine material, while perhaps enjoyable, is not fantastically edifying to the mind. Number 2: Up to 70 percent of a magazine is advertisements and they are updated every month, so you don't need to keep them. You can go through a trade journal or newsletter in minutes, scanning the headlines. If there happens to be an article you want to read or save, tear it

out and read or file it, and throw the rest away—it's pure junk. Yet people store tons of magazines. What value is a ninety-pound box of 1968-72 *Better Biscuits and Garters?* Seventy percent is out-of-date ads; most of the rest is obsolete or out-of-style ideas.

When it comes to magazines, a little hard thinking while you're poised over the order blank can save a lot of guilt and accumulation later. Are you *really* going to read it? Or do you just want it to be seen in your mailbox?

And because you paid for it doesn't mean you have to read it. If you miss something, there's a good bet you'll be able to read it a year later in the doctor's office, because he keeps his even longer than you do.

Bills The most dreaded. In almost every home I cleaned in twenty-five years as a professional, there was a little den or pile of unpaid (and unopened) bills. Always open every bill immediately—never pitch or file one because you haven't the money to pay. Many of us have suffered for this. I had one for six months; I didn't open it 'cause I didn't want to know how much, and when I did it was worse than I thought. In fact, it was a ripoff on some construction work done for me. I yelled my head off about the $250 they had overbilled, but to no avail because six months had gone by—wheat had grown over the proof. I "hid" another bill from myself for months when cash was desperately tight; I worried, sweated, and finally opened it—to find it was a credit of $200, asking how I'd like it, cash or a check. If you can't take care of all your bills, at least be aware of to whom, how much, and when. Instant adjustment to the shock is less damaging than long-unknowing suspenseful agony. Don't keep bill stuffers; they're bulky and usually irrelevant—all you need is the statement or invoices, and if you insist, the envelope.

P.S. Unless you're into calligraphy, writing out return addresses on each bill envelope by hand is a junk pastime, so keep your eyes open for some tasteful means of "automating" it (a stamp or stickers).

Contest mailers Ahhh, just rub off the plastic cover, peel to reveal the hidden code, or simply match the numbers. And what do we win . . . a drawer full of false hope . . . junk paper. We keep the labels, cards, and coupons, peck out the jingles, and peek out the window to see if the mailman is bringing our $50,000 jackpot. He isn't, but he does bring us more and more and ever more junk mail, as our name is computer-plucked from contest rolls for future junk bombardment. When a real opportunity for fame and fortune comes to our door,

we miss it because we can't see over the pile of entries on the kitchen counter.

Sorry I'm so opinionated on this, but I think mail contests are almost immoral. Giving nothing and getting lots just doesn't work and never will. Hoping for something for nothing, which most contests encourage, will junk up your life. We waste a lot of valuable time and emotion dreaming and hoping—and even if we were the .000001 percent that won, our troubles would just begin. Many of the prizes are junk we don't want or need, and winning a vacation (or a lifetime) with nothing to do would ruin most of us. Complete the following sentence in twenty-five words or less:

Junk mail abounds in my abode because _____
_____
_____ .

Deals and Offers

When people have to solicit us for a deal, it is definitely not as neat a deal as we could go after on our own. There are plenty of deals in the mail, good and bad ones among them.

Have we got a deal for you: *COME TO LONE PINE CONDO* and be the first to get in on this time-sharing opportunity, for a tiny down payment, you'll have part ownership, horses, pine trees, privacy, swimming, friends, and quiet . . . all for $5,000. You'll get a FREE prize, free dinner just to come and look.

The best land deals and investment opportunities seldom come announced in bulk mailers. Most of them you can pitch, especially if they start: "You have been selected. . . ."

There seems to be magic in the word "investment," especially when we read rags-to-riches stories, how-I-gained-power tales, and "how by investing five minutes a week I made a million dollars, a master touch on the piano, this bustline or that bicep."

In this frame of mind we're set up for a plunge into the pool of gimmicks, not investments. Our world has fast become one big sphere of promise. Almost every person, company, group, organization, or government is constantly, twenty-four hours a day, trying to get us to invest in something. In the course of an average week in our life we'll be exposed to three hundred opportunities to improve life, gain a friend, see the world, master our emotions, or make money. All we have to do is say "Yes," then pay up, and wait for our ship to come in. . . . A great opportunity? No! On many of these investments there isn't even a ship sailing—you can be swindled. It happens fast; it happens often.

Make-money-at-home junk mail is awesome. There are hundreds of such schemes. When someone promises to make you a Rolls Royce-driving millionaire with no work, no investment, no selling, no risk, for a $10 formula, you are being insulted, not approached. If small fortunes were being made quietly at home raising earthworms, knitting nosewarmers, or stuffing envelopes, it wouldn't be a secret long.

A U.S. Postal Services expert testified in a TV interview that he had not seen even one of the hundreds of mail-advertised "make money at home easy" deals that he'd investigated work. Yet thousands of people respond in hope of financial solutions and send in some of the little money they do have, as the ad asks them to. Be careful—a dotted line can make a junk transfer in seconds.

Many of those direct-sales, "pyramid" fortune-building outfits promising something for nothing are among the biggest junk concepts in the world. Few ever make it. But homes and offices are littered with glorious brochures showing smiling families posed in front of their big shiny car and landscaped yard, proof that by using others you, too, can build a fortune.

Welcome to the (Clutter) Club

The most exhausted moment of my life was an evening I staggered to the bunkhouse after rounding up, on foot, a big herd of our cattle from a 640-acre pasture. The agony and fruitlessness of the whole job could all be traced to a single pin I had carelessly left unlatched on the gate. All was well, the stock were mooing and grazing where they belonged—until one cow leaned against the unlatched gate and it swung open. One started, they all followed, and then they all had to be rounded up. I thought I'd learned my lesson, but no—a pen the same size as the pin opened another gate . . . to a "Book-of-the-Century Club."

I read the coaxing, colorful ads for years and finally one book popped up that I wanted. It was free just for joining. I signed the coupon and the gate swung open and those paper dogies didn't stop. I'd read the bulletin buildup and find nothing I wanted so they'd send me *their* choice (*The History of Masking Tape*). I'd get so irritated that on the next offer, before they could just send me *A Rudder Study of the Great Sailboats*, I'd order it. I tried to get rid of my book club inventory as Christmas gifts, but others were doing the same and I ended up with gift copies of the same books I'd gleefully given away.

I stuck it out with the club for five years—do you realize how many months there are in five years? The books and extras were pretty, but seldom really edifying (or read). It was hard to get out because I still felt guilty about getting that free book up front, but finally, after being thoroughly junked, I withdrew.

Feeling relieved, de-junked, unburdened from that monthly pressure,

I still hadn't learned my lesson. A business book library offer came (what a clever way to disguise the *real* name—book club) and I fell for it. These were different, however—they cost $39.95 instead of $9.95 each and my corporate name was peddled to every mailing list and merchant in America. I really opened the gate this time—I had catalogs arriving hourly selling surplus Army jeeps, sexual aids, pewter paraphernalia, electronic dominoes, desert land, and ocean bottom. I never did read any of the big complicated business books, but the catalogs usually each had one item I might buy someday, so I kept them. In two years I could have opened my own publishers' clearing house—90 percent of the material, no matter how beautifully printed and presented, was junk.

Catalogs Allowing sleek, slick catalogs, large and small, to steadily enter your dwelling is like touring the bakery to start a diet, or opening the gate for a stampede of junk to follow. Remember the run on the L.L. Bean Company? L.L. Bean, known for years as a supplier of quality outdoor gear, was spoofed in a takeoff of their popular catalog that featured a bunch of adorable little items like doggie brassieres, a steal at $7.75 . . . sheepskin-lined cases for

canned tuna, $5 . . . even genuine edible moccasins for $41.75. The response was overwhelming, orders poured in, the phone lines were clogged.

Our fascination with the glossy anthologies of clutter called catalogs knows no bounds. The new ones pile up and take time we don't have to go through and discover new things we wouldn't have needed or wanted if we hadn't seen them there in all their full-color and backdropped glory. The old ones pile up because we never get around to wading back through them to weed out. And the clever companies who send the same catalog with a bright new cover four or six times a year (how can we throw it out—there might be *something* different in it) really thicken the stack. Catalogs not only add to our *paper* clutter, they have (in those innocent-looking little order blanks) the incredible potential to multiply every other kind of clutter on our premises astronomically.

Men who criticize their families or friends for having old papers or magazines around will have literally hundreds of pounds of old parts or equipment catalogs—you know, the looseleaf kind the parts guys thumb through on the counter. Every salesperson in the world must get a commission for the amount of ring-binder catalogs he or she unloads. Most are obsolete in a year or two. Once I bought an old bankrupt lumber store and found two pickup loads of binder catalogs dating back to 1947. I kept half a pickup full of the binders for four years to hold all my papers—and finally ended up dumping them. You'll never be reincarnated as a purchasing agent, so dump those old catalogs right now.

I haven't missed those books or catalogs since I de-junked them, and I sure love the space in my life I have left to pick what I want to read when I want to, and the space in my home to store the things I really want to keep.

Letters Open immediately, and if the address and date are on the letter, pitch the envelope. Read the letter, and if it doesn't call for a response, pitch or file it or save the address or make out a check or whatever and move it out. If it needs an answer, carry it with you until you answer it. That will be the best disciplined and most efficient way to be sure you do.

One of the most valuable skills of time management is learning to use time fragments—the ten minutes waiting in line, the twenty minutes waiting for a meal, the thirty minutes riding somewhere, etc. Letter-answering is an excellent way to do so. An unanswered letter is a prime candidate for mental debt—free yourself and your life!

Old letters aren't always clutter, neither are special cards and notes and postcards—they are human history. The letters that bring tears to our eyes and a flood of memory and love may be old and yellow, but never junk. Meaningful writings are easy to store and the amount of feeling they hold is well worth the space. If necessary, trim them down to get rid of the bulk.

I cut out the most meaningful parts of my favorite letters, laminate them, and insert them in books as markers. When I open the book—monthly, yearly, or every five years—there the letter is, in perfect condition, to remind me.

Calendars You only need a couple of calendars in a house, yet after Christmas we have one for each month. Because of the friends who gave them, or the fact that they came in the mail, or were given to us *free*, we feel obligated to keep all calendars and they end up being clutter. Our digital watches, TV, and newspaper remind us almost hourly what day and year it is; don't take or keep calendars if you don't need them—they cost the distributor a bundle and you'll never be able to throw them away because of all those pretty pictures.

Calendars—The Bigger the Better

The "big calendar" concept used by home efficiency expert Gladys Allen and others is a wonderful way to eliminate junk mail, unnecessary phone calls, and clutter.

A big calendar is one with the days marked off in squares big enough to write notes inside. Purchase the one with the largest squares you can find. Hang it on the wall next to your telephone and bulletin board (if your bulletin board isn't next to the telephone, move it!), near the heaviest flow of communication. Mount a pen or pencil on a string or in a slot beside your calendar. From now on, as soon as invitations and announcements arrive in the mail or are brought home, instead of hanging onto them (but never being able to find them when you need the information), simply transfer the data (address, time, etc.) onto the appropriate square of your big calendar, then toss the card or mailer out before it can clutter your house—and clutter your mind trying to keep track of it!

Place a wastebasket on the floor beneath your big calendar and watch the basket fill up with that flurry of junk you formerly had been saving, shuffling, hunting for, and worrying about. Things like wedding and party invitations, notifications of events, schedules, appointment cards and reminders, loose addresses of places you're going, assignments, instructions, letters containing specific information, etc., etc.—often we have our desk drawers stuffed full of this junk. We cram these things in our wallets or purses or stack them on the refrigerator to "remind" us of things we need to do. It's so messy and confusing—and so unnecessary—to keep it all around.

A great feeling of power comes from feeling in control of your life's events, from knowing what's coming up and where you've been. Big calendars can help you achieve that control at a quick glance.

If your mechanic tells you the brakes should be checked again in six months, flip ahead on your calendar and write in the checkup date. If your insurance comes due twice a year, don't always be caught unawares. Page ahead and calendar in reminders to yourself so you can budget ahead and have the money available.

Calendar in important birthdays and dates a year ahead, then mark reminders to yourself a week before so you can get the greeting card off on time.

Hang onto your big calendars and file them. They're a concise record of family history. They tell you everything you and your family did all year and exactly when you did it. Take the time at the end of the year to review your calendar month by month and write up a brief recap of your life for that year. It's easy with all the data right there to remind you.

File It Doesn't Mean Pile It. . . .

Files are one of the greatest repositories of "invisible" clutter going—just because it's alphabetized and tucked away in a drawer doesn't mean it isn't junk.

My values and needs change, as yours do, as the years pass and the thrust of my life changes, but seldom do I (or you) go back into my files and throw out the clutter and stuff that no longer applies. because "it would take forever." And besides, you say, you can throw it out when you happen to run across it going through for something else.

Well, it won't happen, and your files will grow into a Pentagon paper storage bank that makes retrieving anything (*if* you can find it) slow and costly. Yet it takes only minutes, while you're watching

a TV show or when you can't get to sleep some evening or your ball game is rained out—to sit down and riffle through some of your files. This is fun, educational, and reminds you how clever you are for saving all this stuff. If you chuck the clutter periodically, your files will stay healthy, and when you need something you won't have to mount an expedition or perform an excavation to get it. Office or home, *you* have to do it: if someone else cleans out your files, that is exactly what they might do—clean them out, and there goes the picture of you forty eons or so ago, the masterful letter that proved you weren't speeding, your grandfather's letter from Teddy Roosevelt. Sift your files yourself about once every three years—it's fun, and emotionally stabilizing.

Without a functional filing system, finding and using can be a maddening and disappointing quest. But there is such a thing as over-organizing—when you have to use a separate set of files to find where something was filed or otherwise put away, that's one step too many.

File to fit your personality and needs—don't try to follow the Dewey system invented for the American University Library. Surprisingly few folders or notebooks can organize almost anything you need and do it well. Don't stuff things in a drawer—that simple file folder, with a title or topic written across the top, will only take a minute to make and cost only twenty cents. When you need it, you'll be able to find it.

"I Know I Kept That . . . ."

1. We see or hear something interesting.
It's so great we want to save it, savor it, share it: a good joke/cartoon, an excellent article, a great idea, an exciting job, an important address or date, an intelligent quote, a tempting recipe, a solution.

2. We start to record it.

Because of the unpredictability of the moment, we often end up with our valuable bit of information written on the back of a used envelope, a napkin, the corner of a program, a candy wrapper, a hanky or shirt cuff, a piece of board, a boxtop, the back of a business card (or if we're lucky, a notebook or phone pad or calendar square).

3. We search in despair.

"I know I kept that . . . it would be just perfect for what I need if I could find it. . . . Where did I put it?"

If we do find it, we can't decipher it—too much time has passed!

4. Or use and share. . . .

This valuable material enhances our lives and others'. (If you are here you can skip the next page.)

Losing track of something we liked and saved is almost as sad as losing a cherished memory of a loved one: snatching gems of thought out of the torrent of life is one of our great pleasures. Develop your own system to be sure you save and *use* them. Your method will have to fit *you*, but it can help to get with someone who's a good "saver" and ask them to share their secrets (99 percent will be flattered to do so).

My system isn't sophisticated, but it works, and here is all I do: I save everything that impresses me (five to fifty tidbits a day). I carry a leather notebook shaped like an outhouse (you can be sure that no one wants to steal it). It has a pouch and a pad—everything I collect or jot down goes in one of these.

My notes I write out on the spot in my notebook on a sheet titled "Write & Record." I write each separate thought out in complete sentences under a key word or topic heading. I don't go into full detail or describe it completely, just enough that if I *do* want to go back to expand on it I'll know clearly what I meant. Writing down the notes only takes a minute, if done right at the moment the thought strikes.

When I get home I drop all my Write & Record notes (snipped into their separate topics) into a box labeled "Write & Record," and drop all the printed materials, programs, photos, documents, forms, booklets, etc., I've picked up into the "Important Paper" basket on my

desk. This way I have all my notes and gleanings in one of two places—not in pockets, bags, boxes, books. . . .

I don't use prime/highly productive/all-cylinders time—such as morning hours—to file the material in these two boxes; this can be done in time fragments, on semi-sick days, while watching TV or tending kids, while waiting for someone, right before and after meals, on sleepless nights, etc.

My files are arranged so that I have a drawer for each of my important interests and one alphabetized "general" file drawer. My immediate-interest projects/current enthusiasms I keep in ring binders—such topics, for me, for example, as The Life Story I Will Write Some Day, Salable Article Ideas (I've accumulated over 8,000 without any special effort to do so), Janitorial Humor, etc.

Ring-binder notebooks are cheap (most of my binders are scrounged "recycles") and simple to use, and you can assemble a useful library of your very own just in your spare time and odd moments.

I use an inexpensive rubber stamp to stamp my name on all my file materials—and I don't loan files! In seconds I can find anything I have and use it.

School Papers and Projects

After investing $2,000 each to bring our babies into the world, then another $10,000 to $15,000 to get them six years old and in school (plus an incalculable amount of love, effort, and emotion along the way), we seek evidence to assure ourselves they are going to be productive people. The first trickle of assurance comes in the form of some scribbled art done in kindergarten, and we snatch it into scrapbook storage. By first grade we actually see intelligent words (even if the letters are a little out of alignment);

every sheet is collected. By the second grade sentences overcrowd the scrapbook and stuff the drawer. By the eighth grade, we have mountains and foothills of evidence that our offspring indeed are literate. Once *we're* satisfied our kids have made it, we still can't dump the stuff because surely our kids' kids will want to see how their parents did—so we keep those school papers for the grandkids!

Kids' or your own, don't try to keep them all—just enough to be a decent sampling—and store the ones you save in a folder. Four Dick and Jane workbooks for every grade will end up flunking you (junking you). A few representative "works" for each grade really should suffice to soothe any pangs for fleeting childhood.

As for your own excess school papers, here is a definite solution. Throw away Cs down through Fs, so if your kids take after you (are just as dumb) you'll be safe. If your kids are smarties like you, you have lots of evidence of their inherited super-intelligence and don't need papers for proof.

Newspapers

A newspaper is an important tool of communication in our lives; it is also one of the most common forms of litter and clutter in our homes, offices, streets, and public buildings. As soon as a newspaper is read (and maybe an article or two torn out), it is obsolete; it's junk. Yet the average person keeps a week's (or a month's or . . .) papers around in case he might want to go back and reread. Who has ever read a newspaper twice? But once you set one down or tuck it away, the chances of discarding it are infinitesimal.

The bad news is that there is no magic formula for keeping newspapers from becoming one of your biggest, most consistent clutter headaches. Newspapers are as dependable as the dawn. If you fall behind in reading them, they will be there in an enormous pile waiting; when you finish, they will be there in an enormous pile waiting to be disposed of. The uses for which old newspapers work *best* are almost nil—counting all the bird-cage bottoms, paint jobs, moving or packing stuffers, window shining (ugh), dog training, and newspaper fireplace logs on this continent—only about .001 percent of newspapers are used after reading.

There is only one way (aside from a faithful paper drive or recycling box in the garage) to handle newspapers and that is *instant* disposal—the instant you are finished reading it. Don't ever lay a read paper down for "later"—the last guy to read it should be the last person to see it alive. If you miss a few days, don't try to catch up; much of what is in a daily paper will be recapped later somewhere else (radio, TV, weekly magazine, conversation) and not much really new or important (except Doonesbury or Ann Landers) happens in a few days of a daily newspaper.

Office Clutter

The words "shop," "industrial," and "office" offer a great (but invalid) sanctuary for junk. Somehow we feel we can get by with piles of garbage if it is hidden away "at work." But don't kid yourself: offices, for example, offer some prime dejunking inventory. Hidden away in desks and credenzas, gathering dust in file cabinets and coat and janitor closets, are massive amounts of clutter.

In twenty-five years of cleaning and inspecting some of our country's largest and most elite office complexes, I've found that a high percentage of cleaning, breakage, fire, and injury costs result from plain unnecessary clutter. Boxes of outdated files and discontinued printing are everywhere, stacked to dangerous heights, inviting toppling and lifting injuries. Extra pencils, pads, pens, clips, and handy-dandy trays are generally overdone at least 50 percent. On tops of desks and cabinets you'll find department store displays of ungodly excess: ashtrays, trophies, commemorative paperweights, cartoons, centerfolds, candy dishes, elaborate nameplates and pen sets, ceremonial letter openers, moldy coffee cups, and outdated paperwork. Though fancy pen sets come in every design and material imaginable, I've never found any that write much better than a 69¢ Bic. Few of us like to carry good pens because the carried pen/pencil mortality rate is about 60 percent. If we don't lose them, some absentminded guy like me innocently rips it off you. So I have many gold gift sets that I shuffle and dust, waiting for the day that I'll write a book in public view. Meanwhile, they're crammed away, jamming my drawers every time I open or close them.

Office junk includes unnecessary furniture, too, because of the unwritten office rule that you never surrender any item of furniture once you get it—whether you need it or not.

Most office storages are blessed with rolls or boxes of fresh new labels (business cards, or stationery) with outdated or misspelled or slightly misprinted addresses. Everything else is perfect—the paper, the stickum, the color, but they are utterly worthless. Keeping them in hope of having a $1-an-hour kid go through and revise them with a rubber stamp will never happen—and if they stay around, someday new office help will find and use them, with some resulting very sad situations.

And why can't we throw out obsolete or disintegrating rubber stamps? It seems that once a name or message is engraved in rubber on the bottom of a wood block, it's engraved in our very souls. I found thirty of those in an old desk I bought, and kept them for years because they cost $5 each now and after all they *did* print. Finally, realizing I'd never use them (I couldn't update their 1940s message to the 1980s), I tossed them! Then at home in my desk I found two others I had made up for a job I held as a representative—no place or way I'll ever use them again. Today as I write this, they went.

Every office has its catacombs of clutter, even a professional cleaning firm like mine (here comes another confession). As our business grew, we kept up with the needed new furniture, forms, and equipment. About twelve years ago, to expedite matters further, we made what we considered a wise purchase and bought two large full-key electric adding machines. You could punch in anything, hit the total button, and those things would snort, whirl, and click out the most impressive rhythms of taps and grinds you ever heard, finally spitting out a tape of the transaction—we thought we had Einstein encased in plastic!

Two months later I was in a friend's office, and he showed me this newfangled electronic calculator, a tiny thing that did twice as much as mine in less than half the time and cost a fourth as much. I thought it was a hoax, and of course you know it wasn't—those amazing, accurate, efficient, and low-priced midgets have since taken over.

And today my two big ugly electric adding machines, still brand-new, sit under the dust and cobwebs in our stationery storage room, poised for the day the cunning calculator might fail and they can be reenlisted. That day will never come. Those adding machines are as worthless as the four chairs with armrests and two casters missing, those balding blotters, the original 1953 carbon dip copiers, the hole-puncher we used three times in five years, the stapler that jammed as often as it stapled, the green typewriter ribbon somebody thought would be a nice change, and the 1979 calendar note pads waiting to be made into scratch paper. I'll cast my clutter out, if you'll cast out yours. Gadfrey, we hate to admit mistakes, especially we businesspeople!

Business Before Treasure

Fancy offices are for ego (or for a cushy prelude to over-billing!), not production. In some offices there are more swords, bits of armor, helmets, sheepskins, ships, tapestries, carvings, and extra cushions than a Viking could carry out on a good day. Others are so loaded with oriental rugs, glowering old oil portraits, and antique English furniture that you're waiting for the hounds and huntsmen to come thundering down the hall. Atmosphere comes more from people than from props—"image"-strewn offices generally house a person with more than the average share of insecurities. (Check out your psychiatrist's office—you might be able to help him or her with a de-junking problem.)

All of this costs money to buy, time to clean, and worry to protect. Office junk costs us a small fortune because we professional cleaners learned that it's just a matter of time until those excess decorations will be destroyed or damaged, or will disappear.

And when you have to wrestle daily with an elegant unwieldy phone, carefully remove a special envelope from a special holder, or come to terms with the fact that your snazzy revolving address file has spilled its guts all over your desk top, *production* is impaired. When arranging the accessories or debating the decor won't allow you to focus on the problem at hand, *function* is suffering.

Walk into any office and inventory the visible junk honestly. Now inspect the bottom desk drawers and cabinet storage areas (careful that the old exit signs, empty boxes, used mailing tubes, retired notebooks and briefcases don't crush you). I'll bet you'll average 50 percent junk. If you don't want to go through this clutter inventory now, just wait until you move.

You'll see! If you are the junkee, repent. If the employer of the junkee, command and demand de-junking. It'll save a fortune in time—and be a lot safer and better-looking, too.

In Brief, Junk

Hope chests, vaults, safes, fruit and wine cellars, and portfolios can all house clutter and few will dare question it. But the most sanctified of all official clutter containers is the briefcase. To carry, or even own one, seems to be a milestone in many lives. You can tell the executive stature by the size and style of the case— the slimmer and more refined it is, the more important the character carrying it. Briefcases and all their brethren are now being designed into junk; we have teak and zebrawood attaché cases and elegant leather ones costing up to $800, not to mention snakeskin, sharkskin, stainless steel, brushed aluminum, plastic, wicker, cow fur and coyote hide—and to carry what? If you looked in most of them, the only briefs you'd find are some worn shorts.

Briefcases are generally full of things people don't use but are supposed to carry—or things they're *not* supposed to carry. I just looked in mine—I am a corporate president, chairman of the board, sit on several other boards, own and run several businesses—I'm lugging around three Hyatt Regency pads and two pens that don't work (I must have kept them to clean my ears), a $400 dictaphone I've used once in five years (though I did entertain my grandkids with it once), Idaho potato pins, toilet keychains, squeegee tie tacks, a harmonica, guitar pick, my Boy Scout merit badges, three procrastination projects, and . . . well, never mind, it's too embarrassing.

No clutter is excused by its container!

On the book spines, from left to right: Manipulate, Don't Merit · Exercise Your Guts Out · You Can Be Thin as a Pin · Encyclopedia of Ecstasy · How to Make $300,000 in 30 Seconds · How to Win at Goldfish

No Book Is Junk . . . or Is It?

Finally inspired to de-junk my large library, I was at the garbage barrel casting a dilapidated book into a blazing fire. My wife and my mother-in-law, returning from the store, jumped out of the car and headed for the burning barrel on the run. "Don't burn that book!" (They didn't even know what book I was burning.)

We all have a certain awe for a book, almost regardless of the contents. A book seems to be an entity or institution in its own right. Maybe because we remember the difficulty of checking out a book past a stern-faced librarian; maybe because our parents or grandparents had only a few books and kept them forever. Or maybe because we associate books with the positives of education, knowledge, and wisdom. Once that mass of paper, regardless of what it says or shows, is bound and titled we feel it's sacred.

My wife pulled on my arm—"Oh, don't burn those books, give them to the Salvation Army, or a friend, or something." Then I showed her the books. They were books I had kept in my library, moved, tended, protected, and cleaned for twenty years (and books are among the heaviest of items to carry or store!).

The first was a 1929 typewriting book,

yellow and brittle with age; you should have seen the whalebone shoes and long dresses on the typists. Then there was *Modern Taxation Moves for a Small Business* (1951), a 1928 book of modern classroom accounting, a guide to gear ratio adjustment on the modern tractor (1934), a turn-of-the-century guide to irrigation systems, a 1947 almanac, *Current Used Car Prices 1963*, a 1971 college catalog, campground guides from the late '50s (I knew these were useless when I ended up camping in a shopping mall), a road atlas from the Pleistocene era, a *Political Geography of the World 1937*, and eleven boxes of other beautiful books that had absolutely zero value to me or anyone else. They contained outdated, incomplete, or inaccurate information, but they were books!

Honesty and My Library

Do you know why I had eleven boxes of no-good books to burn—why I had kept them, bought them, sent for them, pulled them out of others' junk piles? It was for ego and show. Most people dream of and plan a family room or den—and true to decorational demand, an impressive wall of books must be there. Those books are seldom opened; they just sit and gleam and multiply and give an intellectual air to the room they adorn, or serve as a reminder to the kids, visitors, and relatives that we have scholastic and educational wisdom in our home. Oh, and we should also have several prestige books worthlessly sunning themselves on a coffee or reception table: their titles— *Early Prints of Andrew Dauber, Great Midwestern Castle Architecture, Lampshades Through the Ages*—are a dead giveaway of their purpose—show! The most handling they get is when they're dusted.

When I ran out of room, when my home office wall was full, did I throw out the worthless books? Nope, like you I bought or built more shelves or boxed and kept them in case I got another office and had to have *two* displays. As a professional, was I backed by layers of deep knowledge in my tax and business-planning books? Nope, because in the fast-moving business climate and fluctuations of the economy, those books are almost worthless a year after I get them. When I need an answer, I can get it current and accurate in four minutes from my banker or accountant.

The Epitome of Book Vanity

I was in a board of directors' meeting in elite Scottsdale, Arizona. The meeting room decor reeked of power, authority, and the deep knowledge of bygone masterminds. The stately bound classic books on the walnut mantel cast an almost oracular spell over the room. During the boring parts of the meeting my eyes scanned the books and rested on one beauty familiar from my teaching days. When break came, I vaulted to the mantel and reached for the treasured book. It wouldn't budge! I pulled hard and it moved, but so did all the others. I jerked, and the whole row of books came teetering down—they weren't for reading, they were for show—all the covers were glued together!

How are the pages of *your* books? Maybe not physically glued, but if you never crack them they might as well be. Showing costs your life. Most of it is clutter!

De-Junk Your Bookshelf

There is no sacredness to books any more: TV, radio, and other media present "live" material we once had to read. Books are available now everywhere, not just in schools and libraries. There are more than 40,000 new books published every year.

Books today are cheaply produced from cheap materials, and printed on large presses that can roll out 10,000 books in a few hours. Most books today are not beautiful and they're not made to last as they once were; even the paper in them deteriorates in an amazingly short number of years.

Many books today are not painstakingly compiled wisdom or information but essentially entertainment. Once the majority of books were educational, uplifting, edifying; now many are strictly for profit—anything that will sell will be written and published. Books, in short, are not the special repositories of distilled knowledge they once were.

Yes, there are still books today that are sturdy, beneficial, and better than the old. I can't and don't want to pass judgment on your books because you can do it perfectly well if you'll be 100 percent honest with yourself: you wouldn't read many of the books on your shelves if you were trapped with them on a desert island.

Yes, Even Cookbooks Can Be Clutter

Two of the biggest-selling types of book on the market today are cookbooks and diet/exercise books. Guess how many are kept: all of them. How many are used? Few. If and when a cookbook comes off the back burner, it is usually just for a few recipes in the entire book. And though a book might be worth buying for one or two items, the other 372 pages of exotic dishes in the large binding are junk. Most home cooks use a handful of recipe cards (or the recipe on the box or package) for their favorite standbys, but *all* keep drawers or cupboards full of cookbooks. (The average home has thirteen; real junkers have twenty, thirty, forty; the record is probably 184).

Cast out your unused cookbooks! But before all of you gourmet cooks baste me at the stake, remember I told you to be objective when de-junking. Cookbooks may make you *feel* domestic, but do you ever use them for cooking? When (honestly) was the last time you used a cookbook? I've posed this question to many a group—silence usually follows, no one can remember. I suggested to one woman, "Have you used yours in the last six months?" Silence. Everybody laughs—someone finally chirps, "I made gingersnaps once." Another says, "When I have lots of friends over." Clip the few recipes you need and meet me at the burning barrel.

When you throw out, give away, or sell those books that have no value, you'll spell relief F-E-W-E-R B-O-O-K-S. Good books that nestle in you when you nestle with them are one of the finest of all gifts, and worth keeping and giving and loving; just don't try to become the city library. (You might try *using* it though—it's one of the best ways to avoid buying the books you'd only read once or only need once in a great while.)

Good reference books, and books, adult or juvenile, that you'll read over and over and enjoy, are worth buying and keeping in fine editions. The one-timers like *Watergate Witchery Volume XIV* or *200 Uses for a Stiff Opossum* are one-time shots not worth $14.95 to clutter a shelf.

Get a $4 paperback and once you've read it, pitch it or pass it on to someone else.

P.S. When de-cluttering, don't forget to check out your "mini-books," too: for outdated government publications and old maps and guidebooks and pamphlets and brochures, instruction booklets to appliances you no longer have, old phone books, instructions for crafts you've given up, etc. And don't be so eager to *add* booklets to your shelves (and suitcases). Are you really ever going to want to read the guidebook to Howe Caverns again?

Shutterbug Clutter

Let's zoom for a minute to the classic picture-sorting situation: one member of the family holds up a picture for the others to see.

"Who is this?"

There is silence, no one knows, but because they have the picture, it must be someone. . . . Finally. . . .

"Durned if I know."

"Seems like I've met them . . . once."

"We'd better keep it; it might be someone we know."

You could drive clutter collectors crazy by slipping a photo of a Brazilian countess into their family album. I bet they'd keep it forever!

Even good and worthwhile things can evolve into junk and clutter your life and environment. A prime example is photographs. What a priceless property our own pictures can be—they allow us to relive precious moments, stimulate memories and feelings, bring laughter and warmth to our families, friends, and co-workers. But if you're like most people, probably 75 percent of your pictures are piled, boxed, buried, bent, or unfindable. *The only value a photo has is in being seen.* If that isn't possible, what good is it?

Slides, even those that will never win a photo contest, can be exciting to family and associates, but most slides are

FORGOTTEN PHOTOS A-L

jumbled and bunched in the box and for the most part we don't even remember we have them. Prints are the same story—if you have to sort, hunt, and dust before viewing them, you'll seldom or never see them. Hence these expensive, potentially stimulating, heart-warming items are junk, litter, clutter to you. For years this has been the case, yet we continue to take more pictures and slides, show them for a while when they're fresh, then throw them in a drawer, box, or pile, thinking, "Someday I'll. . . ."

Photos aren't junk; don't let them become so. Transform them into a treasure that will bring joy into your life and others'. In a few spare evenings or Sunday afternoons, you can de-junk a lifetime of pictures.

My father-in-law, Jerry Reed, is a mobile portrait studio and darkroom. He carries a 35mm SLR, a 16mm movie camera, a Polaroid, and a video camera.

He uses his pictures to change lives and entertain; we love him for it—his pictures have enriched our families' lives and built worth and confidence in our children, neighbors, and relatives. It took me a long time to realize why he and his pictures do so much good, since everyone has tons of slides and photos. Jerry simply makes his pictures *accessible* to family, friends—even strangers. In his car or house, even standing in the doorway visiting, you can always see one or more of his pictures. They're on the walls, in handy slide trays, in neat folders, or in his well-organized video library. In a flash you're enjoying new or vintage photographs. I learned much from Jerry and converted my photographs from stored junk to meaningful, enjoyable displays.

Let me pass on what I learned to you. First I had, with my family, a day of "Sort."

Create some categories that fit *you,* such as:

Family Your immediate family, old and new, group and solo shots. Maybe include here also your home(s), pets, vehicles, and all "family feeling" things.
Friends All the friends and places of your wider life—high school and college, colleagues, buddies from service or single days, friends of the family, neighbors.
Vacations That California, Nova Scotia, or Mexico trip, the grand excursion to China or Israel. Keep the pictures from each trip separate within this category. You might want to make a category for:

Special occasions or **one-time events** Special ceremonies, weddings, bar mitzvahs, milestone birthdays or anniversaries, special celebrations or parties.
Other categories Could be business- or career-related, a group or organization you are involved with, your hobbies, sports, certain types of shots you like to take just for the fun of it. Fit the categories to *your* life, because you'll be using them.

Eliminate bad or unwanted pictures.

Discard ruined shots, blurred and cut-off shots, too dark, too light, slips, bad photos (except maybe for your only picture of Cousin Lula, hazy as it may be), and *those totally black slides and prints!* You'll never use them and besides, they insult your photo prowess.

Give away You may have lots of pictures (good) that have little or no value to you, but may be of interest to subjects in the shots. Give or mail them to people who might want them. This will give joy to others and make you friends for life!

Sort all the remaining pictures into the categories they fit—you'll probably find yourself adding or changing a few categories as you sort through. You might want to identify all faces and places while you remember who they are.

143

Now decide on the medium to best display your pictures. Remember, a picture's only value is to be *seen*. You want yours to be protected, but easily located and displayed and organized so new pictures can be added easily.

Prints can be mounted in sturdy, durable albums—you have hundreds of choices of types. If your albums are composed well, they'll be looked at and enjoyed often.

I like the ring-binder albums with looseleaf plastic pocket pages. These are inviting to use and practically indestructible. The prints are nicely displayed (and the pages can be handled safely even by little children, who get the most out of pictures).

Mounted on the wall your pictures can be enjoyed more by you and others than any other kind, at any cost!

Mounting and displaying pictures doesn't have to be expensive or difficult. Frame shops will do it.

True, they charge, and if you can't hack it, there are frame-it-yourself centers that offer inexpensive guidance, and department stores—even nickel-and-dime stores—have a selection of frames and mats in which you can in minutes mount your pictures and hang them. As a cleaner, I really like things hung instead of placed (on pianos, etc.). If you have to move Grandpa every time you clean or dust, you grow to dislike him!

Store negatives in manila envelopes in a handy file so you can get at them easily to have copies made for the friends and family who want them.

Slide trays are neat, really worth the money. They simplify not only storage but use. I like the standard 140-slide tray; it's easy to store, use, and add to. In slide trays your pictures will be permanently organized to look at again and again. Label the tray with the category or identification. These slide boxes can be stored in, on, or under anything and still be usable in seconds.

You can even make your own cassette—voice or music—to go along with some of the trays.

Make Your Own Slide Show

With a little imagination and effort you can place the best action or most expressive slides in a tray in a sequence that tells a story. On a piece of paper write a caption or comment to go with each picture (funny or clever is usually the most interesting kind); this only takes a few minutes and adds a lot when you show the slides. I leave the "script" in the slide tray and read it as the projector rolls out the pictures. Recording the copy on a cassette is simple, too—clink a spoon or something for the slide-change signal. Anyone can use and enjoy a slide tray with a cassette, and will do so, over and over again!

A book library? Why not a "photo library" of photo albums or slide trays?

Video is a fun, clever way to keep, organize, and enjoy photographs. It's really quite simple. Use your own video camera, or rent or borrow one. Load it up with a cassette, lay your pictures out, and simply film these in sequence as you would scenes with a movie camera. You might even play some music with the filming. You can't go wrong. Your pictures are all stored in one small cartridge and the investment is small. In twenty minutes you can put literally hundreds of pictures on a video disc and play them over your TV. Most families will like them better than a losing football game or situation comedy reruns. Video players will be as common as stereos in the home in 1990, and many of us have them now.

CHAPTER 9

Dress Less for Success

(So Your Clothes Don't Wear *You* Out)

Isn't it strange how some little scene in a play or a movie will stick with you forever? One of my "never let go" screen glimpses came in *A Connecticut Yankee in King Arthur's Court*, starring Bing Crosby. Toward the end of the movie, Bing was forced into a showdown with the most ferocious knight that ever rode. Bing was prepared for battle, fully suited in his armor; as he moved the armor swayed and creaked and his voice sounded like he was in a tunnel. Mounting his horse and riding to the battle station was practically impossible. And when he stepped backward off a step, of course, because of all those pounds of armor, he teetered, fell over, and jangled and clinked rhythmically down the stairs like 600 empty pop cans. Realizing that his dress was so heavy and restrictive that he could hardly move, he de-junked himself of the whole cumbersome outfit, leaped on his horse, and, armed with only a lariat, was able easily to out-ride, out-maneuver, out-dodge, and finally topple the nasty knight of the court.

Nothing better describes for me the futility and frustration, the drawbacks of overdressing than this memory of Bing rolling helplessly down the stairs and landing in a huge heap of scrap. All of us can relate to the feeling Bing had when he suddenly discovered that he had so much to wear it was in fact a liability instead of an advantage. In the Dark Ages this excess of wearing apparel was justified by the word *protection;* today our excess of wearing apparel is justified by the word *fashion.* That magic word keeps the factories and looms of the world rolling by making sure, with semi-annual changes of style, that things keep coming in and going out.

We make it through the "Twiggy" look, and go from "mini" to "maxi," then we layer minis *over* maxis, the next year leathers and silks are in, then tweeds and knits, then it's on to "Ivy League" or "Preppy." Suddenly we're back to 1940s "hot pants"—that is, until we jump to designer jeans. We buy it all—and if we manage to resist, our kids, cousins, and friends buy it for us. Somehow we gather and keep all these clothes, compacting them tighter and tighter in our ever larger (and then extra and portable) closets and wardrobes with no hope of ever wearing them out. How many neckties or scarves or, for that matter, suits have you heard of (or owned!) that ever wore out? Style has generated more waste than any single word, when it comes to wearing apparel.

Fashion seduces intelligent human beings into paying ridiculous prices for clothing that makes them all look the same. The word "wardrobe" convinces others that they need platoons of shoes, racks of dresses, squadrons of suits, shirts, and blouses.

If our good sense starts to take over and says, "Hey, I don't really dig these saddle oxfords and this slick silk shirt," we can rest assured that the media will quickly come to our rescue—and present a parade of skinny strutting turkeys whirling around on some big-city stage. We sigh and say, "Who am I to question?"

While most of us stand by like a bunch of mute mannequins, somebody out there is piling clothes on us unmercifully. They are piddling around with our hemline, neckline, bustline, waistline—and most of all, our credit line. They take straps away and we buy and keep; they add straps and we buy and keep; when they can't alter the style any more, they change the colors by the year, and then the season.

*O*ur beautiful apparel . . . clutter? Not a chance—it's necessary for image, employment, affection. . . .

Did you know (a look at your apparel inventory will verify this) that *you*, all by yourself, have more clothes than the whole general store in an early western town? That could make you right proud, pardner—but it doesn't, because for months and years already you've known in your heart that your inventory's overstocked. It's worried you, caused agonies of selection, taken room you didn't have, been a pain to move and clean and protect—and you have a small fortune sunk in your wardrobe. You sincerely tried to dress for success and ended up with a closetful of clutter. Now let's try dressing *less* for success. Throw some of it out (you want to, anyway). Clothes clutter affects your life in more ways than how hard it is to fit another hanger in the closet.

I've known many a dignified, wise country gentleman who always looked clean, neat, and presentable—but who never owned a suit. Some tog-touting relative will always come on the scene and say, "What! Zeke doesn't have a suit? Why, *everybody* has to have a suit!" Zeke doesn't agree—he hates suits and places that require suits—but the relatives work on the wife and convince her and they both browbeat Zeke into getting a suit. He yields, gets a suit, satisfies his wardrobe antagonizers, but never wears it. This piece of junk in Zeke's life now is fresh bait for the neckties, hankies, suit socks, watch chains, cufflinks, and suit bags that pour in on birthdays and Christmas. Since Zeke never wears the suit, his family gets him a sport coat, though old country gentleman Zeke needs a sport coat about like he needs another ailment. The sport coat inspires a similar flood of holiday receivership and he receives more accessories and footwear to match. With no room in the closet now for his overalls and boots, Zeke up and dies. Of course for his funeral the suit is out of fashion and he needs a new one—but his family keeps the other one, because "after all, it was never worn."

Apparel that is neat, attractive, comfortable, wears well, protects us, and helps us project our feelings and physical self is a worthy investment. It's the clothes that over-decorate us, strain our personality and our pocketbook, that are clutter.

Most of us don't need clothes to take over for us. When you consider the power of the eyes, facial expression, voice, and body movement in the sum total of what makes a person "attractive," anything else seems insignificant. Yet we hang incredible arrays of fabrics and leathers (and if we can afford it, precious metals and stones) on ourselves. Draped over or fastened onto our bodies, they take hours and hours of our lives, not only to pay for, but to wear and care for. (Not to mention to sort through and argue over.)

For everyday living these "overdone" fashions will hobble us. And how foolish we are to spend what we can't afford on too many, too-fancy garments.

> *W*hen the best dressers are dressed, no one even notices what they wore.

We've all known people who have so much to put on and take off every morning and night they spend hours of their life doing it. When they travel, their suitcases and ditty bags are bulging with garments, accessories, and personal appliances that they need for their daily assembly and disassembly.

I've seen people so hung with elaborate material they look more like the living room drapes than a living person. Others are in clothes so styled, tailored, and tight—like old Bing in his suit of armor—

they can't sit, run, or breathe deeply (though they can stand and rotate). They are literally wrapped in junk, and no matter what their trappings cost, they look like an overdecorated tree.

Why should we clog our closets with things we wear rarely or never, that don't keep us warm or cool or dry when we need to be, and don't permit any comfortable movement ever?

Unclutter Your Closet

I once cleaned a woman's closet that had ninety-four blouses; her husband wasn't far behind with fifty-five slacks. Most were out of style or didn't fit (that's why the others were bought). And I was astonished once to discover that people even keep sections of clothes by size in their closet; one woman had a span of five sizes so she'd have something to wear at any weight she might be found at.

Most closets have enough garments to insulate the whole home; some take security in such inventory, but the opposite is usually true—it's a mark of insecurity and indecision. No amount of clothing and trimmings can substitute for real personal confidence and self-worth.

Before we know it, our life becomes as jammed as our closets and our dresser drawers. Much of it is of little value to us. Most of us only wear about 20 percent of the clothes in our closets. But we have to sort through it *all* (100 percent) every time we go to get dressed—hunt, ponder, weigh, decide, and worry about when, how, and what we should wear. Excess clothes clutter our life with unnecessary stress. Like other junk, their ownership obligates us to use them. And when there are so many to choose from, we're almost always troubled by the possibility that perhaps another choice would have been better, and so we don't enjoy the choice we've made.

Be Careful with Apparel You Have to Be Careful with

Many people praise my wife because no matter where, when, or what the call for her help, she can be out the door in a minute for any emergency or for a three-week trip. Some of us take hours, days—even weeks or a month to get ready to respond to a sick friend, a sudden move, or a family crisis. The secret of her quickness? I think it has a lot to do with her wardrobe. . . .

Out of ideas for a nice birthday gift a few years ago, I asked my wife how she would like a beautiful fur coat—she turned me down! Her logic for the decision was excellent: "A fur coat, I'd have to be very careful with. There aren't that many places I could really go in it and even then I couldn't sit in it because the back would wear out. Knowing it was so expensive, it'd be hard to relax in it and I'd have to worry about it being stolen. I'd have to avoid Sue and Mildred, two friends who are allergic to fur. The

grandkids' burps would ruin it and hugging babies feels better than any coat. And I'd have to keep it in a special place in the closet, have to put it in cold storage and insure it and mothproof it and even worry about looking ostentatious." It wouldn't be worth the things she'd have to sacrifice for it.

She brought the same principle to my attention when I returned from a business trip with some white cotton shirts. I could care less what kind of white shirt I wear, but as I was buying a new suit, the pencil-moustached clerk and my district manager informed me that cotton shirts were the "in" thing—that anyone with any class wore only cotton shirts. I went along with this, but when I unpacked those dudes, my wife questioned my sanity. She didn't care what the stylish salesman said; the labor and money (ironing, starching) it takes to keep a cotton shirt looking nice was ridiculous. "Look at the one you wore home." I took my coat off; the sleeves were so wrinkled, it looked like a calf had been sucking on them. She was right, and they didn't look a bit better than my old Dacrons, which could be maintained in minutes.

So many of us weigh ourselves down with apparel that does as much damage to our freedom as hanging a millstone around our neck. Take a good hard look at those suits and skirts and slacks that only look good for the first half hour you wear them, and then sag and wrinkle and crush and embarrass you for the rest of the day . . . at those blouses and shirts that will never look good without dampening and starching and a good twenty minutes bent over the ironing board (a twenty minutes you're never willing to spend) . . . at the filmy numbers and special fabrics that have to be run through the dry cleaner after *every* wearing (how many times the price of the garment will you end up paying in "maintenance" fees?).

Unadmitted "Obsoletes"

Most of us have a small universe of things inhabiting our closets that we've outgrown, physically and mentally, or that are just outright unusable, but we haven't gotten around to admitting it yet. These are among the prime contributors to closet crowding, and can actually be rather easily de-junked if we force a (one-sitting, or keep-it-up-till-we've-worked-our-way-entirely-through) showdown with them.

Rare is the closet that can't be de-junked of darling little dresses that were *very* becoming on us (fifteen years ago), formals that have sat in their plastic wrappers for the last ten years (and will for the *next* ten), ugly old coats and bedraggled beloved bathrobes, ties that are out of style (or in style but we don't like them anyway), clothes that shrank or got iron-melted (but we couldn't face throwing them away right at the moment of trauma), too-small belts (or belts so exotic we'll *never* find something to wear with them), stretched turtlenecks, broken necklaces, disintegrating bras, mateless gloves, more "shirts and pants to wear when I'm painting" than a lifetime of remodeling will ever require, pantyhose and tights in colors we'll *never* want our legs to be, jumpsuits and floats we always admire but we keep shuffling past when it comes time to pick something to actually wear.

Impulse Clothes

The clothes we wear the least are often the ones we bought the fastest. We really didn't need or want them, but the mood of the moment mesmerized us. We've all done it—a drive through Dallas and we emerge with some Western duds, a couple of evenings on Oahu and we own aloha shirts and muumuus, not to be worn again until the next trip twenty years later. We can't get out of Wales without four wool sweaters to take home to Phoenix, we couldn't exit Acapulco without an incredibly embroidered stiff canvas shirt. Let a World Series or major tournament come anywhere near our area and we have an instantly outdated T-shirt and matching warm-up jacket. One visit to *Raiders of the Lost Ark* and we'll unflinchingly spring for a smelly leather jacket.

An excellent example of passing-fancy apparel is the cowboy hat. Almost everyone has to have one, because they travel West, live there, or were turned on by Gene Autry or Clint Eastwood. Cowboy hats are a true white elephant for 96 percent of their owners—clumsy and obnoxious inside planes, buses, auditoriums. They get ruined easily and take up a lot of space and almost as much time to care for. Real cowboys (for whom they were designed) shielded themselves from the sun with the hat's wide brim, clamped it over their ears and neck in blizzards, and used it to beat off mosquitoes, kill horseflies, fan fires, and feed their horses. (They also didn't care if their hats got stained or smashed.) We shuffle and protect ours to wear once a year to the rodeo—is it really worth it? My father—and other real cowboys who live on large ranches with lots of mooing cattle and shedding horses—never owned a cowboy hat!

Clothes bought in a hurry—for a party, trip, or new sport enthusiasm—are often an impulse purchase and often end up junk (yes, even jogging suits and "outdoor outfitting").

Costumey/quaint/outrageous/gift clothing often falls into this category, too. Okay, it's arty-looking and it was a great buy, but is *your* husband going to wear that beret? (Maybe if you buy him a mask.) Your wife *might* look great in that red satin Chinese dress slit to the waist, those rainbow-striped harem pants, or rhinestone-studded boots—but would she be caught dead in them? It's sometimes a nice idea to give gifts your loved ones would never indulge themselves in, but don't let your impulses and fantasies override their self-image—you might end up making them feel uncomfortable and guilty, in addition to junking up their lives.

THIS SPACE AVAILABLE

Lettered T-shirts "It's just a T-shirt," you think. "That's not so extravagant." But to be the bearer—on body or clothesline—of an offensive or just plain inane motto or message is the height of pure junk ownership and display. When people can't manage to attract attention with their words, looks, and manners, they resort to buying and wearing a billboard. It generates junk reactions and junk opinion of self, costs far more than it's worth, and crowds the drawer. (Just how often can you wear an I'M A VIRGIN or THIS IS AN OLD T-SHIRT T-shirt anyway?)

Unused impulse clothes are among our most conspicuous clutter. They cause family fights and are a waste of money (and make ridiculous spectacles of us if we do wear them). Go to your closet right now. . . .

Pick out all your impulse clothes. . . .

Don't ask yourself "Why did I do it?" We're all weak. Ask yourself, "Why do I *keep* it?" Then you know what to do. (Aloha.)

Whittle Down Your Wardrobe

No matter how rich you are, whether it was a gift or not, non-used clothes are clutter.

When you have so many clothes that they can't fit into the normal closets of a normal home—mobile, condo, dorm room, or apartment—you have too many! Remember, there's only one of you—and if you have to stash and box and truck clothes away to get room for the ones you're actually wearing, *you have too many*. I'm not in any danger of being elected to the ten best-dressed list, but I try to always be presentable. After I de-junked myself, all the clothes in my section of the closet took up only two feet in width. I do farm work, hundreds of TV and in-person appearances a year, attend church, play sports, and lead Scouts, and everything I need only fills up one-third of a normal closet, as do my wife's clothes. I've been a lot happier since I decided I had better things to do than sort through a dry-goods store inventory every morning just to get dressed.

Know yourself, and think use. . . .

1. If it's not flattering to you—the color or the cut is wrong—pull it out.

2. If it doesn't fit or it's not comfortable—you have to suck in your stomach, you can't bend over or move your arms, or it's itchy—pull it out.

3. If it's too complicated—if you have to wrap or tuck or tie it just so, or if you have to remember to straighten the sash or pull the bodice up every ten minutes, pull it out.

4. If it's too fragile—if you can only wear it where there won't be food or drink or animals or children, where it won't be too hot because you don't want to sweat in it or too cold because a coat or jacket will wrinkle it—pull it out.

5. If it's badly damaged or has an important part missing that you probably won't be able to replace—pull it out.

6. If it needs to be altered or repaired before you can wear it—pull it out.

7. If you wear it never or very rarely (because your lifestyle has changed or it just isn't called for more than once a half-century), or if you can only wear it with certain things (that you don't have or really don't like to wear)—pull it out!

Leave in the closet everything you wear consistently and feel good in; and make two piles of all the rest.

ONE

Needs to be cleaned or repaired—there's some practical reason you're not wearing it.

TWO

Is out of style or doesn't fit or you've decided you just don't want to fuss with it any more.

Take Pile 2 to your favorite charity, or if you're not tough enough, to the garage. In four weeks you'll get rid of it easily because it's been so nice having it out of your way in the closet. . . .
  Pile 1—clean or fix (several of these pieces, when you look at them closely, will join Pile 2). Arrange what's left in the closet according to color coordination and needs. (And when you see something on sale, think about how it will fit in with your basic wardrobe and how *often* you'll wear it—not just how much you'll save.)

Down at the Heels: Junk

No more astonishing proof of human devotion to style at the expense of utility exists than in the case of our footwear. Shoes way down there on the grubby ground house our far-from-delightful feet and are a necessity to protect them. People possess shoes by the piles, many never worn more than a few times. Shoe buyers stalk, parade, twist, rotate, and jig in front of shoestore mirrors for an unbelievable length of time—not concerned with comfort or durability, but with how they'll look to others.

The lowly shoe is responsible for a lot of physical torture, too. The vast majority of shoe styles—men's and women's—are somewhere between uncomfortable and painful to wear. Trying to figure out why a woman would willingly subject her feet to a 4-inch spike heel—so she can't walk, but must wobble and hobble and lurch around—would boggle the finest mind.

Even being a conservative in the shoe style parade, I slid around in sleek slip-ons for fifteen years, because they matched—not my feet, mind you, but the other ridiculous apparel some rich designer designed. Even so, it was hard to buy a shoe I didn't have to snip the bells, buckles, and beads off so I could wear it discreetly. Some near-falls onstage and during TV appearances inspired me to seek a sturdier, more practical shoe. I bought a pair of plain ole "mailman" shoes, and gadfrey—my feet thought they'd been resurrected. I de-junked all my "sophisticated" ones, realizing it was better to plop a little than flop a lot.

How you dress your feet is probably more important to your spirits and physical well-being than anything else you wear. If your feet hurt at the end of the day, or after the first hour, it's time to retread your shoe wardrobe. Comfortable shoes are available for every occasion; it's worth some time, money, and trouble now to invest in a few basic pairs of sensible shoes. And throw out (or give away) all those pairs you aren't using. You'll have more room in your closet—and you'll be able to stride down the street, skip up the stairs, and whistle right past the corn pad display.

And All the Trimmings

Just as the just-right color and just-right amount of trim can make a plain house come alive, too much and in the wrong place can make the same house leap off the lot at you.

So it is with clothing and accessories. Just right is beautiful. Too much is clutter. There are "trimmings" complementary and even necessary to human beings—and there is too much. "Best-dressed" seems to get confused with "best-decorated." Over-dressing, like other junk, detracts because it makes us forget that it's *us* we need to present, not what we're wearing.

I heard a jeweler remark once in a convention address that when some men achieve "success" they buy big cars and nice homes. After discovering, however, that today many people, rich or poor or middling, have nice cars or big houses, they find a different way to flaunt their money: they buy their wives a giant diamond. It's not for the benefit of the wife, you understand, but for *him*—he's just using her to advertise, so people will say, "Boy, Harry is certainly successful, look at that diamond his wife has." Precious stones can be a good investment, but there are better ones—especially if all you're doing is feeding your ego. Jewelry has to be guarded, insured, duplicated, matched, and serviced—it often puts more junk than joy into our life.

Think about your jewelry—your baubles, bangles, beads, and bands. If you have to take them off when you wash your hands or try to work on something, take them off every trip through airport security, take them off when you're in a big city, hide them before you leave home, hide them while you're traveling, and hide them in a bank box the rest of the time, maybe it isn't worth it. It's just another thing to worry about and take care of.

And besides—what woman or man really believes that a flashy object dangling from ears or neck enhances personal appeal? What is it that people want most from each other? Warmth, affection, love, and feeling. What does $30,000 worth of the goldsmith's and silversmith's art do for a cold blood-vesseled hand? People wear jewelry more to impress than to attract, in sober fact.

The most beautiful jewelry is usually utterly simple and expressive of something meaningful; a mass of gaudy stones draped in six strands of chains is a great place to start de-junking.

A lot of our unused jewelry clutter originates in the strange notion there are certain trinkets we can't live without. Looking back thirty-one years, when class-ring-buying time came around to our high school junior class, $28 was a small fortune to me, and working in grease, on machinery, etc., as I did made ring wearing questionable. My announcement that I didn't want one was met with a barrage of opposition: "How will you remember your school?" "How will you identify your steady girl?" "How will you remember the Class of '53?" When they finished, I felt like a traitor but refused to buy one—I bought instead a catcher's mitt that served me well (in fact, I still have it). I never miss the ring, nor do I miss having it cluttering up my "unworn jewelry" case, like all the rest of the Class of '53. Know yourself and please yourself—don't worry about satisfying society's "supposed to," "ought to" traditions, styles, and fads. Most of it will end up junk to you.

Your Crowning Clutter?

Amazingly enough, some of our clutter is literally "home grown."

Anything hairy has caught our fancy in recent years (King Kong was born thirty years too soon). Hair gets more attention, care, coddling, consulting (and chemicals) than any other part of the body. People will let their lungs, heart, stomach, eyes stand last in line for expenditure—hair rates the first slot of value. We spend millions of dollars and hours of time daily to tend it, display it, repair it, enhance it. We nurture face and head hair to the abundance and extent that we have to hire artists to groom it for us.

Yes, it's been called the "crowning glory," but like anything too complicated, hair can be clutter. Nice clean hair, flowing or curled, *is* attractive, but when it takes more from us than it gives, it begins to dictate our existence. It's sad indeed when fear for our hair keeps us from swimming, out of wind and breezes and sun and morning dew, robs us of sleep (those cursed curlers), rules out warm hats, determines what we will do when, causes constant compulsive mirror checking. Hair care for many has become so dominant that our daily schedule revolves around "hair time." (*When* it has

to be washed, conditioned, set, styled, and for how long, etc.) At least the "greasy kid stuff" allowed kids time to be kids! Work, errands, weekdays, and weekends are altered and arranged for hairy reasons—not to mention the actual time taken up setting and grooming.

In most of our lives hair has become a taskmaster, as we spend up to two hours a day curling, straightening, washing, conditioning, tinting, bleaching, blowing, brushing, massaging, teasing, ratting, or otherwise styling it. And that's just *head* hair. Chin, chest, lip, or skull, it takes its toll of our hours and affections. Many a sexy sideburn and macho moustache takes precedence over concern for others' needs. Incredible how the output of an epidermal gland has somehow become the ultimate expression of our masculinity or femininity. Do you *really* feel your hair's worth an hour of your time a day or $50 a month to maintain, not to mention storing and thrashing through all the tools to groom it (or the devastation all that fussing inflicts on once-healthy hair and scalp)? A sane and simple hair style is an easy way to de-junk.

Boot Your Baggage!

Once we've de-junked what we wear, we'll want to do the same for what we carry. Wallets, purses, and bags are stuffed with clutter, necessitating a sorting exercise every time we need something.

No wonder people fumble. You're in a line and the customer just ahead of you, completing his or her transaction, reaches into wallet, pocket, or purse for money, checkbook, credit card, I.D., keys . . . and can't find it. Out comes every imaginable piece of junk. The fumbler can't find the needed item and frantically begins to fling things and rummage through every pocket and personal carrying space while the other people in line begin to mutter at the line blocker.

At an all-day seminar once I asked the audience to gather just the junk they were carrying with them (pockets, purses, briefcases), offering a prize for the most unique collection of clutter. They initialed it for identification. My son passed around a large drawer and in minutes it overflowed. What did I get, you wonder? Used flashbulbs, a 1976 calendar, old speeding tickets, partly eaten chocolate-covered peanuts, a hacksaw blade, a roll of toilet paper, three-year-old food coupons, rocks and pebbles, expired membership cards, half a sock, antique Christmas lists, broken compacts and empty lipstick containers, plus some censored items—and I suspect they held back plenty on me! The woman who won had a whole bulging handbag full—and she was the best-dressed person there!

Do you really want to be muttered about? When you find yourself throwing an extra comb in your handbag because you know your chances of finding the other one in there are slim, that's a clear signal that it's time to streamline the stuff you carry.

Lugging too much around with you can actually be dangerous. A young woman from London told me she had carried an "assailant protection" whistle in her purse for years, and one dark night when she was pursued—you guessed it—there was so much clutter in her purse she couldn't find the whistle. Fortunately, the would-be rapist, intrigued with her junk thrashing, tapped his toes at a distance for a while, then left.

Portable Compacters (Wallets)

We're all wowed these days by demonstrations of how much information can be stored on a tiny computer chip. But far more impressive is something we've managed to do all by ourselves for years—how much we can store in a tiny wallet. I've seen wallets that are so crowded, they actually issue a sigh of relief whenever they're opened.

Once a friend at dinner entertained his guests by going through the small compact leather container. There were six-year-old business cards (from two jobs ago), stashed cigar bands, 1977-78 fishing licenses (this was '83), a YMCA pass from a state he no longer lived in, and of course a complete portable picture gallery.

The weight and bulk of all this is phenomenal . . . and most of it is packed so tight the wallet itself is bulging and distended like a colicky cow. The contents themselves are all bent and frayed and blurred. If you want to have fun at a party, have a wallet-stripping contest. I'll wager 75 percent of your entries are either clutter or something you clearly don't need to be packing around.

Clutter Is Not a Credit to You

Among the real prestige clutter is the credit card collection. People love to open their wallets and purses and fan out a cache of credit cards capable of purchasing anything from a shrimp cocktail to a whole cannery—department store cards, discount store cards, check-cashing cards, gas cards, charge-everything cards, card protection cards—twenty, thirty, even more cards. All this demonstrates, of course, that they have fabulous credit (or are poor managers and have to charge everything on installment). Extra or unnecessary cards are junk, *plastic junk*. You don't need all of them; if you lose your wallet or purse your risk is compounded twenty times, besides which they are awkward to carry around. When I decided my clutter was killing me, my boulevard of credit cards went; for ten years now I've carried only two—and I've traveled the world over, bought dinners, lodging, gas, tickets, supplies, gifts, and never (even once) needed any more. It was one of the most delightful de-junking moves I ever made—try it! Plus you'll pay fewer card fees and spend less money on junk that was easy to buy with all those cards that made you think you were rich.

CHAPTER 10

Junk on Wheels

Some Junk . . . Drives You Mad

Because we all spend so much time in the confines of an automobile, cars carry some of the finest, most concentrated, and damaging clutter collections in the world. Vehicles are a mecca for junk congregation because we secretly believe that once we're outside our homes, our garbage is someone else's responsibility. When we leave the car and go inside the house, we feel our junk is safe in a sealed vault. So we can ignore those diapers fermenting under the front seat, the empty bottles rolling on the floor, the pits and dried peels, decomposing apple cores, broken dimmers, thermostats, and mirrors, the map of Yellowstone Park stained with sour milk right on the bear's face ("We might go again, after all, it's been five years"). The key ring is so heavy it throws off the power steering—it's filled with the sacred collection of Grandma's house keys, the keys to the broken lock on the storage shed, the bicycle lock, the executive washroom key, the key to the car sold four months ago, a can of Mace, a miniature (nonworking) flashlight, a plastic toll coin holder, and a magnifying glass with a screwdriver in the handle. Some cars in their senior year of clutter accumulation are eligible to graduate to garbage trucks.

Cars were never meant to be four-wheeled files for old parking stubs and unpaid tickets, antique gas receipts, peanut shells, pop cans, crushed fast food containers and tissue boxes, candy, gum and film wrappers, directions to past parties, single-lensed sunglasses, flattened matchbooks, partly peeled flares, dried-out first-aid kits, and non-fitting fuses. They're junk—why carry them around? I recently heard two Catholics discussing the fall from grace of St. Christopher, whose statue once stood fast on every dash—I'll bet the real reason was, the clutter competition crowded the old saint out!

Any time you eat in an auto, 23.7 percent of it ends up on you and the car: you get 3.7 percent; the car interior, the rest. (You think I'm kidding?—think again. A few years ago the growth of the fast food market forced the auto industry to make a big adjustment in their upholstery fabrics.) If you scanned the interior of most cars with a moldy food detector, it would light up like a pinball machine: there's relish on the running board, ketchup on the keychain, mustard packets lubricating the power seat mechanism, rigormortised french fries and sesame seeds lodged in every crack, baby slobber down the front and back seat, all-day suckers stuck to the instrument panel—food of all kinds slung, dribbled, and embedded so long that selling the car is the only way to clean it.

The junk problem in vehicles escalated when motor homes/vans came out. Like homes in miniature they have all the same junk hazards, including the literal kitchen sink that attracts dozens of ditsy little accessories, from spice racks and scouring pad holders to elaborate utensil collections: bagel slicers, cheese cutters, garlic presses, pastry crimpers.

One car can generate more junk than forty kids rummaging through neighbors' junk piles. Every vehicle somehow manages to sprout a bumper crop of extra rims, hubcaps, jacks, and yes, even those bug-spattered and gravel-dented old license plates. You finally sell the beast or drag it off to the junkyard, but the shrapnel of its demise remains behind—dispersed into every corner of the garage, attic, basement, and tool box. Certain that no one else would properly value the treasure that decorates your trusted transportation, you take hours to strip it of the decals, stickers, waving hands, fuzzy dice, leggy deodorant strips, broken scrapers, monogrammed floor mats, back seat clothes hangers, and as a last act scoop up the oil change stickers on the doorframe. Then, in the middle of the

night, at the sound of a police siren, you realize you forgot the play fireman's blinkers and the extra flashing built-in brake light.

The epitome of car junkdom is keeping the whole car when it expires—people often do this when it's too far gone to trade in. They feel they owe old Betsy a decent home or, eventually, burial. Now, when a hungry car dealer won't even give you a trade, that's a pretty strong hint that what you have has moved beyond clutter, to *menace*. But we tow the clunker home and park it. The tires go flat, birds use it for a target range, the sun bleaches the upholstery and cracks the dash, the windows get broken

mysteriously, friends scavenge off parts, our teenaged son backs into it twice with the new car, our neighbor's kid smashes his tiny finger in the door, a mother cat converts the back seat to a maternity ward. The hood, wide open like a begging alligator, matches the sprung-latched trunk. The old car is totally shamed and demoralized, but illusions of antiquity now cloud our judgment—we keep it.

Our three-year-old is now sixteen, and, growing up in the shadow of our shrine to Detroit, has become a car jock. He needs a part off the bottom, so he and five friends roll the car over on its side—and leave it. The oil drains out and stains the sidewalk and kills four imported African droop lilies. Seeing how stoutly the undercarriage is built, we fall for the most hypnotic junk phrase in the world, "They don't make 'em like they used to," and we decide to rebuild and restore it. The divorce threat following our announcement steers us reluctantly, at last, to the local car crusher, who when he comes nods his head, muttering, "Poor sucker—what a mess." We step forward to ask him to please not insult our cherished deceased property when we suddenly realize he isn't talking about the car. . . .

If a car won't run or isn't used, why keep it? It's taking space and junking up your yard. Unless you're restoring an old classic for a hobby or using a clunker to teach your children car care and hard work (or plan to throw it in a gully to check a flash flood), it can only clutter your life.

What is *your* opinion of car jocks—of car worshippers, of car clutter collectors, of junked-up cars, glove compartments full of junk, trunks full of junk—repulsive, aren't they—aren't *we?*

Few things are more unimpressive than a cluttered car. When we see a messy mobile unit we have a tendency to treat the owner as slouchily as he treats the car. And a seedy front seat tends to be a tipoff to a junked-up home or apartment—have you noticed how copiously crudded cars and sadly junked-up dwellings seem to go hand in hand?

The (Wrong) Automobile in Every Garage

Most people make poor decisions on automobiles, both owning and buying. A three-bedroom motor home is impractical for the average retired couple, a velvet-seated Lincoln is not the right transportation for a shepherd with four dogs and a sick sheep forever in tow, a slick two-door sedan is not the smartest way to haul four kids to Little League and newspaper routes (though a nice tough station wagon might be). A convertible is not the car for the avid skier—there's no place for the rack and in high country those babies are cold!

When you get a vehicle for show or ego, it usually ends up junking up your life—it doesn't serve your needs and you don't get the full benefit of what it *does* have to offer. And affordability isn't only a question of economics—many rich people can't emotionally afford the vehicle junk they have.

The pleasure of driving a fine machine isn't the main reason most people own a glamorous gas guzzler—they often only want to own one so they can be seen parking it, sort of like a big metallic piece of chic outerwear.

How often have we seen a struggling family—a young wife with several kids, barely able to pay the bills and keep the kids clothed, while her husband has to be the overloaded macho man with a giant jacked-up nobby-tired pickup or an impractical sports car loaded with options (junk) strictly for ego.

Car sales (and prices) soar when the manufacturer adds "XY-3," "WHIZ," or "Fireball" on a strip of plastic chrome. The reason dealers display their "play" line in the showroom is to get men (who are far weaker than women when it comes to cars) to come in and look, and imagine themselves careening past crowds of admiring onlookers as they maneuver this magnificent powerful machine through life. Entire families' future health and education (and many other things) are suffering because of poor judgment when buying a mode of transportation.

Four-wheeled junk We tread in sacred mud puddles when we question the value of 4-wheel-drive. While there are a few important farm, sport, commercial, and military uses for 4-wheel-drive vehicles, for most of us they're a junk power symbol: the need for 4x4 drive in this country now (especially in downtown

L.A.) is almost zero. I have lived in both the desert and the highest, toughest mountains—7-foot snows in winter—and I've never needed a 4x4, and I've never been stranded for more than a few hours because of weather. Four-wheel-drive costs about $1,000 extra, gives you an extra drive train to tend, and uses more gas—for what?

Paying extra for safety or comfort—maybe even power—on your vehicle might make sense, but most "extras" sooner or later become junk to you.

Consider that classic of conspicuous consumption—fancy hubcaps. You buy an economy car, standard shift, with a smaller, more economical engine—then get $400 worth of wire, turbo, or mag wheels on it. These are absolutely no aid to travel, and are easy to lose, hard to clean, and expensive to insure (and as a Portland accountant pointed out, "I get no enjoyment out of them. I have to stand in the front yard and have someone drive my car by so I can even *see* them"). The fancier they are, the more mental and financial concern they cause. Who (besides other car junkees) really notices or cares about hubcaps anyway?

There is always a sickening feeling about overjunked car purchase and ownership. The newness wears off in a few weeks and the reality of thirty-six, forty-eight, or sixty months of payments sets in—just for something to take us places. Transportation.

It doesn't really matter how sexy or classic or convenient the vehicle is, we bought it to drive and now, for a long time, we *will* drive it. Many of us try to get even with the car that bought *us* by never washing it and leaving junk in and on it, but it's really only we who suffer.

The time, money, and emotion spent on an automobile—a piece of plastic and metal—is incredible.

A businessman noted for the accuracy of his financial analyses produced some interesting facts about the "average" person. The average person who has a $385,000 lifetime income spends $81,000 of this on his automobile (more than on food or shelter!). One transportation analyst claims that the typical American devotes more than 1,600 hours a year to his car: sitting in it, hunting for parts and parking for it, working to pay for it (about 28 percent of his income). True auto eroticism can be found in some exclusive sections of this country where the average car is owned for about eleven months (a bit longer than the average house is retained in the same areas). An automobile is merely a mode of transportation, yet it has been designed and marketed as a status symbol, personality outlet, aggression releaser, and pacifier. People spend almost twice as much as they need to for a car, and brag or talk about it more than about family, friends, or personal health.

People can easily find hours to wash, polish, and baby a car, yet can't find minutes to floss and brush their teeth. They can make a staggering payment on a car, or spend $5,000 more on a prestige model, yet not be able to afford a weekly long-distance call to Mother or Dad or a $2 donation to the Girl Scout cookie drive. They will know every engineering wonder and calibration of that special model and not even know their nieces' and nephews' birthdays, or what time to be at work. Do you want to spend all that emotional, spiritual, and physical strength to sustain a *possession?*

Maybe It's *Not* Time for a Trade

One day a friend of mine mentioned that since he'd been married (he has seven children, three of them now in college), he'd spent a total of only $13,000 on automobiles (and he's always driven a safe, handsome, fully-paid-for vehicle around). That didn't seem possible to me

because for some time now those nice autos have been costing $9,000-$15,000 each. His simple secret (and what I do now): he waits a year or two, watches the paper, and buys a nice clean sound $10,000 used car for $3,500 direct from a first owner or wholesale from a dealer— and then keeps it maintained and de-junked. It lasts many years and will usually be running well enough to pass on to his children, who drive it another five years. Impossible, you may say: "My car wears out." Not really—we just get anxious for something new and begin to look for excuses to trade the old car in. Once we *want* a new car (slick TV and magazine ads help us out here) the justifications come easily enough. We've only got 30 or 40,000 miles on her, we've just about paid 'er off, and we're ready to leave her behind.

How did I decide to overcome this expensive habit of mobile mothballing, like we all ought to?

During a 300,000-mile publicity tour for one of my books last year, I asked an Indianapolis cabby (driving a plain old 1979 Plymouth just like we drive), "Hey, buddy, how many miles on this thing?" "275,000," he says, "it's about broken in!" Wow, what a blowhard, I said to myself— I thought people only lied about gas mileage. When I got to St. Louis, I asked *that* cab driver, "This thing got a few miles on it?" "325,000," he said. "You're kidding," I said in the back, trying to keep the disbelief out of my voice. "Sure it does, we have two Novas with 225,000 and [some other ordinary cars like we own] get over 400,000 miles—some of our cabs in New York City get 600,000 and over." Positive that I'd met two truth-stretchers in a row, in the next four cities I asked all the cabbies about their cabs and got the same answer (some of them owned the cars they drove). Their secret, I found out, is taking care of things—not necessarily overhauling, but routine maintenance and fixing problems as soon as they come up—and, of course, keeping the engine warm and going helps a lot.

I went back and reviewed the autos (business and personal) I'd owned since 1957 (sixty of them), and almost every one, once I sold or traded it, was run for years by the next owner and more years by the next owner. I figured the new owners must have rebuilt them entirely, but not so—they just replaced a belt and gasket or two and cranked 'er up. Once I bought a '54 panel truck with 70,000 miles on it, beat it up hauling cleaning gear for five years, and put another 70,000 miles on it. I figured it must be dead (the battery was weakening) and sold it to my neighbor for $25. He replaced the battery, fixed the door handles, and drove it for five more years. It finally got so ugly he figured it was dead, and sold it to a high-school kid. One day three years later, when I was doing my Christmas shopping in a town many miles from here, I saw the old '54 Chevy, same dents, my faded Varsity Contractors logo still adorning the doors, parked right with the Cadillacs and luxury Jeeps. A kid came out of the mall, jumped in, and drove off, smooth as silk!

When I sat down and thought about it, the reason I got rid of cars was usually that a latch was broken, the clock stopped working, the glove box light went out, a window stuck, or there was a rip in the upholstery.

Don't do it! It's a poor investment. Sit down and calculate your vehicle purchase and operation costs for the last ten or twenty years. Now figure what you could have done with that amount of money if you'd followed a more practical course.

The adjustment to a whole new way of thinking about vehicles is a shocker, but it will pay you some amazing dividends. I wasn't at all sure I should keep driving a vehicle when it reached the 100,000 or 125,000 mark. I'd start getting nervous and say, "Surely I better get a new one." I could scarcely believe it was still

running well, and pictured myself driving somewhere and the whole motor or transmission suddenly disintegrating or dropping out on the highway—but that nightmare never comes true. I'm just being seduced by the new-car enchantress.

Yes, I do have a little fix-it problem once in awhile, but the glory of no payments, low insurance premiums, and all the other nice paid-for sensations more than make up for it. *All* my vehicles have over 100,000 miles. They are real luxury units—I can relax (even leave the keys in!) when I park them or when someone spills a milkshake, jump in and take off without a thought in my grubbiest work clothes—yet they run and do everything the $15,000 models do.

Since I kicked the expensive habit of mobile mothballing, I've been constantly reassured it was the best de-junking move I've made—cars don't wear out as fast as our resistance to new models. Cars don't drive me, I drive them, and I love it. Your car can go to 100,000 miles— oh yes it can!

When Adding Subtracts. . . .

Some of the best designers, engineers, and decorators in the world work for automobile manufacturers, expending great research and effort to make cars efficient and beautiful. They work for years to achieve precision and balance in a car model's power, mechanics, size, and weight for maximum durability and safety. Yet when ownership falls into our hands our impulse to clutter it up is surpassed only by our urge to redesign it. We think we can grossly improve the unit by adding extras (junk)—and we succeed! We modify pipes for more noise, rip off the hood so everyone knows there's a motor in there, jack up or weigh down the frame, reshape the grille, install miniature traffic lights in the rear window, add larger tires, bigger carburetors, giant plastic bug guards, racks, winches, and a horn that plays "Dixie." As a final touch we have to play police with whipping antennas that get ripped off by every car wash and kid in town.

Few of us are convinced the auto company's gearshift handle designer is as smart as our local hot rod parts salesman and so, before our $14,000 vehicle can operate, it needs a genuine gold-plated goosehead gearshift knob. The goosehead is a bit awkward to handle and too bland for some real mover with silver-studded driver's gloves. He's more likely to reach for a German Luger handle, a dagger, or a replica of Mae West's bosom. And of course in the *real* macho car you'll find a scented satin garter clasped around the sun visor.

While serving briefly in the state legislature, I rode home on weekends with a fellow legislator. The view out my window was somewhat obstructed by an obnoxious black box fastened to the dash—a radar detector. My colleague proceeded to drive 80 miles per hour, the detector of course functioning to intercept any police radar, at which he would slow down to the lawful 55 miles per hour. He apparently felt that it was his right to break the laws that he was, as a public officer, on his way to enact.

The ownership of such an instrument is an admission of intent to break traffic safety laws. The speedometer gave him all the information he needed; it's designed into every car free! It's a great example to friends and family, too: "This is Daddy's sneaker cheater lawbreaking helper." If a kid cheats on a test, lies a little, or dodges a household duty, that same father comes unglued.

Junker sticker An ugly 12x4-inch piece of glue-backed paper, generally containing some unimportant poetic or political message, plastered on automobiles and other conveyances to get attention or create a distraction. Bumper stickers are a hard-to-equal demonstration of bad manners (even more obnoxious than blaring exterior loudspeakers). What's worse, while you're driving, than having a message preached at you off the back of the car ahead? One car reads "Honk If You Love Jesus"; the next, "Honk If You're Horny." Be it political or moral persuasion or the crudest "Get Off My _____," bumper stickers are junk, in bad taste, and (with the possible exception of "I Brake for Animals") *impair passenger safety.*

Decor Can Be Dangerous

Somewhere in the process of junking a vehicle we forget its original purpose—transportation. A telephone or stereo in an auto is often useful, but once we start in making our car a home away from home we add a TV, a bar, an icebox, venetian blinds, clothes hangers, footbaths, extra clocks, makeup mirrors, compasses, cup holders, thermometers, and cassette sorters. The car looks and feels obese—becomes unwieldy to operate and maintain—and unsafe. The last three times I've run into something on or off the road, I was watching out for, fiddling around with, trying to eat, or adjust a piece of junk.

Our efforts to decorate our vehicle and give it all the comforts of home are often at the expense of important and necessary equipment like safety flares, flashlights, first-aid kit, chains, jumper cables (that *work*), blankets, a shovel, etc. The food-stiffened seat belts are tangled and unfindable amid the rubble. Visibility suffers, too—there are gaudy souvenir stickers on every window, dancing dice, miniature teddy bears, dubious deodorizers dangling in the driver's line of vision; bobbing-headed dolls and stuffed snakes bring up the rear (window).

The tissue holder on the dash ends up poked down a defroster vent (which makes it a lot less likely that we'll ever get the frost out of our faces). The FM radio and tape player may make staying awake on long trips easier, but the moment we're dawdling with the dial and fumbling with cartridges could be the fatal one.

For a clutter-free vehicle:

1. Keep a garbage can in the garage or driveway area. This will help keep clutter from infiltrating your car and make it easy and convenient to de-junk when you pack up or unpack.

2. Be sure you have any necessary tools, shovels, emergency flares, chains, etc., in a sturdy box in your trunk. Better still, roll them in a pad. This keeps tools compact, quiet, and provides a nice mat if you need to crawl under or over the car.

3. Keep some small (11x17-inch) plastic trash can liners handy and as bits of food and other refuse build up on a trip, put it in the bag immediately. Odors and stains that junk cars usually result from *left* food, not the act of eating itself.

4. Carry a Masslin® dustcloth (see *Is There Life After Housework?*) in the glove box. It will pick up the dust effectively. I also carry a spray bottle of alcohol-based window cleaner and a cloth in the trunk for spills, mud on lights, and other instant cleaning needs.

5. Don't screw, bolt, or glue cheap accessories and gadgets all over the vehicle.

6. Clean and wash the *inside* of the car occasionally, too. A wet/dry vacuum and a hand brush will clean seats and floor mats easily.

Modern transportation offers us tremendous advantages and conveniences. But a vehicle is not an extra house, room, shed, or a mobile dining car. It isn't a trophy wall, moving van, or a six-cylinder billboard. *It is transportation!* One of the biggest destroyers of human life today is the automobile used for things other than reasonable transportation.

DRIVE DE-JUNKED. The skin and sanity you save will be your own.

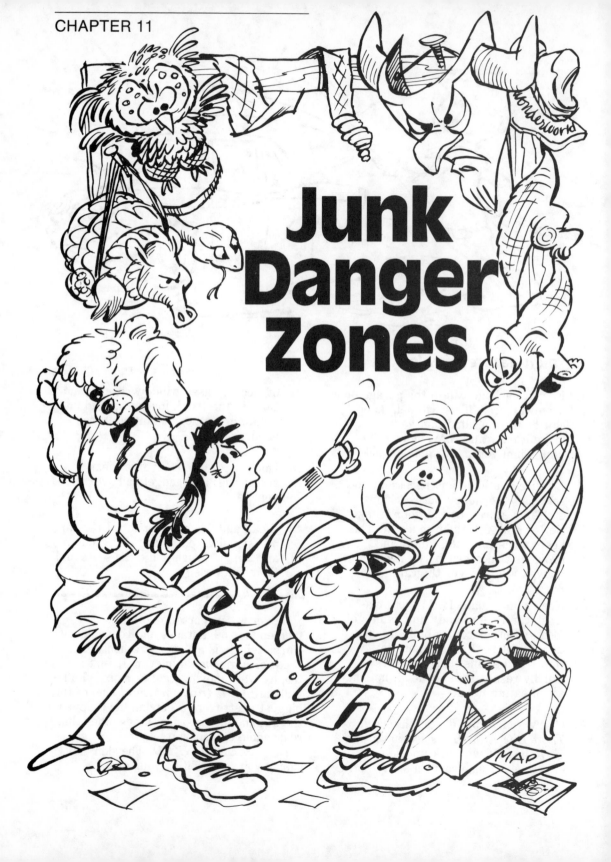

CHAPTER 11

Junk Danger Zones

Junkee Safari

Maybe we saw too many Tarzan shows in our youth, felt excitement stir in our veins as the great heroes and hunters stalked the field for trophies. Now we imitate those events perfectly—alone, in twos, and in families. Father and mother are the great "white" hunters (there's no minority edge in cluttering). The kids are the caravan led into the distant wilds of amusement parks, national parks, ballparks, state fairs, toll road restaurants, and gift shops anywhere.

Suddenly we see it . . . through the trimmed hedge . . . the "Congo Curio Cache." Our pulse is pounding like drums as we peer at: a granite gazelle, a teak tribesman with a bone in his lip, a brass camel nutcracker, a genuine jade juice glass, a varnished driftwood thimble holder and—hold it—a 6-inch alligator of glued-together guava pits (tremendously valuable—even more valuable than the sunflower-seed owl we got in Phoenix). We carefully examine the base of each unit, which identifies the country it was "homemade" in and what machine it was "handmade" by. Our chest swells with pride as we boldly pass up a eucalyptus umbrella stand and a set of tusk toothpicks. Then we find "it"—an ivory unicorn with obsidian eyes. How could we have lived without one all these years? Into the bag it goes. What fun it will be finding a place to display it!

We are finally exhausted pawing through the fifty of each of these "one of a kind" items, but wait—look! Colorful carved candles. "Who do you think would like one of these?" mother hunter asks, running an appreciative eye over them.

Father hunter says, "There must be somebody!" Kid beams a "beats me" look. They all think, but can come up with no one immediately needful of an elegantly carved candle. "There must be someone . . . I've got it! . . . The Jones kid is getting married. What a lovely gift."

(They'll have to put a note with it, telling the Joneses never to take the cellophane wrapper off, to be careful not to dent it moving it from display area to display area (for surely it's too pretty to burn), to store it in a cool place so it won't melt, and to be sure to pack it up in a big padded box when they move. . . .)

Have you been on a junkee safari lately? Examine your trophies—maybe you should have stayed in camp.

Location Lurking

If it's a forbidden or dangerous place we all have to go there—call it curiosity, inquisitiveness, or exploration, it's all the same. My mother always warned me to "stay out of the sagebrush, or you'll get ticks on you and catch spotted fever." As play at home in the yard dulled, the brush brightened, and sometimes I would drift to the edge—no spots appeared and not a sign of a tick! Soon I was playing in the brush, enjoying the challenge and mystery of it all (and still no spots or ticks). I would return from the forbidden fascinating location thinking I'd gone undetected; I didn't realize the rule of location lurking: it always leaves its marks on mind, body, wallet, and suitcase. When I'd get within twenty feet of Mom, the tangy sage smell would give me away: "You've been in the sagebrush, haven't you?" Fearing her apparent omniscience, I'd 'fess up. And as she'd pull off my shirt there were those tiny ticks all over me; my record was thirteen!

You might not collect any fleas from a flea market, but you'll pick up a bargain or two while you're "just looking" and enjoying the atmosphere. You snicker at fools who bid their heads off at auctions—but if you hang around or attend many, you'll be one of them. At a garage sale your inquisitiveness will soon evolve to acquisitiveness and you'll find junk tucked proudly under your arm.

There are some locations we have to frequent less or avoid altogether if we intend ever to be cured of junkitis.

Frequenting shopping malls (plazas, squares, centers, complexes, or any of their other aliases) is location-lurking suicide: even an innocent amble through will insinuate some junk into your shopping bag. Never go to or hang out in such places if you don't need anything.

Next time you go to a shopping mall, before you buy or look, sit down on a bench and watch the customers. You'll notice the majority of them shuffling along purposelessly, often not after anything in particular, just looking for what they *might* need. The displays, decor, and smell of a mall seem to have a hypnotic hold, especially when people, like overpowered hot rods on a Saturday night, travel up and down the aisles looking for action.

The media—and perhaps our parents, teachers, and friends—have inadvertently taught us that happiness comes from

things: that's why when we get "down" or depressed and want a lift we often seek to buy something. That's why people wander aimlessly through malls and curio shops—they don't even know *what* they want. They just crave the experience of buying a new thing every so often. The minute they buy it, the time starts ticking down till the next time they have to do that. And when they do get something, it just triggers the urge for the next and next—all of which compounds accumulation. Just picking up "one little thing" here and "one little thing" there is where the pile of clutter came from.

"Recreational" shopping is a mistake. If you need, want, or have to have a specific something, go for it, but just poking around in shopping malls (or anywhere there is a glamorous array of goods, food, or whatever) is a temptation you don't need. It will seduce you into acquiring things that will needlessly clutter your life.

The Languid Locations

Some locations are particularly perilous because they have a very high clutter quotient or actually *specialize* in things that are junk to most of us (scarcely or non-functional, largely decorative, often expensive "stuff"). Fortunately, we have a clue to this before we ever enter by the very name of the place.

Any place with the word "gift" in its name.

Ye Olde, etc.: when Old is spelled Olde . . . watch out! (Anything with an extra "e" on the end is probably a junk dive.)

Anything with an animal in the name: The Busy Bee, The Bashful

Bunny, The Fragrant Frog, The Rumpled Unicorn . . .

Anything that sports an ampersand, or has an "N": (N'Stuff, N'Such) is a dead giveaway.

Anything that substitutes Ks for Cs: The Kozy Korner, The Kountry Kobbler, etc.

For that matter, anything with "Country" or "Corner" in the name.

Trees or plants in names are also suspect: The Tulip Tree, The Boysenberry Bush, The Sassafras Shrub.

*H*ave you ever gone back to an old junk-purchase stomping ground, shuddered, and asked yourself, "How could I ever in my right mind have bought that?" It seems we have to buy a certain amount of trinkets a certain number of times before becoming immune. If you haven't reached your junk saturation level yet, *don't wait for it!* It might be years of unhappiness away.

Garage Sale Sickness

Garage sales have increased about 800 percent in the last decade—the ultimate public confession that the house runneth over, a family fight is inevitable if the junk stays, or they need cash to buy different junk.

The display of all of your junk right in front of your house takes real guts. I couldn't do it if they paid me double the price. A quiet classified ad at least has a little dignity (only people might match your phone number with the worn mattress, the highchair without a tray, or the "like new" exercise bike). The allure of a garage sale is unreal: I've seen people become totally distraught when they hear another garage sale is going on while theirs is in progress. It's not the competition that causes the concern—it's the fact that they can't leave and get in on the goodies at the other sale! Garage sales are *the* place to give you a double-whammy dose of junkitis virus. There seems to be something inflammatory about the sight of someone else's junk all spread out on open display (and for such cheap prices, too!).

It's truly the Great American Junk phenomenon—how ordinarily intelligent, discriminating consumers will suddenly abandon all reason and begin to scoop up armloads of the most absurd stuff imaginable:

- Old half-used bottles of aftershave
- Dilapidated parlor games
- Burned-out appliances
- Tent dresses and double-breasted suits
- Half-dead houseplants
- Moth-eaten uniforms
- Mismatched dishes
- Parts to extinct autos
- Leaky hip boots
- Abused toys
- Obsolete textbooks
- Run-over shoes
- Holey Levis
- Shorted-out electric blankets
- Bald tires
- High-water pants

You name it—and it's selling like hotcakes at your nearest garage sale. It's not amazing enough that the junkee shells out perfectly good money for this trash—

he or she actually experiences euphoric feelings of cleverness and joy at having scored such a hit. These feelings usually dissipate by the time the victim reaches home, however. Having by now returned to full consciousness and taken a second look at the plunder, the hapless junkee goes into a fit of depression.

If you're serious about saving yourself from junkicide, garage sales may well be a pleasure you might wish to forgo.

The garage sale has a few relatives also worth sidestepping. The *rummage sale*, for example, is an increasingly rare species that still lingers on in church halls and school basements, often heavily inhabited by charming chirping ladies. The rummage sale abounds in shabby but genteel junk—worn books, limp afghans, faded plastic flower arrangements, and frumpy 1950s clothing. The *flea market*, on the other hand, is a vigorous and fast-growing hybrid that springs up in shopping malls, parking lots, vacant lots, fairgrounds—anywhere there is abundant open space for display and parking. Here the innocent is adrift in a sea of separate booths featuring a breathtaking variety of junk—old, middle-aged, and even brand spanking new. Velvet paintings, Last Supper rugs, log-slice clocks, hubcaps, novelty booze bottles, comic books, used paperbacks, tattered girlie magazines, and printed T-shirts of every description are standard flea market fare. You even stand a good chance of being able to lay your hands on a genuine ($5) Sears wrench for only $6.50.

Some junk danger zones are less widespread than others—not everyone passes through them—but they're no less deadly for being less trafficked. If you're due to travel these zones soon, begin preventative therapy *now*.

Convention Clutter

Have you ever watched crowds at a convention as they scoop up all those buttons, brochures, booklets, pens, posters, stickers, swatches, samples, and special-release records—and cart them home? We even save the plastic bags they gave us to carry the clutter in, and our plastic badge holders to remember the glory of our name in lights (or at least felt-tip marker). Maybe someday we'll have enough to slip in new cards and reuse them to run our *own* convention (the annual Junkman's Convention?). . . .

Convention "fall-out," by and large, just litters drawers and punctures fingers—how much of this stuff do you have squirreled away? I'll bet my whole stack of play money any of you who've been to a convention or trade show within the past year *still* haven't gotten around to using (or even sorting) the junk you hauled home. Embarrassing, huh?

Sick Junk

Even sick, we aren't safe from the junk virus. Isn't it odd that people keep their hospital junk? As we check out, we clutch our flattened bed fleece and all those little pitchers, pans, and cups, plastic straws, and wristbands—after all, we paid for them—so we load them up and take them home, and never, never use them. They're the sickest green you ever laid eyes on, and every time we see them they remind us of the hospital—the shots and the nausea and that miserable operation. (And how many homes need more than three pairs of crutches?) Why do we keep them? Trying to get our money's worth out of that $2,600 hospital bill? Forget it. If you're saving the stuff for the next time, forget that, too—they'll charge you for it again, even if you bring your own!

Passing Fancy Junk

In the moments when clutter begins to overwhelm us, we never ask, "How did I get all this?" We know exactly how! We instead ask ourselves, "*Why* did I get all this junk?" The answer is often—we fell for the old "fad" or "get in the swim" trick.

When any type of craze sweeps the nation, committed as a lynching mob, a big percentage of us join in. We buy fast,

pay more, and then fizzle out. Homes and cars are stuffed to the gills with seldom-used "good as new":

aquariums	gerbil cages
jogging accessories	hula hoops
video games	food processors
fondue pots	fad style clothes
ceiling fans	movie cameras
string art kits	weaving looms
massaging foot-baths	yogurt makers
wood-burning kits	hot tubs
pet rocks	macrame makings
diet books and plans	hurricane lamps
weights and exercise machines	guitars
metal detectors	trampolines
ceramic molds and kilns	CB radios
pasta machines	walkie-talkies
organs and pianos	slow cookers
stereo headphones	popcorn machines
rock tumblers	wood-burning stoves
adult bicycles	ice cream makers

Most of this is bought on the spur of the moment and before the new smell has vanished, so has our interest. As costly as it may have been, it's now a burden to us. How can we poke fun at the snake oil salesmen and claim-salting victims of the Old West when we're suckered out of millions of dollars daily on things we don't need, or that we use for an hour and keep for a decade?

Beware the "Danger Days" that accelerate the accumulation of clutter

If you think avoiding gift shops, shopping malls, and even garage sales alone is enough to keep you safe from junk, you're riding for a fall.

Custer came to an untimely end because he unwarily rode into an area where the opposition outnumbered him; our clutter defeats are caused by a similar unawareness. When you stop and think about it, we're surrounded by specially scheduled days that circle and bombard us. Study your calendar the way Custer should have studied his war map.

JANUARY

NEW YEAR'S EVE

We insist on starting our year off miserably with too much liquor, rich food, tootie horns, stupid hats, streamers, pages of unresolved resolutions and twenty-seven more calendars than we'll ever use.

FEBRUARY

VALENTINE'S DAY

This high holy day of accumulation rolls around just about the day the last piece of Christmas clutter finally disappears. We only prepare for it a week or so in advance, but manage to swiftly replace the missing Christmas junk with frilly paper doilies, cheap candies stuck together in a gaudy dish bought for the occasion, over-frosted cookies that hang around for weeks in drawers and on shelves, shiny cupid-shaped cake pans to be tucked (or crammed) into storage for next year . . . and who with a grain of romance in their soul could throw away empty embossed candy boxes with lace and ribbons?

APRIL

EASTER

Think of all the awful Easter bonnets and broken Easter baskets, battered chicks and bunnies, baggies of plastic grass, and picked-over jelly beans stashed somewhere; along with the leftover egg coloring kits and peekaboo candy eggs that we'll never eat and never throw away.

MAY

OPENING DAY: FISHING

Full-grown adults (especially the males) become insane weaklings on this day, so hide the checkbook. They buy assorted rods, reels, creels, lures, and hooks, fish-fooling and -finding gadgets, books and bait incubators, tons of real and artificial foodstuffs, attractants, repellents, and special fishing togs, 80 percent of which are expensive (and ultimately destined to dry-rot in the storage room).

JULY

FOURTH OF JULY

We always get twice as many sparklers, wienie buns, coolers, and charcoal briquettes as we need, and more suntan lotion than we could use in three summers—and then spend the rest of the year trying to keep it all out of sight.

OCTOBER

HALLOWEEN

We buy racks of creepy costumes, a bale of orange-and-black napkins, a six-foot paper skeleton and witches for the walls, keep a 50¢ mask with our kid's first trick-or-treat candy crushed on it—and then at the after-Halloween sale buy four more plastic lanterns to store till next year.

NOVEMBER

THANKSGIVING

Got to have ugly miniature turkeys, six extra giant platters, assorted relishes in assorted little awkward display dishes, shedding centerpieces and door ornaments, and an extra meat thermometer in case the other three extras don't work. (And we'll keep those gap-toothed Indian corn ears and dried-up gourds into infinity.)

DECEMBER 25

CHRISTMAS

Keep the wrinkled wrappings, crushed bows, and snarled ribbons, sagging Santa candles, frayed pine cones, faded wreaths, broken bulbs and tree ornaments, every tree stand we ever bought, and the last two surviving pieces of the Nativity set (even if Joseph's head is missing).

SOME OTHERS TO BEWARE OF:

Mother's Day—Father's Day—Memorial Day—birthdays—weddings—anniversaries—any opening day—reunions—graduations—Election Day—St. Patrick's Day—Washington's and Lincoln's birthdays

For some reason we can't just enjoy the spirit of the day—we have to "thing" it to death. It's as if we have to *prove* we're loving or patriotic or happy or thankful. But the proof is in the feeling, not in the accessories.

Celebrity Clutter

Billie Bicep eats Soggie Doggie Flakes, so millions eat Soggie Doggie Flakes. Many don't even know Billie Bicep, or if the flakes killed him, or what—but they'll buy and eat. Miss Doris Dottungorto wears purple pump shoes exclusively—so millions of teens buy (but seldom wear) purple pump shoes. Endorsements and testimonials from the most famous "personality" can't convert junk to jewels: because a guy hit fifty-eight home runs doesn't make him an authority on what to drink or eat; because a woman has traveled to the moon doesn't mean she knows anything about luggage. We are as much authorities as anyone on ourselves and our world.

We seldom see ourselves as celebrities, but we are, all of us—only our degree of exposure varies. You are admired and looked up to by someone—probably scores of someones. When you begin to realize this, you won't be such a victim of celebrity clutter. Don't let yourself revere any mere human to the point he or she can dump junk into your life.

I love heroes—they have been and still are some of the greatest inspirations in my life. When John Wayne died I felt like laying down in front of a truck; when Sophia Loren appears on the screen, my nostrils flare. I think Walt Disney was one of the greatest geniuses who has lived on this earth—but they are just people like you and me, and your friends, relatives, and family. I don't need John Wayne saucers hanging on every wall, or a Sophia Loren T-shirt (it wouldn't fit anyway), or a pair of mouse ears in my closet. My Roy Rogers capgun was my pride and joy, as was my Captain Marvel code ring, when I was a kid, but we all grow up (we hope) and take a saner view of celebrities.

Let your heroes and heroines fill you with feeling, not load you down with junk. Anyway, think how disrespectful it is to blow your nose right in the faces of your Beatle hanky, chew on the eraser of your president pencil, or sit on your Elvis Presley pillow. (And an autograph on something only *guarantees* you'll never use it.)

Endanger Junk? . . . Never!

If you're a tender-hearted junkee you may worry about becoming so junk-free that junk will become extinct. It won't happen. As hard as you may be working to pitch it out of your life, 40,000 companies are actively working to lay more on you. Have you ever noticed when anything reaches the "endangered species" state how it suddenly multiplies? Newspaper headlines now read:

*SNAIL DARTER
ENDANGERED SPECIES!*

Overnight, snail darter plates and coins and memorial mugs and spoons appear in gift shops and in mailings. People stampede to buy them so they'll always keep in touch with the snail darter (whatever a snail darter might be). Soon there is tons of snail darter junk, though no one remembers or cares about the real, live, almost extinct little darter. Other creatures, famous/infamous people, places, etc., are handled just the same. As soon as something is winding down, the media and manufacturers pump it right back up. Don't have junk paranoia—there'll always be plenty if you get lonely!

Media Mania

Every time new heroes come on the tube or screen we fall in love with them, but the experience is so passive that to keep our love alive we have to shower ourselves and our shelves with the flood of trinketry that follows. The whole environment is remade in the image of some fictitious creature: rings, T-shirts, notebooks, pencils, ponchos, perfume, candy, sleeping bags and sheets and pajamas, watches, shoes, decals, games, books are everywhere. Can you believe it? We pay for it! $10.95 for a $1.99 T-shirt with some nonexistent primordial amphibian silkscreened on the front. It all ends up junk as soon as the theater changes the marquee.

Imagination junk We snicker and chuckle at the kids being suckered in on movie and TV junk (toys and souvenirs), but they can't really hold a clutter candle to our acquisition of imagination junk, whereby we buy miniature replicas and play models of the things we want but can't afford. Thus we have Mercedes and Porsche keychains, Ferrari eyeglasses; if we can't have a boat in the bay, we have one in a bottle; if we can't be a real cowboy, we get the buckle, boots, spurs, hat, and often a bronze stallion for the shelf.

The really gross junk in the line of things we want but don't always get is *women's figure junk*. Anything made to resemble a woman's body, some men will buy. Thus we have female torso drinking glasses, bottle openers, ice cubes, swizzle sticks, toothbrushes, chess sets, ashtrays, and even tire irons. Talk about imagination junk! Can you imagine being eager to use Marilyn Monroe boat bumpers or a Dolly Parton parcheesi set. . . . Gadfrey, I can't "bare" to go on!

Beware of These Junk Seduction Words . . .

All of us are lambs when it comes to the seductive words and phrases that convince us we can't live through the day without knowing what _____ feels or tastes like, if we can't own a _____ of our own. Before soft messages and signs croon you into the arms of Old Mother Junk, make sure you translate them.

The One-Word Wonders

Selected: *Everything* is selected—it could be selected out of the reject pile, the failure file, or the trash barrel.

Imported: Just about everything is "imported" from somewhere—how far away doesn't matter much any more.

Premium: Could be a way of marketing something, not an indication of worth or quality.

Limited: They don't say limited to what or where, or how many.

Model: A small imitation of the real thing.

Special: A term of timing—not value! In the right time or circumstances *anything* can be special.

Exclusive: They haven't dared try it anywhere else.

Handmade: A hand touches the tool or mold that makes everything.

Homegrown: Everything is homegrown (even if it's been shipped in from 4,000 miles away).

Free: Law of the Universe: There is nothing without a price.

Revised: It didn't work (or sell) the first time.

Quality: Quality is just a state (it could be good or bad).

Priceless: Smiles are priceless. People are priceless. I've never seen a *thing* that is.

Distinctive: Distinguishable from other things—isn't everything?

Authentic: Genuine junk!

Reduced: Same junk with a different price.

Layaway: Get it now and let it grow on you before you have to pay for it.

Clutter by Any Other Name Is. . . .

We've evolved gentler, more indirect, euphemistic approaches to most of the unpleasant things in our lives: we can say "portly" instead of "overweight," "sexually active" instead of "immoral," "legally detained" for "in jail." Thus of course we've found some soothing clever names for clutter, too—so we don't have to come out and call it "junk" or "trash" or "clutter" or "worthless objects."

You can do a fairly good job of identifying junk by its nicknames—and they are legion. Cast a harsh eye on anything that you find yourself (or others) calling:

doodads	trifles
odds and ends	trinkets
curios	baubles
knickknacks	gimcracks
gewgaws	folderol
paraphernalia	doohickeys
collectibles	thingamajigs
bric-a-brac	watchamacallits
whatnots	

The Phrase Fresheners

Sometimes, no matter how seductively junk is marketed in the first place, it just doesn't sell. So the advertising people are called in to revamp the campaign and they come up with ploys like these.

On Sale: The most desirable things and places don't have to go on sale.

New, Improved: It failed, and we want *you* to guinea-pig the second round.

Once-in-a-Lifetime: You can be sure that after getting stung this time you'll never do it again.

In Style: It's time again to tell people what they like.

For a Limited Time Only: They've only got a few more left to dump.

May Never Be Offered Again: There are two lawsuits pending.

Backed by _____ Years of Integrity: "The more he talked of his honor, the faster I counted my spoons."

Top-Rated: Only means that it's popular—doesn't say why: it could be the only one in town.

Double Your Money Back: If you can find them.

Only One per Customer: Offer to buy a hundred, they'll love you!

Our Only Concern Is Your Satisfaction: Your money will satisfy that concern.

Ten-Day Trial Offer: They can depend on your procrastination.

Not Sold in Stores: We decided to hit you suckers direct.

First Edition: Is always the worst—mechanically and structurally. All first editions are prototypes, experiments—which means they don't have the bugs worked out yet.

Space-Age Material:	Most likely plastic, sometimes stated as "Space-Age Technology."
Years Ahead of Its Time:	Just hope it doesn't need a part not invented yet.
World's Thinnest, Lightest, etc.:	They made it as cheap as they could.
Doctors Use:	Doctors make mistakes and have bad habits, too.
The Next Best Thing to _____:	Please buy this second-best.
No Artificial Preservatives:	But surely lots of natural ones.
Factory Outlet:	No retailer wants it.
First Class:	Should be the standard, not a degree of excellence.
Grand 2 for 1 Sale:	Easiest way to get rid of two pieces of junk simultaneously.
Custom-Made:	The factory made an error.
Order Toll-Free:	Junk is only a phone call away (we'll include the toll in the purchase price).
Special Edition:	Every edition is special in some way.
For Adults Only:	If you're a twelve-year-old with fuzz on your lip—you're in!
Train or Truckload Sale:	Just about everything travels one way or the other these days.
Laboratory-Tested:	It could have *failed* the test.
Made from Selected Raw Materials:	Probably a tuna can you threw away a month ago.
Largest Selection Available:	Nobody else in the area carries any.
New Fall Colors:	The same old colors with new names.
Almost Too Good to Believe:	It almost fools you every time.
At Last, a _____:	It never was really needed.
Order Before Midnight and We'll Include. . .:	Will you accept a bribe for junking?

Everything tagged with these teasers isn't necessarily junk, but how often do we let phrases like these inflate an object's value—and how often do we end up with clutter because of them? You hear people (who have no idea what that might entail) say, "But it's Swiss-made!" So what? Do the Swiss (or the Japanese or the Swedes or Guatamalan Indians) have a corner on quality? The fact is, well-crafted items can come from anywhere—and so can sloppily built things.

CHAPTER 12

You *Can* Take It With You (Clutter!)

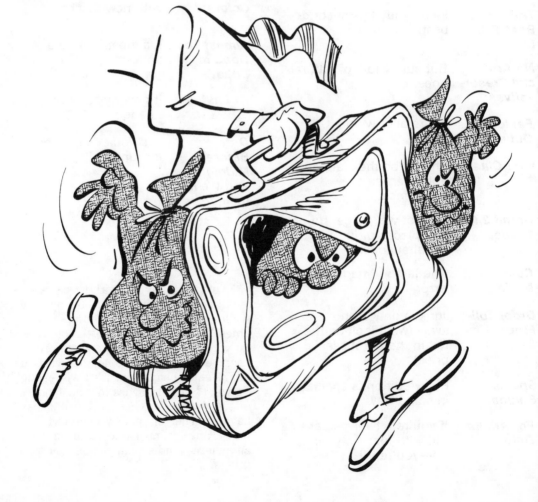

At age fifty-seven, my wife's parents, Vera and Jerry, were comfortable, their family was raised, their health good, they had plenty of friends, and Jerry had a good job. They had just built a little house and I guess you might say they had it made—they could live out their lives in a secure and honorable fashion. But to them, as to most of us, there's more to living than room, board, and a job. Although their situation was pleasant enough, they got to thinking of the routine they'd established in the past twenty years—it just wasn't going to be as exciting for the next twenty very important ones. They'd watch the same trees turn, the same people cruise the neighborhood, go to the same bowling alley (and get the same score), have the same hamburger every Tuesday, the same chicken every Thursday, go on the same vacation every year, suffer through the same weather, and so on. Secure—but dull, unchallenging. Routine, too, can become junk.

Of course, we know we don't have to change geography to change routine, and that problems can travel with us to the farthest mountain cabin or desert isle, but sometimes a change in location, leaving the junk of routine and place behind, can force a freshness into your life that will make your heart beat with joy again and arouse new feelings (and revive some old ones).

One evening, during the same conversation during the same visit to the same house at the same hour with the same people, Jerry's drooping ears heard someone mention a possible mechanic's job in the wilds of Fairbanks, Alaska. The job wasn't for sure, but for a qualified mechanic chances were good—and Jerry was the *best* mechanic. Three weeks later, eyes blazing, possessions loaded in a new Ford pickup with a camper shell, Vera and Jerry, at an age most people would hole up in fear, left their home of forty years and went to Alaska.

When my wife and I visited them three years later, we discovered a miracle had occurred in their lives. Both looked forty, both bubbled with enthusiasm. We stayed with them two weeks, and every place and person they introduced us to was stimulating and life-brightening. They had experienced floods, dog races, record cold, wild animals, glaciers, and the most majestic mountains in the world. They were irresistibly alive—it was almost impossible to leave them when our departure time arrived.

After ten years Vera and Jerry retired, and still with only a pickup full of possessions, came home (grandkids are hard to resist). Their lives today still have a zing from those ten years of new experience and challenge. They still have the love and associations of their home and friends of forty years, and now hundreds of new friends and memories from Alaska.

When our realm of experience is too confined, we lose confidence—get cluttered. (Isn't just about every unconfident person you know intensely territorial?) We don't give new people or places a chance to touch our heart.

We can have the same experience twenty times—or twenty different experiences. I'm not saying old friends or good old places are junk—just that we need to always be progressing and expanding. We can't stand still and savor a situation too long or it loses its savor. We have to go forward; we'll get junked standing still.

Reflect on this some evening after you arrive home from a twenty-same-experience activity. Maybe a trip to Africa or Australia or South America is out of the question, but if you curl up in your den of routine and security too long, your mate, family, peers, employers will see the junk of routine making you into a dud.

The same goes for the clutter of constantly returning to old stomping grounds and scenes of former glory. Junk locks us into the old; it gives us false security.

It's like that spark of hope we carry around of revisiting and reliving the past. Life doesn't have any reruns: all those people and places didn't go into cold storage the day we left; like us, they grew and changed. And when we go back, the miles are shorter, the hills smaller, the old buildings replaced by new, and no one is in near the awe of us that we expected. We had the chance to wave our banners once; the second time around will bring us little or no applause.

A return to jog memories or show the kids or friends is sometimes beneficial, but make it quick and move on. I used to long at least once daily to return to the ballfield where I once had the ability to bring the crowd cheering to their feet. Thirty years later I did return for a big ballgame—and they could have put a tent over me and sold my performance as an act. I was ill-timed and awkward—when I left in glory I should have left it alone.

Things evolve, turn over—the new comes and the old dies or is left behind. Growth is all! Junk prevents growth, change, moving on ahead to better—in love, jobs, friendships.

There is always more ahead than behind; the past can become clutter to us if we don't learn to live it and leave it graciously behind.

You Can Take It With You . . . But Please Don't

We Americans are a mobile society; if we want to, we can move around pretty easily and change our life experience. We can travel anywhere, any way, any day. We travel to and from work, to and from college, to and from relatives, to and from the places we go just for the fun of it—"vacations." We ride thirty different modes of transportation—even go as far as the moon. We spend more time on the move than in our permanent living quarters, called home. The average one of us moves from one home to another about fourteen times during a lifetime.

Most of this mobility is for a few basic reasons:

1. To have new experiences.

2. To meet new people.

3. To expand ourselves.

Much of our mobility is a quest for self-discovery and self-expression, but most of us don't really gain the advantage of our movement, or reach our real destination, because we're too weighed down by the clutter we carry along.

Most of us who want to get away from it all end up taking it all with us. The very things, the very people, the very thoughts that have ruined our nerves are packed (as much as possible) in the car or suitcase and taken along. And then it has to be tended, sorted, and worried about as much in Mexico as back on the farm in Iowa or the house in Baltimore.

We can't change, expand, meet new people, see new places, or have new experiences when the old junk that inspired us to get away is traveling along with us. Consider a simple trip into the country: we prepare for a three-day trip for five days—not what to do when we get there, but organizing to get there and back in comfort. We end up packing so much there's no place to sleep or ride. Excess baggage always dampens travel; much of it is clutter and ends up detracting from the destination. Truthfully now—when you see someone staggering along with piles and piles of baggage, what do you think? You don't like them, do you?

Where you're going usually has a kitchen sink of some sort, so don't take yours along. The more junk you carry on your journey, the less vacation you'll have from junk.

JUNKEES ARE ALWAYS PREPARED—ESPECIALLY ON VACATION. THEY CARRY WITH THEM:

- **four outfits** for each projected day of vacation—clothes for all different temperatures, weather, and moods
- the **dashing outfits** they never have the courage to wear at home (and won't have the courage to wear there)
- more **perfume** and **jewelry** than they ever wear at home
- **clothes** that are too tight for them at home (and will be even more impossible to wear after several days of vacation feasting)
- at least two **fancy formals** "in case they decide to go to a nightclub"—

but they'll never get off the beach, as usual
- **ten pairs of pantyhose** (after the first sunburn, they won't be wearing any—though they *could* use them to hang themselves)
- **wide-brimmed hats** (hard to carry or pack without smashing, hard to keep on, will block everyone's view if they do wear them and the car's rear window if they don't)
- **food** (in case they get stranded)
- a **can opener** (and an extra can opener)

- a **bathrobe and slippers,** plus
- a **dressing gown** (and high-heeled mules)
- an **extra purse**
- extra **heavy coat** and an extra raincoat
- all the **shoes** they never wear at home
- three **swimsuits** (different styles)
- **umbrella** and backup umbrella
- four boxes of **Kleenex**
- the **multi-vitamins** they never take at home
- six pairs of **sunglasses**
- a **sun lamp**
- a **heating pad**
- **towels** they won't need
- a fold-up **exercise bench**
- **curling iron** or electric curlers (they'll be too busy or too lazy to use either)
- a **flashlight**
- **pruning shears**
- a **croquet set**
- the **craft project** they never get to at home (that somehow they're going to get to amidst the exotic sights and sounds and happenings of wherever they're going)
- the last six months' **newspaper puzzles**
- the copy of *War and Peace* they promised their teacher they'd read back in high school
- their **butterfly/stamp/coin collection**
- **unanswered letters** and undone personal accounting
- three **legal pads** for the short story they're finally going to write
- a **diary** with only three pages filled out (that will return with only three pages filled out)
- an **extra suitcase** (to lug home all those souvenirs)

And we wonder why we come home tired.

If you take it all with you, you might just as well as not go. In fact, a better idea: once you have it all packed, just send all your junk on vacation—you'll both be better off.

If you de-junk your travels, you won't need to bring along medicine for:

- Backache (you'll be carrying a light load)
- Headache (you won't be thinking of junk)
- Indigestion (you won't be eating junk)
- Sore feet (you won't be searching for all that junk)
- Nerves or sleeping (you won't be worrying about junk)
- Waking (you'll be eager to get up)

When you're planning your next trip, take a hard look at what you take and what you bring back: remember, the reason we move or go places is often to get away from the things that make our life cluttered and uncomfortable. Our urge to take our clutter with us destroys the very reason for the change. That's why so many people who run away from troubles at work or home or school don't find any peace or easing of pressure. The very things that caused the problem are still tagging along. We aren't talking here only about the tangible things that fit in a suitcase, car, or moving van, but also junk of mind and heart and habit. Before you begin a project, a relationship, a journey, first get rid of the stuff you don't need to take into the experience with you—it's just excess baggage. It's a lot easier to enjoy life without it.

A few tips for de-junking a suitcase:

1. Remember that just about anything can be replaced easily en route—except maybe eyeglasses and medication.

2. The dry cleaner (or laundromat) where you're going can lighten your load on an extended stay. If you try to bring enough for the whole trip, it'll just crush and wrinkle, anyway.

3. Don't bother to pack *food*—there's just about nowhere in the world you can go and run out of food. The golden arches are everywhere your fallen arches can walk.

4. Don't load up on film—you can buy film even at the edge of the Grand Canyon, the entrance to Nairobi Park—*every* junk stand has it. And are you sure you shouldn't just buy postcards? (Let *them* take the pictures.)

5. Pack it all up and try to carry it for two blocks—then start eliminating.

Don't Forget the Bags You Carry Every Day

Make it a tradition, before you leave on any trip, to clean out your pockets, pocketbook, and/or wallet. This will work wonders: (1) you'll leave clean and organized; (2) you'll be reminded of how much junk you already have, and how much money you have to spend, just before you head off toward all those souvenir stands—it's a great junk inhibitor.

Souvenirs

In 1976 I took thirty-eight Boy Scouts to the National Scout Jamboree in Moraine Park, Pennsylvania. En route to the camp we toured some famous, picturesque, and historically interesting places like Niagara Falls, New York City, Philadelphia, and Washington, D.C. The boys had paid about $1,000 each for the trip, which included everything—food, admission fees, transportation, etc.—and all had, as recommended, brought $100 spending money. You could more accurately have called the $100 their "junk money," and indeed, it ended up almost dominating the whole trip.

At the spectacular Niagara Falls I observed only one boy once looking over into the awesome roaring tumble of water, absorbing the grandeur and the mist; the others—you guessed it—were lodged in a souvenir store line, shoving to latch on to gaudy mementos of the Falls. When the bus pulled out, hardly anyone had spent any time at the Falls or noticed the breathtaking flowers, trees, and buildings of the park grounds. They were all sorting through the flags, pennants, pens, pencils, mugs, beanies, whistles, and other cellophane-wrapped trinkets stamped out in the Orient. Fifty percent of it broke before they got home, and 95 percent of it was entirely worthless a month later. One boy had bought a two-pound brick of chocolate that demobilized him at future stops; he was so sugar-junked he couldn't walk far enough to watch a 300-foot ship be spectacularly raised to the Lake Erie channel. In New York, few boys had time to look up at the Statue of Liberty, they were so busy buying little metal models of it. In Philadelphia, Liberty Bell frisbees eclipsed the Bell itself. In Washington, some boys, bedazzled by the souvenir shops, sidestepped the Smithsonian. They were so busy collecting junk they missed the collection really worth seeing.

But my Scouts were only small-time clutter collectors compared to us adults. During a trip to an historic Alaska town I noted that the majority of the people who had spent thousands of dollars to get there spent most of their free time wandering the shops, buying expensive souvenirs. An elderly couple from Colorado bought a rare Inuit seal-skinning knife—absolutely no place for anybody else in the world to legally use it—while their companions invested in some intricately carved caribou-antler buttons. ("Hey Betty, can you and Jim come over tonight and see our authentic caribou buttons?") Gilded gold pans and little plastic bags ($1) of Mt. St. Helens dust were also selling briskly—and we wonder why our lives erupt with junk! But the epitome of valueless souvenir collecting was well represented by a couple of prime little items people flocked to buy—actually paid good money for, and carried home to show friends or set on the shelf. One was a lump of horse manure, sprayed with varnish—with a few wires for legs, wings, and a beak, it was selling for $5.99, a genuine "Turd Bird." In the next town the gift shop stocked a genuine varnished moose dropping, likewise wired for antennae, wings, legs, etc. It was a "Moosequito," a better bargain at $3.99.

Many of the souvenirs we buy and lug home are of about equal value.

We are souvenir-aholics; we feel we must buy. But almost everything we buy on vacation is junk—or ends up that way. We go to travel, to see new and different cultures, people, lands, places, scents, sounds, and to store the experience in our being—to replenish our souls, not our shelves.

We often are so obsessed with mummifying memory with a souvenir that we're oblivious to the actual event or place we want to remember.

Often I've seen the spectators at big-league games so buried in buying (beer, popcorn, programs, hats, bats, helmets, badges, pins, keychains) that they never see the game.

Disneyland is one of the most fascinating places I've been; yet I watched three-fourths of the visitors there spend the majority of their time and money in the junk shops buying food and trinkets, letting the genius of the operation go unsavored.

Once I was with a couple of other cars full of tourists at Needle Rock on the island of Maui. The air was clean, the mountain and jungle enthralling. Three large tour buses drove up—and right behind the three buses came four van-type pickups. They shot in like race cars, the drivers jumped out of their vehicles,

folded down the sides, and opened up built-in cabinets and display cases. Zap—four instant souvenir shops. All eyes left the natural beauty of the land and like possessed spirits, the visitors stampeded, shoved, and pushed to get at the counters of the very same things they had in their hotels and on every street corner at home in San Francisco. They loaded up on cheap jewelry, enameled rocks, smiling sea shells, plastic leis, and shark combs, and wrestled their treasures to the buses, forgetting the reason they came to that spot in the first place.

Souvenirs not only dilute the rapture of the moment, they cast their shadow over the entire trip. What is it, as you are flying or cruising, you suddenly worry about in one of your twelve suitcases? A $75 shoe getting crushed, a $350 suit getting damp or wrinkled? *No*—it's the $2.25 glass souvenir or the swan-shaped bottle of perfume that keeps you awake in the stateroom at night.

Commemoratory Evidence

Perhaps we think people won't really believe we were there, at Famous Fountain, so we feel we must return with evidence. We think about taking a picture or making a sketch—but that doesn't seem to have the whammy of a genuine commercial item, so we buy and return with some ridiculous commemoratory samples:

■ a **lava cinder** from Craters of the Moon Park

■ a genuine **Japanese fan:** You can buy it cheaper almost anywhere (including Sioux Falls, South Dakota).

■ **sand** from Death Valley: Could you or your friends tell it from sand from the Indiana dunes or South Carolina?

■ a **piece of bark** from an Australian Eucalyptus: Long Beach Park has 500 matching trees—with bark.

■ Dodge City **Saloon mug:** A perfect replica of the one Whiskey Pete spat in just before he shot Mole Morgan. One Wheaties box top and 50¢ will get you a matching set!

■ a varnished **redwood plaque** with a maudlin Moon-and-June message: "God bless this little house of mine, that tolerates this tacky sign"—bought at Whitewater Falls, West Virginia.

■ a **can opener** proudly imprinted "Carlsbad Caverns": Is this something you'll want to look at every time you reach in the drawer?

■ a genuine carved gritstone **chess set:** Those knights and kings are really demonic-looking, but no one else has one even close to this baby.

■ a complete annotated **tour guide** to the Old Trojan Mine: A little gem to show your friends who can't understand a bit of it without seeing the mine. And of course *you'll* never read it again, but it can go on the shelf.

■ one adolescent **orange tree** or sawed-off saguaro: It wasn't easy to get home to Wisconsin through quarantine and customs, and should last at least three days before the north wind nips the life out of it.

We buy all manner of often expensive souvenirs to prove to friends we were there. It would be cheaper and more legally convincing to carry a pocketful of 25¢ affidavits and get them signed by the locals.

Show-and-tell is great—for third graders. What do you end up doing with all this?

Not All Silly Souvenirs Come Off the Shelves

A sharp English editor friend of mine pointed to a grotesque piece of driftwood decaying away at the back of his house. "We got that on the north shore of Ireland, carried it on the car, when we ferried, and onto the train. Riding I had to carry it under my arm to avoid poking someone's eye out. It sat too tall on the luggage rack for parking garages, it shed all over us; what a tussle it was getting the bloody thing here, but finally we did. It's a prize piece of grotesque driftwood, but what to do with it, I don't know." (He seemed to have just shifted its rotting spot.)

When we seek to crystallize an experience in things, it's always disappointing. That hunk of rock from the ridge has no grandeur on an end table; those multicolored pebbles leave their magic in the stream bed we plucked them from. That beautiful little bird's nest just sags and gets wispy on the shelf.

And sometimes the "free" souvenirs we labor to acquire (that cactus by the roadside, at the risk of a fat fine and gravel scrapes on our new pumps, not to mention the chance of being flattened by a passing semi) are as costly as the boughten extravanganzas.

Some friends of mine have a summer cottage on a river that feeds into Lake Michigan. They also have a beautiful old wooden powerboat—a classic. One day they were toodling along the shore of a cove far upriver, spotted a large and very nifty-looking log—and decided it would look great in front of their rustic cottage. After securing a line to it they revved up the boat (powerful enough to pull three skiers) to yank the log off the beach. They did manage to get it off the beach— but in the course of pulling it home they pulled the transom off the boat, to the tune of several thousand dollars' custom boat repair work. The log looks real nice in front of the cottage.

MADE IN OHIO

Souvenirs Cost

The big cost over the course of time is the amount of our life's energy spent caring for them—but oddly enough, when it comes to "souvenirs," we lose all price perspective, even at the point of sale. We'll pay $5 for something worth 5¢; I've watched people pay $28 for a cross-eyed bear that cost $1.50 to produce.

Even the best-controlled junker weakens when in another country—we'll travel a thousand miles to buy something that generally was available in our hometown, pay twice as much for it, and protect it on the trip better than our own health.

A 98¢ shirt will go for $10 with 3¢ worth of ink and a message on it. Cheap travel bags worth $2.49 at the five-and-dime store at home will cost us $9.95 away, and we pay it gladly, because it has a garish silkscreen of El Capitan on it.

Would you go to a tourist trap in your own town and drop four bucks on a raccoon tail or a varnished beach rock? Would you spend $10 on a plastic model of your city hall, or the big cloverleaf and overpass outside town? Of course not.

Don't buy junk under the guise of souvenirs! On your next trip try to bring home more memories and less memorabilia.

Bursting the Rubble Bubble

Remember when you finish a vacation and come home and sort through all the things stuffed in your bags and suitcases and one by one retrieve all the souvenirs you so carefully selected? As you take each out of its now-ripped and wrinkled paper bag, your heart sinks lower and lower with every one you lay out on the bed. The glue on some has already crumbled. The eyes have already fallen off the rubber snake, the water is leaking out of your little snow scene, the musical pencil sharpener is already out of tune. As you appraise the lot of them, you see a collection of 100 percent clutter—how could you have been so stupid! Now you have to tend these things, clean them, store them, make excuses for them, and try to figure out what to do with them.

Clutter Bugs

We can clutter ourselves and take our own luster away or throw it in the environment and do the same. I walked the shore of a lake in the Northwestern Rockies and the sights and sensations of this beautiful spot were despoiled with (I took out my pad and scribbled a list on the back):

cups   old tires
caps   straws
lids   broken pens
candy wrappers
chewed gum
butts
matchbook covers
crumpled cellophane
used Band-Aids
lumps of Styrofoam

Ran out of room on my pad. . . .

How do you feel about these additions to the landscape? A walk down the beach, street, or through the neighborhood will be a great incentive to de-junk.

Animal Litterers

Before all you animal lovers see what's coming and refuse to read on, let me bare my soul about animals. I've raised, fed, cared for, and been around more animals, birds, and fish than most people see in a lifetime and I love them. I think children need a pet as much as they need a good breakfast. I've fed rows of pretty kittens in the barn with warm squirts of milk from the cows; I have huge trout in the pond out back that I like too much to catch and eat. I don't even kill bugs—I capture them and turn them loose outside. The friendship of animals does a better job of restoring us to our senses than most things, but in some environments and situations, pets get cluttered and cheated and the junk that results outweighs even the love we get from them.

Recently we drove through the Canadian Rockies, and more awe-striking, sweet-smelling country I have never set eyes and lungs on. While everyone stretched when we stopped at a rest area, I did some people-watching. Sixty percent of the cars or motor homes that stopped would let out a poor cooped-up dog or cat. Then their owners walked them over to the nice lawn and shrubby rest area to do their little job of pooping or piddling all over the place ("Not on *my* tires—over there so other people can step in it"). In one area, nine vehicles with animals stopped and everything from Great Danes to pet panda bears pottied on and over everything. Remember, this goes on all day, every day. It's likely that more than 200 sweet little pets did unsweet things to that area in one day, and the next and the next. Have you smelled a rest area, park, or pet-walking street lately, or tried to get through one? It's like an obstacle course. I'll admit that inside the restrooms where the humans do their thing isn't much better, but at least it's *contained*. The sanitation and health requirements for a house with two people living in it are an engineering nightmare of a septic tank or sewer systems. Yet in many places animals can clutter and litter and junk up yards and parks at will.

Carefree strolls through the park, lolling on the grass, playful tussling with your toddler are just a few of the joyous activities greatly inhibited by the junk left by dogs. No wonder some states require owners to recover their animals' nuisances.

199

CHAPTER 13

Getting Off the Excess Express

No matter what we get, or where we go, our goal of "having it made" always seems beyond our grasp. That happiness, excitement, inexhaustible drive of youthful thinking and wanting and doing is gone—we don't have it. We want to get off, walk away from it all, maybe start over. . . .

But someone or something has convinced us that we have to have a luxurious apartment, condominium, or home with all the trimmings to be happy—and maybe two of them, one in a warm and one in a cool area of the world. A "nice" home was once interpreted as a comfortable, pleasing, convenient dwelling. Now a nice home is "Junk Plush," with hoarded or collected things propped up and hung all over in displays.

When and if all this is obtained, most people find that the effort of maintaining ownership offsets the benefits. If all of us honestly reflected back in our lives to the time of greatest satisfaction and enjoyment, when everything seemed to vibrate with feeling and freedom, it was when life was simplest. Joy, energy, and motivation come from relationships, discovery, creativity, and accomplishment. All of these somewhere along the line were squeezed out by piles (or structures) of junk.

Not satisfied with one house full of clutter, we dream of another, which in itself becomes clutter.

The Second Home

Ex-junkees can produce more impressive testimonies than active junkers, so here comes a personal experience. During our senior year of college my wife Barbara and I picked out a beautiful sixty-acre place in southern Idaho, and in the next few years built a pleasant home in which to raise our children. We had everything—creek, springs, trees, snow, hills, good neighbors, clean air, an unequaled view of the mountains—even mosquitoes! But all that time we were thinking (as millions do): Wouldn't a *second* home in the mountains be nice? A good contract for my cleaning company made it necessary to move to Sun Valley for the summer. We left our sprawling new ranch house behind and stayed in Sun Valley six years. We decided to build another house there and did so, drawing up the plans and doing all the work— plumbing, electrical, carpeting, etc.— ourselves. When it came time to return to the ranch, we decided to keep our Sun Valley house as a second home; we could afford the payments and had hundreds of friends who could use it for ski trips. We kept it one year and ended up paying much more than the mortgage.

That house ended up robbing me of more emotional energy than anything I've ever owned. As I'd be winding up an evening prior to bed, instead of thinking about how my son and the Cub Scouts were doing, how my daughter was doing on her new job, how my wife might be feeling, I'd be thinking about the house— and wondering if the users had flushed the toilets, if the sprinkler had been drained, if the gate on the creek side was closed, if the beetles were boring the pines, if the last mountain storm had done any damage to the antenna. The house was out of sight, but ownership kept it from being out of mind. I felt compelled to rent it and use it simply because I possessed it; all I seemed to have was unappreciative borrowers and non-paying renters. When I finally de-junked that house from my life, gadfrey, it felt good!

Since then I've paid special attention to the topic of second homes. Almost everyone dreams of one, and almost everyone who has one spends every spare minute worrying about, and spare dime fixing and paying for it. Only once in awhile do they experience the pleasure of relaxing in it.

Millions of people who feel they're on the merry-go-round of life, the Excess

Express, want to get off: they think they want to live in a little cabin in the hills. What they're *really* saying is that they want to be de-junked of their dreary routine and hangouts. If most of us de-junked our homes and lives, we could have that little dream cabin right where we live now—and it would cost us nothing.

The Drive to Have and to Accumulate

Everyone wants more, better—and often faster. Someone once said that hell is full of people who were never satisfied.

Never being satisfied can be a virtue—if the longing, the lust, the living is for things that are meaningful to you personally and to those you love. Too many people judge worth almost entirely by accumulation. It takes a lot of whacks on the side of the head before we finally realize that many of the things we've accumulated, at great expenditure of effort and time, are and only end up to be clutter. Things are seldom permanent and unless used are worthless. But accumulated good health, talent, friends, experiences, and sensations are stored in us and are always there to reinvigorate and renew us all the years of our lives.

I heard a farmer who already owned 1,500 acres say, "I don't want all the land in the world—just all that borders me." That of course included all the land in the world, because it *all* bordered him. A certain maturity comes with accepting the fact that we can't have all the land, sex, food, money, and power in the world. We probably have more of the "all" than we can handle now, and anything beyond what we can use is junk. Sharing of self is the greatest satisfaction of all, and making better use of what we already have is the highest standard of living. Go for quality—not quantity!

Get it out of your head that you need a

large selection to be happy. As a professional painter, I found that the more color chips I brought on a job the more indecisive the people became—and when they did choose between three shades that no one would ever be able to tell the difference between, after it was on the wall they always whimpered around about which of the other two colors might have been better. One paint company recently came out with 1,322 new colors; I'll bet the psychiatry business boomed when they hit the market.

Clutter doesn't enrich life, it ends up confusing it. Happiness comes from loving and being loved; a giant selection of *things* just exhausts our spiritual, physical, and emotional energy. Sorting and decision-making can occupy our every waking minute.

"Things" always complicate matters. When the last rumble of the latest earthquake here in Idaho subsided, and the costs were counted, no lives were lost—but there was $500 million worth of damage. And it was labeled a "natural disaster." Had the same earthquake occurred in the same area one hundred years earlier, the cost of the damage might have pushed $500—and it would have been called a "natural tremor." Most of the destruction was to property—

buildings—and their contents. No lives were lost because the worst-damaged buildings were unoccupied. The tremors only threatened a mass of *things*.

Increase is a confusing thing to deal with, because we must, to be happy, *increase* our wisdom, knowledge, friends, travel, experiences, opportunities, abilities, sense of self-worth, and security. Increase is growth, and our possessions do sometimes have to increase with our growth—individuals, families, minds, and businesses that do more usually need more tools, space, and options. But somewhere the "more" becomes extra and then a normal natural occurrence—like the earthquake—because of our junk becomes a disaster instead of an experience.

Be Careful with "If I Could Only Have. . . ."

Generally, by the time you can afford it you either don't want it, haven't the time or energy for it, or it means nothing to you.

I was raised with enough things, but never any of the "extra" or "nice" things that other kids seemed to have. Like you, I always figured that if I had more and better stuff I'd be happier and all-around better off. When I went to the movies every couple of months I was always captivated by the big glass candy counter. Why, that thing was ten feet long and two feet deep—many times I pictured myself lying in there slurping and munching all I wanted. But I could only do some vicarious inner slurping and walk by.

For years I worried and wished, wished and worried about all that candy. Then, when I was eighteen, I worked at night in the movie theater in a nearby resort—was entirely in charge of that gleaming glass counter and instructed to help myself to whatever I wanted. I went elbow-deep into those brimming containers, gorging myself on an array of formerly unattainable goodies—only to discover they were more exciting to look at and think about than to eat. I never again craved candy.

How many hours of life, mind, and emotion we waste wanting and wishing for things we don't need; 99 percent of the time possessing it wouldn't make us happy.

Next time you're driving through countrysides or cities of plenty, run this thought through the "acquiring" section of your brain: If every person in the whole world disappeared and suddenly everything, I mean absolutely *everything*, was yours—fields, factories, bridges, buildings, ships, planes, vehicles—what would you do with them? What good would they do you? If you think it through, you'd realize you'd mainly have the problem of trying to figure out how to use and care for all this.

A friend of mine once thought up an idea to raise our awareness of what we Americans possess, rich and poor, compared to "poorer" countries of the world: he talked an ordinary family in India into moving every single thing they owned out onto the road in front of their house, after which he took a picture. It didn't take *them* long, but (the horrifying thought now crosses your mind) how would you or even *could* you do the same with all your own? It would take weeks; you'd need a wide-angle lens; you'd have to do it house by house in each

neighborhood, each on a different day, because there wouldn't be room in the road for both your and your neighbors' junk. And then would you actually have the guts to stand in front of it for a picture?

We are a society of surplus—most of us have more of everything than we need: food, money, possessions, time, and attention. And after we've used what we need, we foolishly spend our time trying to use the surplus. I've watched people slave and scrounge and pinch pennies and hoard to earn more than they need—then spend the second half of their lives trying to protect the surplus from robbers and taxes. For some reason, when people finally get some security or a little ahead, when they're finally in a position to have more choices, they inevitably—instead of choosing the avenues that would give them more ease and freedom to enjoy things—begin to fill up their homes and yards with expensive porcelain dolls, extra TVs, prestigious books, overpriced paintings, high-powered guns, complicated light fixtures, dozens of extra cooking and eating utensils, hot tubs, automatic barbecues and yard luxuries.

They take others out to dinner and "show" (off their art collections, houses, and cars) because that's all they have to offer. What do you have to offer—a gem of thought? counsel? example? encouragement? companionship? Or just some worthless *things?*

> "*O*ne day I had the sudden realization: If I stopped buying things right this moment, there is no way I could ever use all I have *now*."

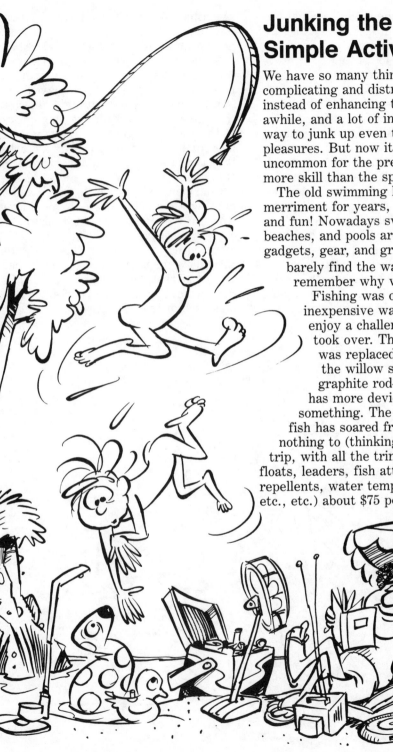

Junking the Simple Activity

We have so many things that they end up complicating and distracting our lives instead of enhancing them. It took us awhile, and a lot of ingenuity, to find a way to junk up even the simplest of pleasures. But now it's not at all uncommon for the preparation to require more skill than the sport or activity.

The old swimming hole was a mecca of merriment for years, not fancy, but free and fun! Nowadays swimming areas, beaches, and pools are so cluttered with gadgets, gear, and grease that we can barely find the water, let alone remember why we're there.

Fishing was once a quiet inexpensive way to relax and enjoy a challenge—until junk took over. The free angleworm was replaced by a $4.95 lure, the willow stick by a $400 graphite rod—and only the FBI has more devices to catch something. The cost of catching a fish has soared from practically nothing to (thinking about my last trip, with all the trimmings—flies, floats, leaders, fish attractants, bug repellents, water temperature gauge, etc., etc.) about $75 per pound. It's not only a project to decide on a place and a means to go fishing—it's hard to afford it, and it takes hours to get our equipment together (including a lot of junk that no self-respecting fish would bite).

We've taken a simple exercise like running and made it seem impossible to do without accessories. The minute we get our okay from the doctor, we begin, from the feet up, to deck our body out with special shoes, cushioned socks, knee braces, all sorts of stylish suits, shorts, shirts, headbands, underriggings, stereos, mileage meters (and would you believe it, the other day I got a catalog selling a "jogging stick" to help you keep your balance when you run, complete with a computer to tell you how far you've run and calculate how tired you are. It has a calendar and clock on it, too, just in case you get carried away in your jogging

overtime). We don't need exercise equipment to exercise any more than we need a uniform to play any kind of ball.

Once *everyone* played baseball—anyone could play, anywhere, pasture or gravel pile, and the game could be played and enjoyed with any old bat and ball. Now the game is called off if the pop machine at the park gets jammed, the dugout gate lock malfunctions, or if there's a crack in the catcher's overpriced and overdesigned shinguard.

Consider, too, the pocket knife and the hunting knife. These two plain old knives won the West and carved the history of early America: skinned wild game, whittled whistles for the kids, and later, cut willow for wiener roasts. Now there are, conservatively estimated, 1,600 versions of specialty knives for the 800 jobs each of the other two plain old

knives did (and still can do as well).

We've even managed to complicate telling time. We worked on the old practical dollar pocket watch for a century and finally got it so gilded and engraved and chained that it was too nice and risky to carry so we had to leave it home and ask our friends the time. (It eventually was used to start family quarrels over who "gets Grandpa's watch.") What a fate for a timepiece! It's nice to have diamonds, peacock feathers, buffalo nickels, compasses, depth gauges, and tiny gold ingots to greet you when glancing at the time, but it sure is complicated.

Glasses for vision correction were so simple at first, we couldn't stand it. It didn't take long for the fitting and selection of the frame to take more time and money than the lenses. Glasses' main function once was improving what we looked *at*—they've become so junked in style and design that now their first thrust is how we look when others see us. It used to be easy to walk into an optician's office and pick out a pair of frames—no more! Now you stand bug-eyed in front of glittering walls full of frames of every shape and color, from the sleek gigolo look to the owly kind only nerds used to wear. You're supposed to own glasses for every wardrobe change and mood—that is, when you're not wearing any of your three different kinds of contact lenses.

Crayons were a delight of all our childhoods—we had enough color in eight little crayons to create anything we could imagine. When the 16-crayon box (double-decker) came out we were amazed—even gray! We didn't use all the colors, but the pack size made us and our parents feel good. Several years ago, though, I saw a sight that stunned me—a package of thirty-two crayons; it had silver and gold and so many reds it shamed my teen daughter's lipstick collection. But today was the clincher: I saw a giant box of sixty-four crayons, big as a lunchpail and full of obscure exotic colors. A kid could get an anxiety attack just picking the right shade.

Toys today are so junked they hardly need kids; today's toys can practically play by themselves. Consider the doll. Dolls have thrilled little girls for thousands of years. My four daughters, even when their dolls lost their tresses, an arm, and the paint off their rubber lips, only loved them more. Then the doll engineers appeared: closing eyes were great, a crying doll was greater; even *I* was impressed with the refreshingly different drinking and wetting models. Then realism began to crowd out imagination; we had walking models and talking models, dolls whose hair could be cut and curled.

Now you don't only need a doll: you need a doll cosmetic kit, a complete doll wardrobe for all four seasons (including resort wear), a sports car, a dune buggy, a convertible, a condominium, a cable TV and stereo system, a digital watch, legwarmers, pantyhose, a pony, a pet, a mini can of Mace, and a male companion for your doll. I expect to see mini cosmetic surgery gear in the next doll kit. But if you give a tot a choice, do you think she'll pick that glamorous robot with the 38-inch bustline? Raggedy Ann will win every time!

Kids don't get much satisfaction out of elaborate toys, because there's really not a lot a kid can do with them—the *toys* do everything themselves. My wife and I learned this the Christmas our six children were aged two to eight. We shopped carefully and bought a mixture of smarty games, a few puzzles, some "think" toys, a couple of somersaulting monkeys, etc. That Christmas afternoon the kids were halfheartedly pawing and pondering their treasures when a friend showed up with a sack of wood scraps for our fireplace—blocks sawed off 2x4s and 2x6s from a new house. He dumped the burlap bag full of plain crisp-smelling wood on the floor in front of the fireplace, and the kids descended on it and began constructing castles, fences, forts, houses, and bridges. For days those ordinary wood scraps held sway over all the brightly colored, cleverly designed toys.

This experience taught us that kids are most stimulated by all-purpose toys that their imaginations can run free with. A Planetfighter Orbitmaster 1234X with whirring engines and battery-operated lasers can't be anything but a Planetfighter Orbitmaster 1234X, and when the kid is tired of outer space he ignores the toy.

Is More Better?

Our ranch has an 1880 log house on it, 36 feet by 15, two rooms and an attic. Driving by it on the way to a concert, affluent acquaintances of ours commented how hideous it must have been to live there. I reminded them that eleven

. . . not having.

children were raised there, with no video games, no TV, no electricity, no ice, no fans, no screens, no bug spray, no thermostats, only one clothes closet, an outdoor bathroom, and spring water—and they were and have ended up to be a glistening, vibrant, healthy tribe that lived long and happy lives with frequent smiles on their faces. The couple shook their heads in wonderment, not comprehending how anyone could exist without the clutter comforts of life. I'm not advocating log-cabin living or camping in the city park, only pointing out that most social and psychological problems, those unpleasant ugly things that suck life and love out of us—like selfishness, despair, anxiety, intolerance, bigotry, financial failure, divorce, embezzlement, theft, murder, suicide, even war—result directly from our honoring of junk, our quest for ever more and ever more elaborate possessions.

Some people will laugh and say, "Simplicity is fine for a change, but I love my luxuries." Next time you hear that,

Living is *doing* . . .

take a hard look at the person who says it, and you'll chart troubled waters. People who have a luxurious life say it's reassuring, that they feel confident surrounded by huge piles of things, even if they don't use them. But are those people really happy—with their lives and minds buried in menu-reading, weight loss, style-watching, color-matching, land-owning, tax deductions, security checks, and their kids fighting over what they have?

I once met a beautiful elderly woman who radiated enthusiasm as she recalled living simply: "We had a lovely, fully equipped home in the city that included velvet curtains and full sets of silver and fine dishes. We had earned that place by working hard at a dry farm in the mountains. The 5,000-acre dry farm had no irrigation (only rainfall) and to operate it we had to move to the old ranch house there and live during the growing season. That house was the opposite of our nice town house. Here were kept only basic supplies, and my husband and I each had one tin plate and one tin cup, a knife, fork, and spoon and that was it—no extras, no luxury." She glowed just thinking about it. "In fact, my fondest memory of my youth and early married life is that old tin cup and plate. Food always tasted good on it, we didn't worry about it breaking or getting stolen, things were so simple, I could enjoy my family, our workers, the air, the leaves. For thirty years the memory of that tin cup has been a source of joy."

She was feeling the rapture of de-junked life.

When the tin cup story is told, I notice everyone in the audience has a longing look. A tin cup isn't necessary for all of us, but the spirit of simplicity is, and will leave a better taste in our lives than crystal goblets.

On the ranch where I was raised, because the main house was too small to fit all our family, my teenage brothers and I slept in a small unheated bunkhouse (I remember the brush cleaner in a glass jar freezing one night). To keep warm at night we'd heat up a little flannel bag of wheat and throw it to the bottom of the bed—ahh, that was nice—and we had outside toilets with all the Sears catalog trimmings.

Since then, I've stayed in the finest hotels, slept in the finest beds, and eaten the finest food in the finest places in the world, but none has ever come close to the feeling of simple freedom of that bunkhouse. A deluxe sauna bath has never felt any better than the No. 10 tub and kettle of hot water (even when I was the third one to bathe in the same water). Again, I'm not recommending a return to primitivism, only reminding you that the things you feel and enjoy the most are the simplest and most basic. Because ownership of them allows you the time to enjoy them—you don't have to spend all your time paying for and maintaining them. It isn't the tin cup and plate that you remember so fondly; it's the fact there weren't cabinets of china to guard and show, velvet-lined boxes filled with silverware to insure, polish, store, and worry about. "We have sufficient for our needs" is a sentence of freedom from the old enemy, *clutter*.

Simplicity doesn't mean hard times; luxury doesn't mean good times. But we too often think of more as better, convenience as comfort—and that isn't so. It doesn't take a padded toilet seat or an electric blanket to mold good character, accomplishment, and feelings of aliveness and personal worth.

You Can Survive on a Lizard Diet

Can you ever! The joy of knowing you don't need junk to survive will be a dynamic motivator to you. When we read those survival stories about people making it through subzero weather with multiple injuries and without food, most of us sigh and think to ourselves, "They must have had incredible nerve and endurance, a super will and sense of determination." Not really. Those people are no tougher than you or me—they simply found out the strength of a human without junk! Allow me to share another anecdote:

I met an energetic, self-assured woman who told me she once felt like a real loser. She was a little overweight and had a poor self-image as she dragged herself around home, job, and school. She had bought everything supposedly needed for a happy life—the best clothes, cars, furniture, vacations, season tickets, the whole gamut of goodies that spell "success." She'd even taken most of the rah-rah "you can do it" courses that try to help you pull your life together to be happy and productive. Looking at her now, I couldn't picture her as the lost soul she assured me she once was.

What happened? Well, it started with a summer course on wilderness survival at a local university. The teacher, a keenly experienced outdoorsman named Larry Dean Olsen, had written a top-selling book, *Outdoor Survival Skills*, and offered a class on the same subject. I'll pass the woman's experience on to you in her own words: "I enrolled in this class and Olsen told us we didn't need much to

survive and live, that as humans we have amazing depth and adaptability. I hadn't tried starvation yet, so I decided to stick it out. After some preliminary instruction, he took us out to the edge of the desert, dressed in the simplest of clothes, armed with nothing but a little knife—no food, no water, no nothing. He then turned us loose in the desert for a week, and we lived! Using nature—the ground, the air, the plants, and all the other things that were just there—to do it. Instead of an unendurable hardship as I had dreaded, it became an exhilarating experience. Self-confidence and self-assurance flowed into me with every drink out of a water cache or bite of a ground squirrel. I once fainted when I saw a mouse; now I was savoring lizard legs. Everything smelled and tasted and felt good because it was just me and what was there. When I finished the desert trip and course I knew for the first time in my life that I didn't need all those *things* I owned to be somebody. For the first time ever I really looked at and experienced the things around me—sunrise, sunset, a cactus flower, the wail of a coyote, the shape of a stone.

"I enjoyed peaceful sleep (even on hard ground)! My hair looked and felt better than it ever had before—without a hair blower or an array of shampoo and sprays and setting lotions and rinses. I felt lean and strong and alert all the time. That course did me the greatest favor of my life. It taught me that *I* determined my happiness and generated my own worth and enthusiasm for life—not all the trinkets, motivational cassette tapes, or exotic getaway places. I got to use what I *was* instead of what I *had*."

That course did only one thing for this woman—it de-junked her. We don't all need to eat lizard stew on the desert—we can enjoy simple meals at home—but maybe if necessary some forcing of the issue might enlighten your life like it did hers.

CHAPTER 14

There Is a Solution to Clutter

In Fact, There Are Many Solutions. . . .

ONE

You could *have your clutter cremated* and have a daily or weekly viewing of the vase containing the remains, if deep feelings are still there for your junk. It can remain with you, in spirit and condensed form.

TWO

You could *microfilm it* and carry every bit of your junk everywhere you go.

THREE

You can *seal it up in the cornerstone* of your new house, and it will finally have value when it's dug out centuries later—as an *artifact*.

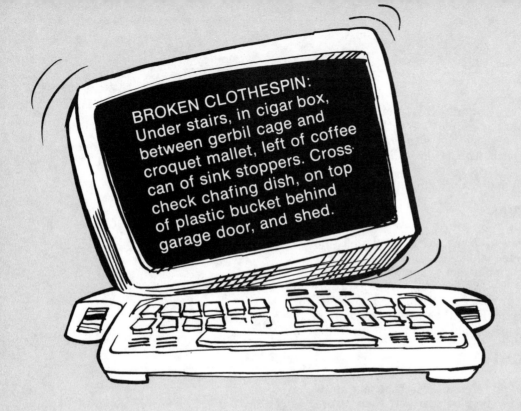

BROKEN CLOTHESPIN:
Under stairs, in cigar box,
between gerbil cage and
croquet mallet, left of coffee
can of sink stoppers. Cross-
check chafing dish, on top
of plastic bucket behind
garage door, and shed.

FOUR

You can *move a lot*—into places that are too small!

FIVE

Our modern computers might be the ultimate solution to the modern-day problem of junk. With a computer you have two choices for keeping track of your junk.

a. You can simply *program all your junk onto a disk*—what, where, when you last saw it, etc.—and when you get to longing for it you can call up that file so you'll know exactly where it is.

b. Or even more useful (because we seldom actually use junk), you can *program all your junk into a visual format*. Then when you get lonesome for it, or want to check on it, you can punch computer recall—and there it is to radiate security and be enjoyed, while taking up no appreciable room.

SIX

You can do nothing. Actually, doing absolutely nothing about the junk that has overcome you is the most common approach. This is also called retreat. It is totally chicken-hearted; you will retreat again and again, and junk will multiply.

SEVEN

Retrench. When any of your junk—things or personal habits—threatens you and your comfort zone, you hide it in a better place, pack it in tighter, contain it like nuclear waste so it won't contaminate its surroundings—thus we become slaves, servants, flunkies to junk.

EIGHT

Planned riddance. Might facing up to junk be the best solution? Face up to it—it won't fade out!

Turn the page and let's get started.

CHAPTER 15

Judging Junk

What is junk?

If we could all throw out each others' clutter, we'd have no trouble deciding, but our own—well, that's a different story.

Knee-deep in our own junk, we are a one-person hung jury. Everything we possess has its attachments—seemingly into the very nerve center of our bodies and sometimes to the rational core of our brains. But we have to judge and sentence our own junk—no one can (or should have to) do it for us.

My opinion of hats, for example, might differ from yours.

Hats

Hats, I feel, exist for three purposes: Practicality, decoration, and to look stupid.

The practical hat is useful, even necessary. These are hats used for building and doing, like hard hats to keep rocks off your head, sombreros to keep the sun out, helmets to keep bullets out, miner's hats to see where you're going and so on. Such hats aren't anywhere near being junk, if they're used for their intended purpose.

The decorative hat (or vanity hat) includes the big parade jobs with "fruit salad" stacked on the head for style, plumed hats that make people in church sneeze, safari helmets or Australian bush hats, coonskin caps, Yukon derbies, captain hats, Sherlock Holmes hats—all of which I feel are a waste of money, effort, and raw material out of their proper context. Unworn decorative hats clog a lot of shelves and closets, but you might like them and use them and they do your psyche a lot of good, so it's hard to make a universal judgment on these.

The "to look stupid" hat I won't even apologize for calling junk. These are wolf faces, pig ears, stuffed fish, bawdy

beercan, or the wing and antler types. Who in their right mind would skull around in one of these? A derby with flipping propellers or deeleybobbers or a baseball cap with curling antennas can only top a total moron, in my opinion.

Pretty harsh on your junk, aren't I? (Thank goodness we can't really judge each other's junk!) If you happen to be a model, an entertainer, or an actor, have grandchildren or like to play cowboys and Indians—or if nothing lifts your heart more than the hat that tops your outfit— many hats in these last two groups wouldn't be junk at all. Only *you* know the immediate and long-term value of your hatrobe and if some are junk you can throw them in the ring to start off your de-junking pilgrimage.

For another example, almost every military person I know has a hand-carved wooden water buffalo on his desk. They're ugly and always dusty and chipped, they always get knocked over and shown off to uninterested guests— but for some reason they're tolerated. If I were to judge your junk and you pastured one of these hideous things, there would be one last moo. But for all I know it may be a sacred reminder to you of the person who saved your life in the rice paddy under machine-gun fire and you'd never part with it.

I also think gum chewing is clutter, that no one with any class would be caught chewing in public. *You* may find it a harmless habit that relaxes you. Fortunately, we don't run others' lives, and must analyze our own selves and possessions to determine what's junk. Some things that keep *your* life fresh might be smothering mine; some things that help keep me well might make you sick. There's no way I or anyone else can assume your junk-judging duties.

Empty tin cans are clutter to 99 percent of us, but not to the person who uses them for constructive projects, or earns money by recycling them. Parties can be total junk, ruin your life—or they can add a sparkle to it. It depends, of course, on the party and its effect on you. *You* have to judge that.

Anything that crowds the life out of you is junk. Anything that builds, edifies, enriches our spirit—that makes us truly happy, regardless of how worthless it may be in cash terms—isn't junk. Something worth $100,000 can be pure clutter to you if it causes discomfort and anxiety or insulates you from love or a relationship.

Most active things are not junk, most inactive things are. But you have to determine the degree of activity that makes something meaningful to you. Whatever contributes to a happy, free, resourceful, sharing life isn't junk to you—but it might be someday. Our needs and values change—with our age, location, mates, and degree of self-development. We should keep our eyes on the new horizon of life coming and that means that some of the tools, places, and things we used to operate in the old horizon, although once good and valuable, might now be junk. As we reach out and grow up, we have to learn to throw out.

The pioneers provide us with an excellent example of this. Heading west, they loaded up all their possessions and precious treasures—including heavy hand-carved furniture, elaborate table settings, trunks of clothes, decorative gates and headboards, and oversized clocks.

When they reached the rough-hewn trails and steep terrain of the hills they were forced, if they were to survive, to lighten their loads, to discard some of their good stuff; it was, although costly, clutter to them at that moment. Others coming along the trail found the valuables free for the taking, but they too had to judge it as junk (and leave it behind) because it stood in the way of their greatest goal—their destiny. So it is with junk: that which restricts our living, loving, thinking, and feeling is junk, be it a thing, habit, person, place, or position. You alone have to make this judgment, because only you fully understand your position in life, your goals, your emotional ties, the time you have available, and the limitations of your physical self and space.

The silliest little trinkets or souvenirs of people or places aren't junk if they give you enjoyable participation. If, on the other hand, you just possess them, they just sit on the shelf and you never even look at them, they probably are junk and should be thrown out of your life.

Consider the story of a family traveling by car on a long vacation to Alaska. At one of the first gift shops, the father shook a wise bony finger at the three travel-weary grade-schoolers and said, "Now don't you kids buy any junk with your hard-earned money, you hear?" The kids bought some beef jerky, a 98¢ travel riddle book, an animals-of-Alaska game, a cheap turquoise ring, and one of those

$3.98 automatic paper birds that fly. While the parents lingered in the gift shop, the kids went out on the freshly mowed park lawn, wound the bird up, and threw it back and forth, screaming with delight, running, jumping, laughing, and breathing the fresh Canadian air. At every stop they did it. The paper bird was the finest thing going. As they rode along, they played with the game and told riddles—thought about and questioned them—and everyone felt and examined the "real" turquoise ring. In four days that bird provided those kids with more exposure to nature and good feelings than they'd had for a long time. On the fifth day, the bird, beat to a frazzle, gave up the ghost.

When they got back in the car, the parents unloaded: "You stupid kids, that's what you get for buying junk, what do you have now for your money, the riddle book is worn out, the bird is broken, and that ring, if you keep passing it around, will soon be gone. Spend your money on something nice like we did. You'll have something to show for your vacation." (The parents at the same stop had bought four cups of coffee, a varnished wall plaque that contained the words "ass," "hell," and "damn," a $2.75 women's glamor magazine, and an ugly $43 etched ivory figurine.) The kids, with downcast eyes, felt guilty and learned there and then that one of the main purposes of a vacation is to bring back stuff (junk). The kids' stuff wasn't junk—it enhanced, stimulated, and accelerated their feelings for each other and the beautiful country they were traveling through. The parents' figurine was packed away and hidden—it had no value; the paper bird beat it a hundred times over. *Junk depends on your use of something, and what it does to your life.*

Don't Let Hard-Earned Cash Buy You a Hard Head!

I wanted a top-of-the-line slide projector. My expert camera man sold me a handsome model and twenty trays to go with it. The unit, impressive as the name engraved on it might be in other circumstances, was a dog—a failure of design. I got annoyed and then angry with it and badgered the company to make it work. *They* were so discouraged with that model, they'd quit making it—or parts for it. But do you think I could dump that bright mechanical dinosaur and all its accessories? No, and twelve years later I gave it to my son-in-law, who now in Skagway, Alaska is beating and kicking and cursing it and trying to decide what to do with twenty expensive-looking slide trays.

One of the biggest reasons we keep junk is that we hate to admit mistakes. Often we acquire a thing, a job, a habit that we absolutely hate the minute after we get it. But we don't get around to taking it back (or quitting, or stopping), though it's a constant pain to maintain, to own, to be around. In general it makes life miserable but we keep it—why? Because we don't want to admit we were wrong or greedy for a moment or made a bad judgment.

Once I bought a pair of "El-Crako" ski bindings and had them mounted. The bindings cost $56.50 and I thought they were great—until statistics and experience showed that they led the leagues in leg-breaking, premature ski releases, and every other binding failing possible, so I took those new expensive bindings off and put on some good Nevadas. But the ones I had removed were so shiny and I'd paid so much for them and after all, they were hardly used. . . . I put them in a gallon can and kept them.

Over time I moved, sorted, and shuffled them from place to place because they cost so much, were nearly new, and I would be admitting I made an error. But I would never use them and it would be immoral to give them to a friend— what good were they except to clutter my mind and shelf? (I finally dumped them while working on this book.)

I've done the same with notebooks. I bought some expensive jobs that looked handy and revolutionary, but the stupid things wouldn't hold standard-size paper and wouldn't open right, so I went back to using a $1.69 one and left the nice leather ones on the shelf. They didn't suit me any better when I tried them again five years later, so I pitched them, wondering why I ever kept them in the first place.

There's nothing wrong with making mistakes—cautious living and five accomplishments only get five things experienced a week. Only those who belt in and do fifty things a week and make twenty mistakes get thirty experiences to the good and gain confidence; they generally end up years ahead in living and enjoying life. Mistakes can be tolerated as building experiences, but don't hold fast to your mistakes—pitch the evidence!

Don't Be Prejudiced by Pride

It was a cool morning and I was dressed for the hike into the hills, when a wiser and older man I barely knew stepped up and said, "You ought to take that last heavy coat off, you aren't going to need it, and you'll get hot later." Like any other twenty-five-year-old I knew how to dress, and what business was it of his? I kind of resented him questioning my decision—so I wore it. Half a mile up the hill, I knew I'd made a mistake, but decided to pretend I was enjoying being overwarm. One hour later the sun was beating down and I was heating up like a pressure cooker. I still hated to admit that his suggestion to shed the coat back at the car was right, so I suffered with it for another hour. I was so dehydrated I felt like a shriveled hide, when about three that afternoon some people came by headed back to camp and asked if they could take the coat back to lighten my load. Humbler than I was in the morning, I gave them the coat and began immediately to enjoy a bright, beautiful, carefree afternoon in the mountains.

When you find yourself resenting having to, or being told to throw something away or give something up, consider first and foremost the reward, the end result—how you and your life will be without it. Nothing is more stimulating than being rid of some thing or habit (or even person) that has held you down. When you pause with the decision in mind or hand—shall it go or shall it stay with me—when logic and even emotion can't manage to help you reach a decision, ask yourself, "What will my life be like without this?" Don't think about *it* (the thing)—think about *you*, your life, your freedom.

Some Junk-Sorting Guidelines

Is it clutter or is it not? Is your de-junking fever being cooled down by cold feet? Are emotional ties and guilt diluting your ability to be ruthless and strong? If indecisiveness sets in, here are some guidelines that may help.

IT IS JUNK IF:

- [ ] it's broken or obsolete (and fixing it is unrealistic)
- [ ] you've outgrown it, physically or emotionally
- [ ] you've always hated it
- [ ] it's the wrong size, wrong color, or wrong style
- [ ] using it is more bother than it's worth
- [ ] it wouldn't really affect you if you never saw it again
- [ ] it generates bad feelings
- [ ] you have to clean it, store it, and insure it (but you don't get much use or enjoyment out of it)
- [ ] it will shock, bore, or burden the coming generation

If you can check one or more of the above truthfully, then it's probably junk. Do yourself, your house, and posterity a favor—pitch it! It's robbing you of peace of mind and space.

IT'S NOT JUNK IF IT:

- [ ] generates love and good feelings
- [ ] helps you make a living
- [ ] will do something you need done
- [ ] has significant cash value
- [ ] gives you more than it takes
- [ ] will enrich or delight the coming generation

If you can check a few of the above comfortably, then it's probably *not* junk—enjoy it and feel good about its place in your life.

The Final Judgment

Let me repeat: I'm not claiming the position of the Great Wahoo of Junk-Judging. I'm presenting some views (perhaps tinged with a little personal opinion) to help stimulate new thoughts in your hoarding soul—but the decision of what to keep and what to dump out of your life is all yours. Age, sentiment, and "I may need it someday" all have their legitimacy. Think about a fire extinguisher—it fits many of the criteria of clutter as it hangs there for twenty years. It's not the latest style, it's ugly, it never moves, it's never used, it costs money to have checked and re-checked— but it's certainly worth having when it's needed *once* in that twenty years!

The ultimate evaluation is up to you. I'll share my observations and others' contributions in this volume, but what is and is not clutter is for you to determine—by the use and benefit an item is to you, the actions it encourages you to take, and the effect it has through you on others. A piece of garbage isn't junk if it enriches the quality of life. And a beautiful, valuable, and expensive thing can be total junk if it detracts from your joy of living and loving.

CHAPTER 16

How to Leave It and Love It (Clutter!)

We wake up one morning and suddenly realize that we're buried in problems—almost insurmountable ones. The more we think about them, the more they seem to multiply. We drag ourselves out into the day, through our home full of things we're struggling to pay for, things we seldom use. Listening to news about everyone else's struggles, we glance in the mirror and see how everything we've eaten over the years has stacked up on us, how everything we hate about ourselves seems to show in our eyes. We get to work, and see the IN basket triumphing unmercifully over the OUT basket. We light a cigarette or go for coffee and a Danish to help us face the work, and we *still* can't face it. When we finally do find our desk top, we find a disconnect notice for a bill we misplaced. At these discouraging times—any discouraging and depressed time, before you reach for more aspirin, a ticket to run away for good, or a shoulder to cry on—reverse it all. Decide to finally get rid of the clutter that's causing your bad day, plaguing your life and mind—all those things you don't need. Throw out your junk first—

before you swing into that miracle plan to rearrange your life for maximum efficiency, or set in motion that complicated strategy of self-improvement. It's as simple and logical as throwing away the shoes that are blistering and cramping your feet, or dumping out the rotten apples at the bottom of the barrel before you try to wash it out. The time you invest in de-junking will pay you back several-fold—you'll save all those *future* hours detouring around, moving about, cleaning up, and agonizing over junk.

It's amazing how many problems go away when junk does. Once something is eliminated, its capacity to clutter and foul up your life is gone. Your life is simplified—and you're free to operate on the important things, not thrash in the piles. Get rid of the clutter that makes you spin your wheels, that causes you the stress, and there'll be no stress left to get rid of. You'll break out laughing when you realize how little effort will be needed to reorganize, restore, regain control of things. De-junking is a true miracle that will happen to you; and I guarantee it's the best antidepressant going.

There's a lot to be said for simplicity—how it feels, and how much we need it. De-junking is the most direct path to simplicity there is. You'll have a wonderful feeling of completion and accomplishment and self-mastery when you hold to an anti-clutter campaign in

your life. Enjoy the most refreshing experience in the world—that great sigh of relief when you're totally (well, 95 percent) free of junk!

Besides, while you're de-junking you'll probably find some things you've been looking for for years—such as the flash unit for the camera, your lower dentures, the hardware for the electric garage door opener, etc. . . .

When Is the Best Time to De-Junk?

When is the best time to rip in and start casting out? Immediately after you've determined that the junk is junk. If you wait for further confirmation, you'll fall back in love with the clutter in your life and keep it. To be more specific, here are some guidelines reported by successful de-junkers:

MORNING:

Light beats darkness for evaluating things. You're more objective in the morning, have more energy to dig and throw. The earlier the better—5:00 a.m. tossing is exhilarating—plus the garbage truck hauls it away at 7:30 and then when you crack in the afternoon and run to retrieve it—it's gone!

SUNDAYS, VACATIONS, and LONG WEEKENDS:

Are probably the best times to reflect, analyze, and file, to review your values and strip yourself of burden (90 percent of your burdens are junk-related). Sunday usually follows a trying recreational Saturday; maybe what caused you to be "overdone" (too much food, too much sun, too much shopping) should go out of your life.

FALL:

As the trees shed at the end of the season, so should you shed some of your worn and tired treasures. It's time to store some, sell some, and dump the rest so they won't press and depress you all winter. Besides, you're going to collect more over the holidays and need some room for it.

On a few of those brisk autumn days or evenings, instead of going "out" and adding clutter to your life, stay home and get rid of some of what you've got. You'll find it entertaining and exhilarating, without any hangover.

MOOD:

De-junking when angry is pretty effective—we need to take aggression out on something. We clean house fast and effectively when we're burnt up over something, and it's when we're angry that we're the least sentimental. However, if you're so mad you're full of disdain for someone (or something) you'll often not make good decisions and will be sorry later (maybe at the dump trying to dig something out). If you're experiencing a peak of energy and motivation (you just got a promotion or lost ten pounds), run with it. And de-junking is the perfect pastime for those moments when you're trying desperately to put off something else.

AGE:

Eight years old is probably the time to start individual accountability for de-junking—and the older you are, the more you have to de-junk!

TODAY:

Is probably the best time to start. Don't wait until your storage runs over or someone is threatening to leave you before remorsefully de-junking, or until you are forced to by some circumstance that won't allow you the time to do it right.

What to Wear:

When de-junking, never wear clothes with big pockets or room to stash. Wear pocketless apparel—like a suit of armor, a bathing suit, a straitjacket, or a hospital gown, and you won't be tempted. And if it's the second time around, wear dark glasses—very dark. In any case, loose-fitting (but not baggy) comfortable clothes and sturdy low-heeled shoes are a good idea, and be sure to wear something you won't be afraid to get messy in the throes of de-junking.

Tune In to a De-Junking Channel

Mood makes a great difference when de-junking. Remember, you aren't just throwing out things, but habits, experiences, places, even people that have been a part of you for years, perhaps decades. Moody, clinging, sentimental music ("Auld Lang Syne," "Memories Are Made of This," "Bringing in the Sheaves," "Send Me the Pillow You Dream On," "They Can't Take That Away From Me," "Carry Me Back to Old

Virginny," sad country western songs or hymns, golden oldy ballads won't do it—put on some rousing music that will make you want to charge, change, chuck, and cheer.

Good music to de-junk by: John Philip Sousa marches, marches from Verdi operas, polkas, "The Good, the Bad, and the Ugly," "Sixteen Tons," "So Long, It's Been Good to Know Ya," the 1812 Overture, "I've Got You Out of My Bin," "Climb Every Mountain," football fight songs, the Anvil Chorus from *Il Trovatore*, the William Tell Overture (the "Lone Ranger" theme), "Fifty Ways to Leave Your Lover," "Burning Memories," "There'll Be Some Changes Made," "Nothing Can Stop Me Now," etc.

Should You Go It Alone?

Most of us don't like friends or companions to meddle in our beloved clutter, but when we're overcome and reach the depths of junk depression, we will perhaps find it advantageous to do a little companionship junking. It really does help to have someone standing by when you seize something and hold it up and weigh its worth. They'll probably say one of two things:

"Gads . . . you'd keep *that* thing . . .?" And it's final, out it goes.

Or as their greedy eyes light up:

"Ooohhh, gimme that . . . can I really have it?" And again, it's gone for good!

If de-junking yourself and your premises gets to be too emotional an undertaking, reformed junkees also testify that it's helpful to find another struggling junkee and trade. Let them have at yours and you have at theirs. It's easy to de-clutter someone else's house; you can be as objective as a ranger roaming a forest marking trees to be felled. You—the ranger—are only using your expertise to identify; you don't have to actually throw anyone else's junk out (besides, you're probably too young to die). Just tag or mark it—and the decisions are made! And you'll probably have to agree with some of the tags on *your* treasures. . . .

One of the biggest disadvantages of being a junkee is that your pack-rat reputation will inspire friends to bring their junk to you, thinking they're doing you a favor. You can become the ammo dump for an entire battalion of clutter collectors. One on one is okay, but I don't recommend a neighborhood de-junking party—with that many people around, it's too easy to get distracted from the objective at hand. You probably also don't want anyone but close friends to see your most embarassing junk. For the same reason, if you hire help, go out of town for the people.

The De-Junking Drill and Warmup

Every great event deserves an appetizer:

Exercise 1. Stand in front of a mirror to give yourself a vivid perspective of how your body junk (and the junk behind you) looks to an outsider.

Exercise 2. Thumb your overstuffed library, or some of those newspapers and magazines you've been saving. This will loosen hand and finger joints and your all-important pitching shoulder.

Exercise 3. Visit one of your storage areas blindfolded. The bumps on your shins, elbows, and head will make you "junk smart" and anxious to get revenge!

Exercise 4. Take off the blindfold. Think of three things in your junk you'd like to find just for fun (or to see if they're still there). Whether you find them or not, you'll be ready to attack and destroy.

Exercise 5. De-junking dry run. If you aren't sure yet that you can depart on a disposing journey through your life and place, try a dry run like the Army does when it trains soldiers: attack some real clutter and place it in an imitation waste container. Practice regularly until your anxiety ceases, then use a *real* trash can.

You are now psyched for the final exercise. I guarantee it will move you to jubilant junk-tossing.

Exercise 6. Pretend the carpet cleaners or the movers are coming in one hour and *everything* in every room has to be up and out. This will force into brilliant focus all those layers of junk that've been there so long they've become invisible to you!

Dis-Count What You Can't Count

One division of my cleaning contracting business handles restoration jobs. In each case the victim of the fire or other disaster is asked to make a list of the items in the attic, basement, or other room that was destroyed. To most that's like asking them if they've memorized the Bible. They know the closets, trunks, and drawers were full, but of what? There follows a week of sheer brain-wrenching, trying to account for what, where, how much, etc., for the proof of loss. It proves that (1) a lot of it must have been junk if they can't remember it, and (2) *after* is not the time to account for your possessions.

Making a list of all you own and where and what is a smart thing to do—start in one room and go through everything. Soon you'll find things not worth the ink or the effort to write down and pitch them away.

Another worthwhile adventure is to rent a home video camera and film all your stuff, simultaneously describing what it is and what it's worth into a tape recorder. This is fun, fast, and effective,

and then you can put the video in a safe deposit box. A two-hour tape should do it, and if you find yourself running into two six-hour tapes and beyond, it'll be good food for de-junking thought. I guarantee that either the list or the video will force a de-junking insight into your life! And you never know, you might get an Oscar or Emmy (or maybe a Cranny) for Junker of the Year.

Pace Yourself

Rome wasn't de-junked in a day. You'll get the bends and terrible withdrawal tremors if you come up through your clutter too fast. A two-drawer day is an honorable accomplishment; a two-drawer-and-closet-and-no-cigarette-or-chocolate-bar day is pushing the limit; a six-drawer-and-workshop/attic/garage day could be suicidal. If you try to do too much at once you'll lose your edge and not be nearly fierce enough to get the job done right.

Pace yourself; don't fall for the old "decoy" trap. When you start to de-junk an area (or habit), get the job *done:* otherwise when you go to throw out that old pan you'll notice on the way to the garbage that the yard needs de-junking. So you stop to do the yard, but notice those faded bumper stickers on the car. You start to scrape the bumper and see the toolshed is a mess, stop to rearrange that and find the plants on the porch have to be repotted, so you figure the pan you were taking to the dump is just the thing to put under the plants . . . and as it turns out, nothing was de-junked.

Vary your attack to maintain momentum. Switch back and forth between outside and inside junk. Every time you have a session of ridding yourself of worn-out tires and shabby coats, turn to your inner junk and get rid of an old unpleasant unkind feeling or a shabby habit. It works! You can lose hundreds of pounds of physical and emotional junk in one day!

How to Get Rid of It

Simply dumping it is harsh and not always the only way or wise—so says Gladys Allen, a well-known de-junking engineer (believe it or not, there are professional de-junkers afoot in this country). I like her approach, which is as follows:

Start with three large heavy-duty garbage bags and one box. Label them:

1. **JUNK**
2. **CHARITY**
3. **SORT**
4. **EMOTIONAL WITHDRAWAL (the box)**

Dragging your bags and box behind you, systematically attack *every* room in the house. Assign every junk suspect—every piece of loose clutter, clothing, magazine, toy, shoe, stray animal, unidentified child, etc.—to one of the bags or the box.

1
JUNK
If it's broken, outdated, lost its mate, out of style, ugly, useless, dead or moldy, then it's junk.

1. JUNK (no good)

DUMP IT

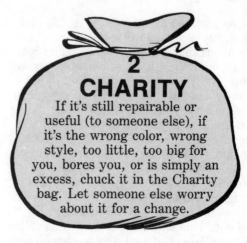

2
CHARITY
If it's still repairable or useful (to someone else), if it's the wrong color, wrong style, too little, too big for you, bores you, or is simply an excess, chuck it in the Charity bag. Let someone else worry about it for a change.

2. GOOD (but you don't want or need it)
   It *can* be used . . . by someone
   It *could* be used . .   for something
   It *might* be used . . . sometime
(means it won't be used—by *you*)

GIVE IT AWAY!

3
SORT
All your loose, misplaced and homeless stuff that is still useful and needed, but that you haven't figured out where to park, put in the Sort bag. Much of this is probably not located in convenient place to use.

3. SORT (want it, but have no place to keep it)

**KEEP—AND
SORT AGAIN
IN A MONTH**

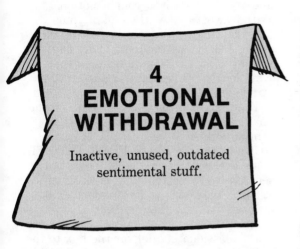

4 EMOTIONAL WITHDRAWAL

Inactive, unused, outdated
sentimental stuff.

KEEP! (in junk limbo for six months)

and then **THROW IT AWAY**

At the end of the junk raid day (or the
end of your de-junking drive) take the
Junk bag to the nearest garbage dump.
Deliver the Charity bag to the nearest
thrift store or pickup point.

As for bag number 3, Sort—it will have
an interesting fate: once it's filled, you'll
let it sit for awhile, as you dread the time
you have to burrow in and assign each
wayward item. The longer it sits, the less
you miss whatever was in there. You're
getting along fine without that whole
giant bag of "good stuff" the longer it
sits, and the less you miss it. Finally, the
prospect of pitching most of it outweighs
the dread of sorting it—and after pulling
out and intelligently placing the things
you do need, it's three bags down and one
to go!

Number 4: The Emotional Withdrawal Box

Have you ever had the experience of
reluctantly trying to let go of the little
hand of your baby so he can climb on the
bus for his first day of school? Or did you
ever try to drop the keys of a faithful old
truck that's been your dependable
companion over many colorful miles into
the waiting hand of the guy you just sold
it to?

These are things you know you have to do, and yet, when the moment to do them arrives, suddenly you're gripped with an ache that almost does you in. Some clutter is like that.

No matter how great our zeal to de-junk our lives, and no matter how firm our resolve to be ruthless and cold as we maraud our cupboards and denude our drawers, still, every now and then we uncover something we just can't bring ourselves to toss into the Charity box.

It's those "emotional involvement" ties again. The funny thing about it is, the object is usually something that would be of absolutely no use to anyone else (and certainly is of none to you), and yet. . . .

Like the day you're attacking your clothes closet and stoically making castoffs out of everything in there except the really current wardrobe. If the hem is too short, out it goes! If the waist is too tight or the lapels too wide or too narrow, out it goes! If it hasn't been worn in the last two years (or the last fifteen), out it goes. If the toes are too pointed or the heels too flat, out they go.

Then, at the back of the closet, you pull out that shortie nightie set left over from newlywed days—a lacy little cellophane number with a matching bikini. "How tacky," you say with a blush (hoping your fifteen-year-old won't walk in just then), and yet—that little reminder from the past will *not* fall out of your hand into the Charity box! You have no intention of ever scampering around in that getup again, yet somehow it seems a sacrilege to discard it.

Do you know the feeling? So what we need to do is get a box and label it "Emotional Withdrawal." Then, when we're mercilessly de-junking with that predatory glint in our eye, and suddenly come upon one of those gripping things that it seems a sin to knowingly discard, then DON'T! Don't upset yourself and lose momentum by trying to argue with your emotions. Just pat it affectionately

and lay it gently into your Emotional Withdrawal box. At the end of your crusade, dispose of your Junk bag, and your Charity bag, and your Sort bag. But write the date in huge letters on the Emotional Withdrawal box and store it away somewhere safe.

Then, six months from the date on the box (or a year if you're really a sentimental slob), go retrieve the box. DO NOT OPEN IT OR PEEK INTO IT. (This is a must!) Because by now, you see, you've forgotten what it was you stuck in there. Or you *do* remember but at least that gripping moment of emotional attachment has passed and you can dispassionately deliver the box to the nearest charity pickup point, or slide it out to the curb on garbage day and never feel a thing but victory—and pleasure over your uncluttered closets and your spacious storage areas.

If you still can't have the Emotional Withdrawal box ripped out of your hands and heart, if sentimental ties clearly demand a retrial, if an appeal to the Supreme Clutter Court is imminent, remark that box "trial pending" and let it sit another six months.

*B*UY—USE—OUTGROW—THROW
Release it so it will release you!

Throw It *All the Way* Away

When I was growing up, we had terrible weeds in our yard, which basically are junk to a nice garden or landscaping. My dad would send us kids to de-junk the pesky plants and soon the spot would be cleaned and looking great. But a few weeks later the weeds would reappear, bigger and stronger than before—because we never did really get rid of them. We didn't pull them up and cast them away as Dad told us to do; we cut them down with a hoe, leaving the roots there to carry on a regrowth. When you throw junk out of your life, don't just wound it like we did the plants—go all the way, pull it out, dump it, give it, sell it, but get rid of it. It's like jumping in icy water or pulling the tape off a bandage—a quick "yank" and it hurts less.

If you don't, the most deadly stage of the junk disease will come the fatal day you creep up on an overstuffed Salvation Army bin. As you step forward to throw your two things in, you'll see something in there you really could use—an old sweatshirt, just right for a car rag, so in go two and out comes one. How much credit will you get for two in and one out? Well, not much, because next time you'll be looking and two will go in and three will come out. That's how junkitis progresses.

The only way to arrest this junker's tendency is, when you decide to do away with something, keep telling yourself how loathsome it is—and tell yourself that all the way to the trash/giveaway bin. If you know you'll weaken, or fish somebody else's junk out, ask a family member (like a long-suffering spouse, no-nonsense teenager, or tough sister) to dispose of the stuff as a favor to you. Or pay a neighbor kid to do it. Be creative—but be ruthless: however you do it, make sure you actually *do* get rid of the stuff.

Here's a scenario of what will happen if you don't.

At long last, that old carpet in the bedroom or living room has to go—it's damaged, stained, and odorful, and you're sick of the color. You select a lush new loom at the carpet store to replace that miserable floorpiece, but whether you or the carpet layers take the old one up, the pangs of pity begin to flow through you. You're suffering, but willing to see it go—until the carpet layer says, "What would you like us to do with this old carpet, haul it away?" Your throat tightens as you look at that neat roll; all rolled up it has assumed the embryonic form in which it was delivered to you ten years ago—a clean edge conceals the threadbare, urine-stained, disintegrating innards. You stammer and then have them drag the moldy heap into the garage or basement. Maybe, just maybe, you can cut out an unworn section or two for the doghouse, the bathroom, the porch, the car trunk. You're so caught up in the concept of using that old worthless veteran, you don't even appreciate your new carpet.

Do you know how many people ruin walls and doors, hurt themselves stumbling over, and get hernias heaving worthless salvaged, worn carpet? If you've fallen for this in the past, don't in the future, or you'll end up with wall-to-wall clutter. Hold your chin high and say, "Haul 'er off, boys," and use your energy rolling on the new carpet.

De-Junk, Don't "Neatspree"

It's possible to be a de-junk hypocrite or fanatic. Remember, the adage "One man's junk is another man's treasure" does have some truth to it. As our lives, age, size, location, and environment change, it all affects what and how much we need. Some real hardhearts say, "If I don't use it for six months, out it goes"; a junkee will bellow in pain at that statement. Somewhere in between you should find the criteria for giving, trading, chucking—or keeping.

One repentant junkee I know got an oversized grill for a wedding present; she threw it in the garbage, right in the

unopened box. In a few years grills were twice the price and there were five in her family instead of two. Think! Just because you don't need it now or have grown tired of it doesn't mean it's junk. Anticipate—don't decapitate. There's always room to store genuinely useful things.

Going on a "neat spree" and throwing out tons of stuff (including valuable items) is thoughtless and stupid. Again, let me caution you not to go on an unmitigated throwout seige just for the sake of taking revenge on a worthless spouse or to work out some aggravation or problem. Some people go on a casting caper and punish themselves by ridding all their (or someone else's) favorite things. Don't do it—think! There's an old proverb about not tearing down a wall until you know why it was built, and that's a saying of great de-junking wisdom. Throwing out the overshoes and umbrella when the sun comes out isn't smart (unless they leak or you've moved to the Mojave).

Recycling— The Great Equalizer

Is ruthless de-junking wasteful? Will you go straight to hell or be pronounced un-American if you trash something worth cash? Nope! A soothing word called "recycling" comes to our rescue here: recycling is the great equalizer, the great escape from bad judgment.

At the age of thirteen I had a serious cash-flow problem and our remote rural location eliminated the prospect of resolving it by getting a job. One morning I heard on a radio show that dried prairie bones (the skeletons of cattle and horses that died on the range) were worth $30 a ton to be ground up and made into fertilizer. Convinced I'd soon be a bone business executive, I threw a couple of burlap bags over my back and began to walk the desert. How many light prairie bones it takes to make a ton (unless you run into a *Tyrannosaurus rex*) is beyond most people's comprehension—I never did get rich, but I felt good because I was not only making a little money, but cleaning up the countryside, and contributing to a product that people benefited from.

Like old bones, much of our clutter can be recycled, and even if we get little or no cash for it, we can help upgrade the environment, contribute to the economy, and have a personal building experience. Just think—those old clothes, papers, cans, and tires you've been stumbling over for years can be reincarnated into a warm quilt, shiny sheet metal, elegant greeting cards, or an NCAA basketball. Glass, paper, cardboard, old cars, lumber, dirty motor oil, blacktop, and numerous other objects can be used again! Think recycle—but be reasonable—don't get carried away into saving credit card carbons and pen cartridges and the little boxes your eyedrops came in. Check with your local recycling center to see exactly what they handle.

P.S. Recycling is a great concept, but when you finish Chapter 18 don't get any ideas—stick to vegetable and mineral discards!

Sometimes the Kids Grow Up Before the Skates Grow Old

I saw that title on an ad in the classifieds, and it made the case for de-junking so eloquently that I clipped it and hung it on my bulletin board. So often tools, equipment, work or play things are still in good useful condition when we outgrow them. But then, forgetting that their only value was in actual use, we feel an obligation to preserve them, as if we were trying to preserve the part of our life that they touched. The longer we cling to them after their usefulness is past, the greater the chance that they'll begin to blot out the good memories they once gave us, the reason for our keeping them. Don't turn them from a positive into a negative. They weren't junk, but

we can make them junk—what a disrespectful end for those beautiful skates or that wonderful bike, to be preserved into eternal inactivity. Use those classified ads and share what thrilled and blessed you once. This way it will live to bless you again and again through others.

Or you can do yourself and someone else a favor—and feel good at the same time—if you box and/or bag up all the things that are of dubious value to you and donate them to a worthy cause— Salvation Army, Goodwill, etc.

I feel particularly good about a certain association for handicapped people I regularly de-junk to: they use the junk as therapy—their people sort, price, tag, and sell it in their own thrift store. It's wonderful to know your old stuff is helping rehabilitate someone (and even more wonderful to know someone else is shuffling it around for a change).

A Solution to Lackluster (or Lost Luster) Items:

One of the toughest de-junking problems we face is stuff that's still perfectly good, but that we just don't need or want any more. In such cases junk transfusion is an effective way to keep those good nonused gifts or other useful items from becoming junk. You simply transfer them to someone else who *can* use and delight in them. If you recycle things this way, at least you'll be helping to prevent the generation of new junk. For instance, I gave my old, too-small, still-snappable portfolio to an outstanding twelve-year-old artist; made my trophies and plaques into awards for little Scouts; and we have a genuine samurai helmet in my family that's in its fourth-generation shuffle.

Old how-to or instruction books can be a difficult cast-away. It seems that we all,

for example, sometime in our lives want to be artistic and end up with a few beginner's how-to-draw or -paint books. We do 99 percent of our drawing or painting the first couple of weeks we have them—but we keep them around for years and years. After finally realizing that mine did no instructing sitting on the shelf, I gave them to an up-and-coming young kid and he shed tears of joy to get those encrusted volumes. This works equally well for those how-to-carve-wood books, those very basic cookbooks you don't need any more, and the foreign language course/tape set we all have stashed somewhere.

A good technique for encouraging such transfers is a "giveaway box." This isn't strictly moral, but it works and keeps clutter circulating. My mother came up with this idea. When over fifty, she realized she had an advanced case of junkitis, but being Danish, she couldn't bear to simply throw out all her useless sentimental holdings. She got them out of her hair—and kept most of them in the family—by creating a special giveaway box (junk box) in which these things would wait for a visit from innocent unwary grandkids or neighbor kids. Like all kids, they loved surprises, and quivered with anticipation on the way to Grandma's—eager to make a selection. (And they try to convince us that our mothers love us.)

If You Can't Can It, Convert Your Clutter

Or if you can't give it away, dump it, or burn it, use a piece of junk to make something useful. Look at it for a few minutes and think: What could I make this into that wouldn't be junk, that wouldn't just clutter my life, but actually serve a purpose?

I made a Mickey Mouse backscratcher into a paint-stirring stick—it then got more comments and generated more affection and honor than its giver ever intended.

I made my old floor polisher into a mailbox.

When something is too dear, too big, or too challenging to cast away, try to figure a way to make it useful that will benefit you and others while it preserves the item.

My wife and I bought our "dream" ranch right after we graduated from Idaho State University. Its only structures were a tiny wellhouse and an 1880s log cabin, said to have been built by outlaws in frontier days. The cabin roof leaked and the windows were gone, so it was valueless as a house, barn, or chicken coop, but we love old cabins—so we kept it and built new fences and barns around it. It became more of an eyesore every year but I couldn't bring myself to burn or bulldoze it down; it even sat right where I wanted to build a machinery

shop—but I could never feel good about leveling it.

So, as a family project, we restored the entire inside and replaced the roof, leaving the outside looking exactly as it did originally. It cost us over $8,500 way back then (not counting labor) to convert that piece of junk—but we now had a delightful guest house (which you'll get to stay in if you visit us). It's now a landmark in the community and in our lives, and not junk any more.

Don't go to the extent of using an old hula hoop for a picture frame, but do be alert to possibilities to convert your clutter.

Miniaturize It

In Chapter 7 I explained the concept of miniaturizing: the simple act of taking something and reducing its bulk but keeping its spirit or effectiveness. I've found that even for things I need, full scale isn't always necessary. I make good use, when I travel, of miniature binoculars, cameras, Scriptures, etc. Even maybe-useful-someday information or oversized worthwhile printed material can be converted, via microfilm, from a clumsy file or ledger to a tiny disk or filmstrip.

I have constant need of names, phone numbers, and addresses as I travel. It was suggested by efficiency experts that I take along a prompter (to whisper dignitaries' names as they approach), a computer, or a preprogrammed personal phone system—all of which threatened to double my mobile junk. Instead, I miniaturized: I typed all my active names and addresses on a few sheets, took them to an instant print shop, had them reduced, and bound them in my calendar. Now I have everything at my fingertips in a few neat tiny pages, easy to use and carry. Names and addresses I need just for a particular trip, I prepare the same way.

The Old Soiled and Spoiled Trick

This is a good technique when you have something that is unquestionably pure clutter, but somehow you just can't get rid of it. It will just lie there in sparkling uselessness and taunt you, because anything physically perfect seems to have an immunity to disposal. Have you noticed how passionately relieved you feel when one day such an object gets defaced—a drop of water blotches it, or it gets stained or wrinkled or stepped on? You suddenly have guillotine gumption and can fling it away with no qualms. Its value didn't change, neither did your attitude—you simply found an excuse, a reason to dump it. The junk is gone with no guilt, because "it isn't nice any more." Even induced defacement is moral if that's what it takes to de-junk a hunk of junk—leave it in the rain or on the counter when you deep-fry, haul it around in your car or with you to the beach, turn your kids loose on it. It's sure to get soiled or spoiled, then it can be easily de-junked.

Apply the One-In, One-Out Rule:

If you can't wade into de-junking wholeheartedly, if you can't completely suppress that itchy urge to collect, an effective compromise or cease-fire is possible that will at least halt the buildup. Apply the "One-In, One-Out Rule," meaning if you bring anything new into your collection, something old has to be removed at the same time. This is a great way to warm up for a full-scale clutter cleanout—and learn basic control.

The Tax Write-Off—Another Great Reason to De-Junk

Some of your heaps and piles of things may possibly have cash value—so get the cash, because if the stuff isn't enhancing your life right now, it's doing you no good. Cash it in, give it to someone who can benefit from it, and if it ends up tax deductible, you'll get a double reward.

A friend of mine had an old classic car he was going to restore and sell— someday! It chugged and snorted but never ran too well so it got little use. He puttered around with it and enjoyed it for a few years, then lost interest—but it occupied a spot in his yard for the next ten years. Finally it had to go. Not wanting to sell a used car to a friend, he donated it to the local Scouts. They raffled it off at a fund-raiser for an amazing $10,000. The Scouts loved him, the town loved him, his wife loved him— and his accountant informed him that under the Internal Revenue Code, he could claim the $10,000 as a tax deduction. He was elated, richer, freer— and best of all—de-junked. Something that had been parked in his mind was gone, and really fulfilling things could move in. Your accountant might be a great help in de-junking: call him or her to see what clutter might qualify.

Overcoming "The Great Junk Standoff"

"I won't budge on my junk until my husband budges on his. . . ." The woman who told me this also admitted being on the brink of separation. They didn't mean it to come down to divorce, but each's

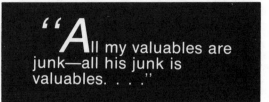

"*A*ll my valuables are junk—all his junk is valuables. . . ."

accumulation began to irritate the other—and the kids aggravated matters further by collecting and keeping an equal amount of junk. Patience and tolerance disappeared with the room to keep everything—so they blamed each other. Each sincerely believed his or her stuff was more valuable, and snide cracks and judgmental opinions of each other's junk soon grew to open animosity: "I won't give up my smoking, every-other-night football, or my cow skull collection until you give up those stupid soap operas and that stinking spaniel." And so goes the

Great Junk Standoff. In a standoff, both sides lose, junk wins, and no one lives happily ever after. Don't force a standoff with anyone in your home, office, school, or organization. Trying to use junk as a weapon on someone else is like shooting a pistol backward—it gets *you*, not them. It's like a kid threatening his parents, "I'll go cut my arm off and then you'll have a one-armed kid and be embarrassed."

If you really want to see results (and get the best kind of revenge on your antagonizer), with great ceremony and enthusiasm, nobly and unflinchingly cast off some of your clutter. You'll disarm your opponent, bring instant peace to you and the situation—and give him or her the guilties. Be the initiator—don't expect anyone else to do what you aren't willing to. Go ahead—start right now with a couple of small things. Make sure everyone sees the junk (thing, habit) go—and then watch—your opponent will

immediately be intimidated and miserable until he or she rids himself or herself of something equal to your sacrifice. This works at home, school, work, social clubs. Try it—quit the threats, cutting remarks, bribes, or any such tactics you are using now to get that certain person to cast off his or her junk. Simply lead the way (and don't overdo reminding the other junker what you got rid of). It's the best way to spread the de-junking gospel.

> "All of humankind is divided into two basic groups, the keepers and the throwers-away. The only thing worse than a keeper and a caster slugging it out is two keepers getting together."

De-Junking Is Not Forever

De-junking is a journey, not a destination; a process, not an end product. You don't de-junk and remain de-junked forever, because new junk will keep filtering in to fill the vacancies. It's like fitness or cleanliness—it doesn't last; de-junking from time to time must become a reflex.

So many of us have suffered from a junk habit or junk object, got sick of it, got rid of it, and felt so good to be free we soon forgot how bad being laden was. So gradually, we reacquire the same problem. Slowly and silently we gain the weight back, start dropping our clothes instead of hanging them. Once we get our noses out of problems, we somehow want to stick them back in.

It reminds me of the time my neighbor's Labrador retriever tangled with a porcupine and came whimpering home with a snout full of quills. I held the dog while my neighbor, using a heavy

pair of pliers, pulled two dozen wicked quills, the dog yelping generously with every yank. Painfully de-junked of the quills, you'd think the dog would avoid a repeat of the adventure. Not so—the next evening a whining and pawing at the door evidenced another losing bout with the porcupine. This time quills were in the mouth and tongue. Sad to say, that dog never learned the value of staying de-junked, and after yet more repeat performances, the canine cashed in.

You're smarter than a black Lab—I know you won't get a new snout full of junk if you do a good initial job of de-junking. Especially if you keep in mind the big secrets of staying de-junked:

1. Avoid junk danger zones (see Chapter 11).
2. Avoid junk activities (see Chapter 18).
3. Avoid junk places and associates (see Chapter 18).

Other than that, the repentant or "on the road to recovery" junkee's very worst enemies are:

1. Moving into a bigger house.
2. Reading junk pornography ("things and stuff" catalogs; see Chapter 8).
3. Reading a "trash to treasure"

book. This little X-rated volume tells you how to take the most worthless clutter and give it a whole new visual identity (transform it into something else you'll have to start all over again to justify the discard of). Worthless egg cartons can be made into a stunning snake—it's clever, it's cute, and it's the same empty carton you were hauling to the trash. Now it might manage to fake out common sense. The sole purpose of most of these books is to provide an elaborate, time-consuming, sometimes expensive way to disguise junk!

"What's Bothering You?"

There's no visible clutter left but you still feel junked in? To find what's been called "inner peace," you have to de-junk yourself of the piles of clutter you carry in your mind, or as some call it, your heart.

This junk got there when you, sometime in the past, did something you now regret. You wish you hadn't. It could be a crime, a putdown, a cruelty, a prejudice, a lie, you swiped something—anything you did or said that now haunts you and you find uncomfortable to live with. We all have this emotional clutter. Like our tangible junk, some of us keep it and tolerate its misery and memory forever, but this kind of junk is embedded in our being and can't be de-junked as easily. Often these are little things—their injury and cost are long gone—but we continue to harbor them, so our guilt and unhappiness about it can pop up again, and again, and again.

An employee of mine, while a young serviceman, like his buddies enjoyed leave—but a shortage of cash often held down the high jinks. As mechanics, they occasionally had extra parts after a job

and smuggled them off the base and sold them, using the money for leave. They were never caught, but years later, whenever any law or military service agent would call on my office for routine employee security checks, this employee would dart out the back door and hide out in terror. I've known hundreds of people who go through the very same thing—avoid people, situations, and places because of a little problem they had years ago. I've watched petty family or job resentments or jealousies totally alienate and choke off people's enjoyment of life. Holding a grudge is no different from holding a bag of junk; one is visible and the other isn't, but both weigh. Both cheat you. Both restrict life. The reason you haven't able to de-junk it (forget it) is because this piece of junk isn't just yours—it involves others. (If it *is* just yours, de-junk it today.)

Emotional de-junking is generally free, but if it involves someone else, pay the simple price of making it right—if you have to come up with a confession, a concession, some cash, a repair, do it. If you can't find a place to start, talk to your religious leader or a friend, but get it out! Go find out the damages, write or call. It will take some nerve initially, but in most cases it's not a tenth as bad as anticipated. In fact, it's often enjoyable—a lifting of burdens, a renewing you never forget. You're free!

The rewards of shedding and leaving behind past grudges, disappointments, and angers are wonderful. Millions of us have stored up and carried such things forever, and because we carry them we nurture them, and like any load it gets heavy after awhile.

Emotional de-junking generally follows a 4-R course:

1. *Remorse*—you're sorry, it was wrong.
2. *Resolve*—you'll correct it.
3. *Restore*—contact the injured party and repair/return/restore it.
4. *Refrain*—from doing it again!

CHAPTER 17

Clutter a la Carte

At age fifteen, for my Future Farmers of America agriculture project, I bought (with a little help from my dad) some baby bull calves. Their horns, at that point, were about three harmless inches long. One day Dad brought home a box of all sizes of steel doughnut-looking weights. He explained to me that the horns of a bull, if left unattended, will grow straight out and up and long and be exceedingly dangerous, causing possible injury to fellow bulls—which even then were worth up to $10,000 when grown. But if weights were fastened on the ends of the horns, the horns would grow downward in a beautiful curve, eventually making the animal both safe and attractive.

As that year progressed, we put larger and larger weights on the horns, and as the bulls grew the weight buildup was so gradual they didn't seem to notice and went merrily along. The interesting event, however, was when the horns were finally curved correctly and the weights removed. As soon as we'd turn the bulls out of the chute with the big weights gone, they'd slowly walk a few steps, shaking and twisting their heads, trying to figure out what was different. They would rotate, lift their heads up and down, first slowly, then rapidly, and suddenly discover they had shed a heavy burden. In noble triumph, they'd arch their heads and tails in the air and thunder off in a happy cloud of dust and glory, feeling a new freedom from a bondage they had never realized they were suffering.

There isn't a one of us who hasn't dreamed of rumbling off in a great cloud of glory—yet in reality, most of us have a hard time dragging, wheezing, waddling, creaking, coughing along, rising in the morning, and getting through each day.

Well, you've already guessed why—it's the same reason we have trouble getting through our drawers, our closets, our garages, etc. Clutter—we eat it, drink it, breathe it. A little here and a little more there, and like the weights on the bull, we gradually build up a burden we don't even realize we're carrying.

Stand there in a swimsuit or in the altogether and face it—many of us are living, walking piles of clutter. Our bodies are like an old junk car; the outside (if patched and primed and repainted) might look good, like those who wear padded or compressing undergarments and coats of cosmetics. But we're running rough, out of tune, out of stride, and gradually putting ourselves out of circulation.

Like our other junk, we can't hide, mint, gargle, or girdle it. It shows on us like a scowl. Who wants or likes a countenance clouded with clutter? A junk body is exactly like other junk—it blocks

us off from the things that generate love and good feelings.

A junky physical condition robs a person of poise, dignity, motivation, self-respect, the joy of work—and believe it or not even affects the mind and the spirit. Inspiration, enthusiasm, and endurance cannot exist in a body or mind struggling to combat the influence of consumable clutter. If we're going to get out of the rut and gain confidence, beauty, affection, exhilaration, we have to de-junk the things that can take it from us.

If there is one thing in life we get tired of, it's people preaching and advising and scaring us about what we eat, drink, and breathe. Even before we were old enough to fully comprehend it, parents and other adults were shaking a warning finger at us and telling us what to eat and what not to eat and even how much and when. As we grew, our health teacher, the coach, the media, and a famous doctor in every issue of *Reader's Digest* were still outlining the perfect diet of life. New fads and health foods and drinks spun by us like meteors, until I really think we became immune to it all. Some great scientist is always warning us of guaranteed early death or disease from

some eating, drinking, or breathing violation. We glance at it and say to ourselves, "Boy, I've heard that before." Ten years ago cranberries were causing cancer, now they're supposed to prevent it; they tell us that we should avoid cholesterol, then that it isn't really necessary. Who can we trust?—and so we shrug it off, maybe filing a little of it away in our minds. And now when we're reading Aslett's book on clutter, in sneaks that message again on food and drink and breathing. Why don't you forget all the advice, hearkenings, and warnings, and for the rest of this chapter, just rely on yourself—who you are and how you feel, and how you *want* to feel. It's surprising just how much you know about yourself and your own health and feelings. For once, listen to yourself instead of the coaching, promising, and prophesying of any outsider—even me.

First, remember your thoughts at the time of sickness (yours or others') or death; the times when you're down and out and feeling draggy, tired, unresponsive; the times you've said to yourself, "How vain and useless all my efforts and plans and ownership are, how completely my values are thwarted and attainments wiped out if I have no getup-and-go." Position, money, opportunity, possessions, even loved ones have limited value if we aren't feeling vibrantly well and full of energy.

When it comes to the things we consume, we seem to have a built-in sense of what is good for us and bad for us. We don't always listen to ourselves, but we do know. Listen for the next few days—and before, during, and after consumable clutter is taken into your life, you'll hear:

"I know this is a bad habit . . . but. . . ."
"I've really got to cut down on this, or quit."
"This is definitely not good for me . . . but. . . ."
"Good thing there are seltzers, pass some more of the. . . ."
"This dessert is divine . . . I'm wicked to eat it, but. . . ."
"I've got to kick this habit. . . ."
"One of these days this is going to do me in. . . ."
"Oh, I really shouldn't . . . you know what it does to me. . . ."

You'll hear a hundred variations of this, but they're all the same. We basically know what is good for us, what we should and shouldn't consume, because we know how we feel after partaking of it.

Doctors and dietitians preach de-junking our life so we'll live longer. A greater quantity of life *is* a benefit, but a better *quality* of life is our ultimate reason for de-junking.

We should de-junk our diet, not only to live longer, but so we can live and feel better *now*. So what if we live longer—if we're miserable and ill-tempered all the time, what good is longer life to us?

Every one of us could sit down right now and make a list of things we're consuming that are junking and plugging the circuits of our lives. We already know, we want to, we just haven't gotten started.

Just as we finish the last piece of candy, remorse floods over us. We're sorry we did it.

Eating Your Heart Out?

I learned an interesting fact about junk food from a park ranger's lecture: "Junk food has weakened the big healthy Yellowstone bears. The bears' natural diet of wild fruits and berries, insects, and fish left them with a thick layer of quality fat to carry them through hibernation. But begging beside the road from junk food-toting tourists, eating potato chips, candy, cookies, white bread, spreads, etc., out of garbage cans doesn't nourish the bears—hence some don't make it through the winter." Besides giving those noble bears sleepless nights, junk food is:

OVERPRICED . . .

OVERSEASONED . . .

OVERSWEETENED . . .

OVERPRESERVED . . .

OVERPACKAGED . . .

It affects us:

Physically We don't have any stamina when we feed ourselves with junk food. Junk food is full of empty calories—high in fat, sugar, salt, and "fillers" that yield little real nutrition. It raises our blood pressure, sends our blood sugar skyrocketing, then crashing, clogs and hardens our arteries, and promotes tooth decay.

Emotionally Junk food either depresses or overstimulates us.

Aesthetically Isn't it ugly to see people gorge, slurp, and stuff garbage food? And to see what becomes of their bodies afterward?

Financially Junk food often costs much (considering what it's manufactured from and what results it yields) but it returns little. And it costs a fortune to manufacture and dispose of the packaging.

Spiritually Junk food encourages undisciplined indulgence.

Full-Course Clutter

Junk food damage isn't confined to making people fat, immobile, and polluted; consumption and desumption have become a time-consuming ceremony instead of a necessity to get on with life. There is barely a place we can go where food is not the featured focus—the main event. Conventions, gatherings, meetings, parties, services, movies, parks—all flash food in our faces constantly. We can't come forth with any genius when our mind is constantly cluttered and interrupted by dining, sipping, slurping, guzzling, sloshing, chomping, puffing, etc. Junkers are always munching, or shoving something in their faces—and trying to shove it in ours.

We spend three or four hours a day in expensive elaborate eating rituals and then have to spend an hour or two (and more money) at the spa or court swishing at tennis balls or lurching around the track trying to work it off—what a waste of life. If you waste just thirty extra minutes at meal time a day, that's enough time in one year to write a dozen magazine articles or go on fifteen fishing trips—182 hours you could have spent with your children or friends or mate.

30 Ways to Ruin
an Idaho Potato

Food in its natural state is full of vitamins, minerals, protein, fiber, and flavor. Processing and overcooking strip food of nutrients and flavor; we then overcompensate for its lack of taste with sauces, additives, and salt, salt, salt. We can junk perfectly good food beyond recognition.

We go to lavish seafood restaurants to savor the fine delight of the ocean, order a dish of "Crab a la Expensive," then dip that good crab in gucky seafood sauce until it's not only coated, but saturated, which leaves the crabmeat totally untasteable. We could just as well have dipped a piece of bread in the sauce and eaten it, we couldn't tell the difference.

Being a potato raiser, I can't believe how a nice Idaho spud (high in protein, iron, and vitamin C) can be transformed into a fried strip of grease or a soggy shell of toppings and fillings. (My next book will probably be *30 Ways to Ruin a Good Idaho Potato*.) In its original splendor it's so good and so simple; junked up, "prepared," or "processed" it's unrecognizable and unhealthy.

Purity and simplicity are everyone's favorite "seek." We travel to remote northern mountains to breathe pure air and fragrant pine, to sip from fresh streams. We enjoy everything in its pure and simple state—but we seem to forget this the minute something is set before us on a platter. On a trip to Alaska once, our guide hauled in some crystal-clear glacier ice, thousands of years old; it looked like a handful of diamonds. As he passed it out for the group to taste, one woman asked eagerly, "Can we put some chocolate syrup on it?" Without realizing it, we've evolved to thinking that any edible thing in its natural state is plain or "bland"—not so.

We're forever fussing with our food— putting ketchup on it, syrup on it, steak sauce on it. I'm not saying we should throw all our condiments and dressings away, but we ought to question why we use so many. Is it just habit? Does food really taste so awful without glop on it? If so, it's probably overcooked or overprocessed—or both.

Those Who Indulge . . . Bulge!

Even good food, like good merchandise, is clutter if we don't need it, don't have a place for it, or can't afford the consequences of it.

Look around the next time you travel, at school, at parties, at supermarkets, at amusement parks, in travel terminals, at the beach, or on the street—people are strained, puffy, bloated from junk.

Pear-shaped spectacles abound on every side—thirty-year-old men with bulging bellies; chubby little grade school kids with chocolate dripping from their lips; overweight women who no longer can walk and now waddle.

It's pathetic to see a woman in gross physical condition spend $100 for a hair and nail job. Her junk fat will be the first thing noticed, completely undoing the superb coiffure and manicure. It's equally sad to see a puffy-cheeked young man, belly lapping over a perfectly tailored new suit, trying to make an impressive presentation.

If we're carrying extra pounds, it's clutter. It will not only weigh us down every step of the way, but very few people have real tolerance for, or faith in, fat people. Alas—poor physical condition speaks for itself, and none of us like what it says about us or others. Making up your mind to de-junk is the best diet plan going. . . .

Savior of the Morsel

So many of us seem to have the consuming urge to devour every ounce and crumb ever placed in front of us. A classic example of this is when we're on an airplane or at a party—we're already so full of food we'd like to lie down, but when the hors d'oeuvres tray or the service cart comes by, we feel we must get our money's worth. The thought of those salty peanuts and sugary beverages and fatty ham bits just lying there and going to waste haunts us to the very center of our junk gland. If we don't save them, they'll go to waste.

Ridiculous, isn't it, that we feel this inner calling to be "Savior of the Morsel."

People are fed three times on the flight between San Francisco and Chicago—it would be more efficient to install self-feeders in the armrests. If the flight were delayed and the stewardess kept serving, the passengers would bloat themselves out of existence. We too quickly ridicule the pig—an intelligent animal that never makes a hog of himself.

De-Junking's Most Dignified Words—"No Thanks"

Just because much of the junk we're offered is "free" doesn't mean we're obligated to take it. No matter what Mother used to say, we are *not* obligated to eat everything set in front of us. Just because the cornbread or the french fries

or the coleslaw "comes with it"—it's not divine edict that we eat until we're uncomfortable. Thousands of restaurants are serving and wasting whether we eat it or not. And we're even *less* obligated to eat beyond capacity at someone's home, where the food is unlikely to be wasted.

I don't know whether it's instinct or conditioning to want to waste food, but we'll go to foolish extremes to keep from doing so. There we were, a vanful of tourists almost upon the Canadian border when my wife announced, "Omigosh, our sack of apples. They're going to take it away from us at the inspection station." The only way to protect our investment seemed to be to consume the apples. We had just eaten—no one needed or wanted to look at a McIntosh—but we grimly figured out who had to eat how many and stuffed ourselves into sickness. The thought of surrendering to loss often overcomes our good sense. The apples had very little value, and were certainly clutter under those circumstances. Leaving them at the border wouldn't have hurt, but isn't it hard to give up something! (By the way, they *didn't* take them and we were miserable the rest of that day.)

The compulsion to "save" it or "get my share" is responsible for a lot of extra pounds and inches.

A hungry snake once trapped and swallowed a good-sized young chicken. This left quite a lump in the middle of his generally slender frame. Crawling between two close-together trees, he found himself unable to pass completely through, because of the lump. The decision to back up was a good one—but just as he was about to another chicken came wandering by. The snake didn't need another chicken, but, like us, he was afraid it would walk away and go to waste. He snapped it up, causing another lump, this time on the other side of the two trees. He was caught—he had junked himself into helpless immobility—and a ferret came along and ate him.

Let's Have a Hot Cup of . . . Clutter?

Let's take a look at the most All-American drink going, good old coffee. Some people really enjoy their coffee and probably will continue to forever, but what do most coffee drinkers, of the thousands we know, have to say in their own words about the habit? "I really need to cut down on my coffee or quit."

Aside from not helping nerves or heart or kidneys or stomach, what does the coffee habit really do for us? It takes hours of time out of our life. We can't do business at home or at the office without the inevitable wait for "coffee." Often the whole operation has to be held up or delayed to get (or clean up after) coffee. "Coffee" often comes before calls, kids, or appointments—shouldn't it worry us that we can't seem to function without it?

It's distracting to meet with or do business with someone who has to sip, stir, gulp, and gurgle coffee down all through the conversation. Or we have to walk slowly alongside as our colleague or client carries an overful cup of it, and it slops onto the rugs, desks—and sometimes *our* good gray suit.

Coffee spillage clean-up in this country (in clothes, furniture, carpets, buildings, vehicles, even airplanes) is a multimillion-dollar job. And with the coffee habit comes all manner of pots, grinders, cups, mugs, filters, strainers, and tools to administer it (and clutter our life).

It's the time they take out of our life that ultimately makes many habits questionable. Watch some of the more efficient people you know work. You'll notice that they aren't necessarily any better or more skilled or faster workers than you—they just don't have themselves burdened with so many junk things and so much personal consumption clutter.

Try to figure out exactly what the allure of coffee is for you. Half the time when you rush to the coffee machine for a "fix" you notice, an hour later, that you never did take more than a sip or two of it. Do you *really* like the taste of coffee? Are you sure a hot cup of anything wouldn't fill the "ritual" role as well?

Junk on the Rocks

Taking a long look at results, can you think of even *one* positive effect that outweighs the harm alcohol does to life and society? (Yes, the industry employs people, but so does disease, war, fires, etc.) The manpower, fixtures, hardware, and utensils it takes to make alcohol available at social events are often more trouble than the food. Yet over 100,000 deaths a year in the U.S. are related directly to alcohol, and the cost of alcohol abuse is a burden on millions of individual taxpayers, families, and businesses, as well as on the government.

Just like junk food and soft drinks, alcohol is full of empty calories. It robs your body of vitamins. Alcohol is a *drug*, remember, and drugs should be used carefully, not carelessly. Alcohol is also a toxin—you can kill yourself with a single bottle of whiskey if you can pour it down you fast enough and manage not to throw up. Why do you think hangovers feel so bad? Your body has been poisoned!

Remember, too, how silly (or disgusting) people who've had too many look and sound: wobbling in their seats (and on the way to the restroom), talking too loudly (and loosely), spilling things, slurring their speech—do you really want to be like that?

No matter what anybody tries to tell you, you don't *have* to drink to be macho, chic, sociable, or even polite. There might be magic in moderation, but remember, "one or two" is only too likely to start a collection.

Carbonated Clutter

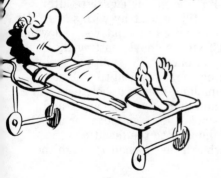

Much of this logic applies also to the excessive use of soft drinks and colas. Of the junk habits I gave up, this is the one I miss least. It was a relief to be able to eat and travel and visit without one of those bubbling drinks forever in front of me.

Do you find a soft drink constantly clutched in your hand? Colas, and other sodas too, inject caffeine, sugar, and all manner of chemical sweeteners, flavorings, and colorings into our system, harming healthy bodies and appetites. I really shudder, though, when I see kids running around with bottles of pop. The sugar rots their teeth and the chemicals make them hyperactive. Milk, juice, or water would be more nutritious—and cheaper.

The soft drink habit is a nuisance to handle and maintain. Pop cans, bottles, and containers, full and empty, are all over the place, filling the pantry, refrigerator, ice chests, cars, and trucks. We get so used to it we think it's an essential part of our life. But like other clutter, it can be disposed of easily, benefiting us immensely.

We get tired of other people harping on what's good and not good for us, but we swallow the advertising that tells us. They even tell us what tastes good and we swallow *that*. I think of this every time "helpful hint" books tell me how great cola is to clean the toilet. As a cleaning expert I have to nod affirmatively—it *does* work. The simple reason—read the can/bottle—is that it contains phosphoric acid. Phosphoric acid is what we janitors use to help dissolve lime, mineral, and hard-water buildup in bathrooms. (I have a friend who even uses cola to clean road film off his motor home.) For some reason I can generate no enthusiasm for drinking a good bowl cleaner.

Mental and physical addiction to soda pop is pathetic—it's just one more cup of calories and carcinogens. The most refreshing thing you can do is de-junk.

Junk Food Generates Junk

The next time you're walking down any street, notice that you're walking amidst litter and clutter and garbage on every side. Notice that most of it is wrappers from junk food, cans and bottles from junk drinks, butts of junk smoking materials, gum from gum chewers. As you look at it, think. As a professional cleaner/restorer/repairer/replacer, I can say from experience that junk habits cause some of the greatest maintenance expenses. And smoking is the most expensive consumable clutter of all.

Incendiary Clutter

Being that we all (even the smokers among us) agree that smoking is a junk habit, let's look at how it branches out to numerous undesirable results.

1. *It hurts you.* Not only is this habit likely to make you die sooner and more painfully, but it will cloud and retard your social life. Fondling, fumbling with, carrying, caring for, and storing smoking materials steals valuable time and image from you (yes, even you sophisticated pipe smokers—smoking projects a negative image)! Smoking can cut you off from opportunities, jobs, relationships. Who enjoys interacting with a person who constantly clutches and nurses a smoke? It has a negative effect on your appearance, as well as your health. It tabs you as unconfident, uncaring—and mates, friends, and bosses will treat you accordingly. Who really wants to see smoking secretaries, receptionists, doctors, cooks, teachers, cab drivers, janitors, companions? Smokers are often avoided or passed over because of their junk habit. (And nobody *really* wants to kiss a smoker.)

2. *It hurts others.* Smoking is unquestionably inconsiderate. Eyes water, lungs fill with smoke, clothes and hair are saturated offensively. Who would consider taking out a miniature incinerator and burning paper, leaves, and trash whenever they got the urge? That's what a smoker does.

Second-hand smoke, as a rule, is worse than the filtered original—and the smoker doesn't give the victim a choice. Most nonsmokers find smoke unpleasant, but for people with respiratory problems—asthma, bronchitis, hay fever—contact with cigarette smoke can be downright dangerous. Many people sensitive to smoke have to avoid restaurants, pubs, and theater lobbies because the atmosphere there is about as poisonous as the surface of Venus.

Lighting up a cigarette in someone's home, car, or presence without asking permission is the height of immaturity. It's plain rude to force ugly, smelly junk on others. And friends and family have to wait on this junk habit: they have to clean up after you, provide you with an area, receptacles, etc., to accommodate your junk habit, and they hate it.

Last but not least: smoking sets an awful example to youth. What kind of parents or grandparents would be uncaring enough to inflict such a junk habit on their offspring?

3. *It damages property.* All of us pay a small fortune for the smoking habit— it costs taxpayers millions of dollars daily. An alarming amount of clutter, litter, and building damage, indoors and out, is smoker-caused.

Smoking also causes a high percentage of fatal and damaging fires, and makes conditions on many jobs unsafe.

As a professional maintenance and cleaning consultant, I'm appalled when I see a person stand on a new floor or carpet, or sit in a nice upholstered seat, and crush and cast one cigarette after another, or fill an ashtray with same. The smoke is dirtying the windows, yellowing the light fixtures above, cutting the efficiency of energy expenditure, soiling and ruining the acoustical tile of the ceiling, smelling up the upholstery, and burning and damaging the carpet and floor. A smoker does as much (or more) physical damage to the facility as the person who throws a chair through the window—yet it's the window-breaker we'd haul off to jail.

Many millions of dollars could go to wages—or profits—instead of cleaning and repairing the damage caused by smokers. In trying to correct the problem, we designate special smoking areas, make better filters, bigger ashtrays, better vents and room deodorizers, better gargles and tooth polishes, develop lung transplants, etc., but this is like building a bigger drawer, closet, or garage when the others get full: the clutter is still there, doing damage, only contained.

The simplest, cheapest, most effective and rewarding approach is to de-junk the habit; then the problem will be cut off at the source. This is the beauty of de-junking. Instead of hacking at the strangling mass of leaves and branches, we cut the root—de-junk!

On Not Being a Dope

Drugs If you take unnecessary drugs, you may be too dumb to de-junk. Pills and powders aren't the answer—look deep into your heart—find *why* it hurts.

De-junk *that* from your life and you'll be able to throw out most drugs, too. It's a very simple fact—though sometimes difficult to accept—that the use of any substance that enslaves us robs us of our freedom of choice. Like all junk, it ends up making the choices for us. Old Shakespeare summed it up pretty well: "Oh God, that men should put an enemy in their mouths to steal away their brains." If you live sensibly (de-junkedly!) and know how to deal with stress (de-junking helps here, too), you shouldn't need uppers, downers, tranquilizers, muscle relaxants, or stimulants. Many physical ailments you're taking medication for might disappear with de-junking, too.

Junk habits seldom reward—almost always let you down in the end.

Stand back a minute and look at the junk eating, drinking, and breathing habits you may have, and measure how much good, how much pleasure they're actually injecting into your life, then imagine yourself without them. When you free yourself of consumable clutter, your personal confidence will double, your popularity will increase, your work and play and home life conditions will improve drastically. And it costs nothing, absolutely nothing, to de-junk.

DON'T FACE IT— TAKE ME

CHAPTER 18

Junk on the Hoof

When you get through throwing clutter out of your drawers, shelves, car, shop, purse, tummy, etc., you'll feel *almost* pure and free; your life will *almost* breathe new meaning. I say "almost" because there's still something bothering you, some junk hovering around somewhere, about to pop into your life and reclutter it. What is it? You can't see a thing hanging on or around you; you've followed this book to the letter. Nothing could be left; why, you're so pure of junk you feel disinfected! You can't figure out what that growing anticipatory ache is. . . . Until **rinnnnnnng**—it's the phone or could be the door. Suddenly you realize that secret irritation's not some*thing*—but some*body*.

Truthfully now, aren't there a few people in your life you just hate to see coming? They might be nice people, too, but when they appear (in person or voice), a shudder or sigh of boredom escapes you, and your good feeling only

comes back when you see their taillights go out of sight or hear the final click of the phone.

There are people who, no matter how hard they try to be friends, clutter your whole being—cause discomfort and conflict in you. They're generally the type who begin a conversation with "Guess who this is" or "Watcha doin'?"—and usually end it with, "Well . . . er . . . could I have/could you spare. . . ." Every day they waste forty-five minutes of your life with phone calls detailing their gizzard operation, their bowel trouble, their gas mileage lies. Their only objective is to use up time or make you aware of their problems (which you could do without). Do you like your life being interrupted, questioned, mooched upon, scheduled, infringed upon by someone—anyone—at his leisure?

No matter how good their intentions, no matter how distinguished their accomplishments, no matter how hard we

try not to come to this conclusion, some people's presence can junk up our life worse than a garbage truck unloading on our lawn.

The little boy who wore the T-shirt that said, "I ain't junk, 'cause God don't make no junk" was right, but man makes junk and plenty of it, and not all of that junk is just the *things* around him. People let themselves get worthless; they do worthless things, have worthless conversations, spend time in worthless endeavors, learn worthless precepts—and although they look and breathe like normal people, are rich or poor, have a high position or low, they can become junk because in general they are useless to most anyone, including you.

Could it be that a friend, a longtime associate, a companion, a fellow worker or board member, an employee, a customer, a teammate, or even a partner could be clutter? It could be so.

Any of These Sound Familiar?

A teammate: at first you thought it was his bad breath, his squeaky shoes, and his horse laugh that bothered you, but every night of league play the glory of the sport is dampened because old Horsebreath is going to be there. He can't keep his hands off you, he can't keep his conversation out of your business and personal life, he never chips in to fill the tank. He's like a cancer, growing stronger—it's time to de-junk.

You went to high school with her and were chums, you both twitted and giggled and goofed around. You parted ten years ago; she kept on twitting, you grew up and got some class. You end up in the same town in the Midwest; she's over every day and wants to hang around and rehash long-gone high school gossip, the style of those cheerleader uniforms, her

new shade of nail polish, her unimaginative vacations, her sexual frustrations—all the while ignoring her four kids playing Tarzan on your drapes. You are either going to lose her as a friend or lose several years of your life: it's time to de-junk.

You come home and see that certain car there, and your stomach tightens and sinks. "Come on," you rationalize, "they're my relatives, God-fearing, respectable—but gadfrey I thought we'd moved far enough away. . . ." You need to de-junk—because that sick feeling won't leave until they do.

You've been an employer for ten years, you've aided, counseled, paid, instructed, insured, etc., a person who seems to steadily be getting more removed from the reality of his job and causing you and fellow employees constant irritation. Soon you spend all your time trying to avoid contact, find no benefit together—it's all agony. He's doing little but take now—taking your emotional energy, not just your financial resources. If he can't or won't change, it's time to de-junk.

You've been lovers for longer than you can remember. He's smart, funny, charming. He also drinks too hard and works too hard and his apartment is filthy. You worry about his drinking, his bad stomach, his insomnia; he tells you you're a nag. You try to help him as much as you can without fussing; but you suddenly realize that he's self-destructive and he's taking you with him. Your self-esteem is zero; you're not doing him any good and it's slowly killing you. Great vibes or no, you'd better de-junk him—you'll save yourself and the shock may make him get the help he needs.

We've all met the "promoter," the high-flying and high-rolling guy who's always letting you in on the ground floor of a get-rich-quick deal that hasn't made him rich yet, but will you. He spends his full time scheming, conning to make the "big buck." He always finds or has fantastic deals going, sure-fire schemes that will return great amounts of money, instant power, and fame. He completely ignores all his previous failures with remarks like: "Well, that fell through because of the change in the economy, but this new deal. . . ." He bleeds his friends and relatives, the old and the young, yet never seems to have anything himself except great enthusiasm to put together another "great and promising" deal. Do yourself a favor and do some de-junking.

Remember that sometimes you can take a reverse approach with a junker who's cluttering up your life. If you're locked in a job, place, school, or association with a person or persons who make your life steadily more unbearable, withdrawing or change might be a desirable or even mandatory de-junking maneuver.

Beware of Chronic Junklings

There can be no valueless or unimportant person; all human beings have a unique makeup and deserve respect and consideration for what they are or have chosen to do with their lives. But there are some people who carry so much junk in their appearance and lifestyle that they need only walk through a place (or a life) to clutter it up.

We usually have a choice as to who we become friends and associates with. If we link up with a person with junk attitudes and aspirations, we'll get a junk relationship in return.

Living to be productive and happy is a struggle—full of tests, obstacles, and sacrifices. Those who have chosen junk standards, who have chosen not to be industrious, constructive, or honest, have chosen a loser's path to travel. They're not necessarily bad people, but they're keeping their lives like most of us keep our belongings—a lot of junk mixed in. This makes interaction with them uninspiring, if not unbearable.

The biggest problem with junk relationships is that they occupy the time when other, more meaningful relationships could be enriching our lives. A person who takes our time and emotion for nothing is worse than an item taking up physical space on our premises. Junk people become psychological leeches— they suck the life and energy and enthusiasm out of us, often just by their presence.

Like many of you, I've been a champion of the underdog as long as I can remember. In coaching, no matter how inept some of those who tried out for the team, I had great difficulty cutting them from the squad. As an employer of thousands of people, I've never found it easy to choose the productive person and send the one with junk ability down the road. I've financed and taken into my home (and still do) people who have severe problems and setbacks. If they tap hidden reserves in you, help you forge new strengths and skills neither of you realized were there—it may well be a worthwhile sacrifice on your part. But too often this is not the case; the "problem" goes on forever till it strips and exhausts you—both your physical and financial resources and your good nature. When you can't help, if they are unwilling at this point to put effort into their own recovery—as un-brotherly or un-sisterly as this may sound, you need to rid yourself of chronic junklings. It is probably the kindest, most constructive thing you can do for them. Being tossed out of your life for awhile might give them the hint to reshape a few things in theirs—and they're the only ones who can do it.

Don't let yourself be dragged down by constant association with junk people. I'm not recommending a guillotine party for all those junk people who've been plaguing you—only that you refuse to let them clutter your life until they show some interest (and action) in contributing to instead of confusing it. It's better to be alone than in bad company.

The ABCs of Escape

De-junking "friends" is not as unpleasant and difficult as you might think; in fact, if you follow some of the counsel in this book first, as you de-junk your home, hangouts, habits, etc., you'll find many of your two-legged problems gone with them.

Here are a few ideas for how to go about de-junking. Some are short-term solutions, some are just meant to give the big hint, some have to be repeated ten or a hundred times, some are plain silly—but most of them work!

Make Yourself Unavailable

This is a sneaky but necessary technique for dealing with many insensitive associates who invade your life. Too many people assume that because they have nothing to do, neither do you. You'll never convince them otherwise; they'll sit or stay for hours (or days) while you try to tear into some deadline work or project; they expect you to tend them, cook for them, and tuck them in bed.

I had a friend—nice guy—but after he finished his eight-hour workday he thought *I* had finished, not understanding I had several more hours of family, church, and business commitments to finish before midnight. He'd wander in at will, often bringing other friends he found junking around. Strong hints and even the suggestion that he come back later didn't register—"Oh, no trouble, I'll just stay." I tried to introduce him to women from the Hawaiian Islands, Israel, and

Canada in hopes he'd move—it backfired, they moved here—and then I had to cope with them too. My escape, when I'd see his car coming down the highway, was to grab a notebook and briefcase and sprint for the sagebrush. Once in the deepest part of the brush, I'd tackle my paperwork; my family truthfully told him that I'd gone for a walk in the country. He'd amble across the creek and through the brush but never would find me. I got the work done and still think I'd rather face rattlesnakes and Rocky Mountain spotted fever than a junk relationship.

If you don't have any sagebrush:

1. Spread out a project and lean over it with a stopwatch lying nearby.

2. Stick a thermometer into your mouth and jump in bed.

3. Change your phone number, get an unlisted one, or a second number just for "nuisances"—you don't have to ever answer it. Or you can give the second unlisted number only to select friends, colleagues, and relatives and instruct the kids to answer your ordinary number; you can frequently be "out" or unable to come to the phone.

4. The telephone answering machine is an excellent means of keeping callers at bay. You can monitor the calls and pick up important ones, ignore all calls, or record a tall tale about being out of town if you want a few days' peace.

5. Switch shifts or get a night job so you have to sleep during normal junkers' visiting hours.

Have Decoys

Some people you're just plain stuck with—there's no graceful way to avoid them. Buy video machines and go-karts, build nature trails, install pool tables, swingsets, etc., so such people can entertain themselves for hours and you'll never be missed. They'll go home satisfied without taking up *your* time.

Start Selling

Insurance, home cleaning products, dishes, cosmetics, real estate, etc., and people will avoid you like hazardous waste. It might be worth getting a license to sell, just for its de-junking advantages. Joining a fringe political group or a religious cult has many of the same advantages.

Make Yourself Repulsive

Eating onions, wearing Mafia-style clothes, and smearing horse manure on your boots are all worth trying, as is

strewing your front yard with rubber snakes and spiders or planting it to poison ivy. Serve unwanted guests the foods you know they hate, or food you think anybody would hate. If your junkee guests are allergic, acquire the fluffiest felines you can find and brush them vigorously prior to unwelcome visits, or sow a stand of goldenrod and incorporate it into indoor flower arrangements.

You can strip your home of extra dishes, beds, chairs, and autos—leaving no accommodation for visiting junkees— or lend them five or ten dollars (it's well worth a few bucks to be rid of them). You might even try freezing them out. One year our furnace went on the blink. We didn't have funds to replace it, so we toughed out the winter at interior temperatures of 44°. We all wore long underwear and sweaters. When real friends came we logged the fireplace; the junkers, we ran cold. As soon as they could see their breath, they left.

Crowd Junkers Out of Your Life

This is one of the positive ways to avoid junk relationships; you can enroll in a night class or fill your schedule so tight that wasteful relationships will have to fall by the wayside. Most junk relationships breed in non-constructive situations—so jog, take a second job, start your own business, or a new hobby—use the time productively somehow. When you're hanging around, you're an open invitation for others to hang on you.

Try to Put Them to Use

Have a few unpleasant projects you need help with waiting in the wings and plow into them when a junkee arrives. You'll get help or get rid of the unwanted guest—either way it's a plus for you. Hard work has a way of turning off junkees.

When junk friends show up, it's simple to say, "Hey, I'm right in the middle of this _____. Would you mind (sorting, shoveling, carrying, etc.)?" By this means I've converted not a few misdirected visitors into productive guests.

Avoid the Places Junk People Hang Out

Trouble and time-wasting and problems brew in certain environments—like the group roaming the hall in high school or the kids smoking behind the fence.

My interest in many sports and social activities was short-lived because they were infested with too many people with nothing to do and nowhere to go. So many "hangouts" are a case of the same time, same place, same old people, same old conversations; coffee breaks and other breaks are always times when tongues and brains are engaged but not in gear going anywhere. Cocktail parties are another place where people spend hours tee-heeing, nibbling, crunching, gulping, slurping, blowing smoke and hot air in each other's faces. Country clubs, too, are clutter to a lot of people who belong.

Too much beach time, bar time, party time, cruising time, theater time leave us without any of our own time. When we spend all our time letting people and places shape us, we don't shape ourselves or make our own mark—we miss out on some of the greatest thrills of living.

Don't Join Junk Organizations

We owe our very history and heritage to the dedication and accomplishments of groups and organizations. But just as a single small souvenir grows into a collection, or watching a single TV game show can blossom into a something-for-nothing attitude, many organizations, groups, clubs, and movements have grown into a large junk experience. There are numerous clubs and organizations that build, edify, and improve life and society, but there are others that have junk meetings and conventions, play junk games, do junk projects, tell junk jokes, go junk places, push junk causes, and help produce junk people.

I had an active college life—was on debate teams, played ball, was in the Education Association; I benefited and the groups benefited. I wasn't interested in fraternities and social clubs because I got all the fellowship I needed from my home and business. When I finished school we moved into a nice community, and a delegation from a well-known national organization soon was knocking on my door. I came at their invitation to an introductory social dinner, taking my wife and six children—we were the only family there amid the drift of cigarette smoke and fog of formal ceremony. I was politely informed later that this wasn't a family organization, and that was all I

needed to know. It was a fine organization but my time was limited and being with my family in the evening was important. I couldn't afford nights frolicking alone in ceremony when the kids and I could participate together in Little League, Scouts, 4-H, Junior Achievement, PTA, and other activities we enjoyed and that I felt changed lives to the good.

Hedge that pledge Because an organization exists, or even because it benefits someone else, is no indication that it is good for *you*. You know what you'd really benefit from joining, and what you won't; you know the limits of your own schedule and resources.

I'll bet every one of you belongs to one or two (or three or four) things that are a pain to sustain and are benefiting you and the cause for which they exist very little. They must go if you intend to free your life. It takes time, energy, and money to belong to the "Thrasharound Association." Gracefully surrender your membership. If you can't see the benefit, don't join in the first place. Like much junk, only *you* know what must go.

Beware of the "Bored" Room

Junk meetings are one of the most efficient collecting places of junk associates. When worthless meetings are cast off, so is much two-legged junk. Meetings—business, church, group, club, school, etc.—can be the biggest junk pastime in the world. People have meetings to figure out when to have the next meeting.

About fifty percent of all meetings can be de-junked; they're only held because they've been scheduled and because "meeting" is a bona fide buzz word of the business world—no one dares question it. A business executive confided in me once that his (major) corporation had made a miraculous recovery from near-bankruptcy; they did it by firing half

their managers. Oddly, they didn't miss them; business picked up! The matter was researched to see what all those hardworking managers had been doing. Guess what was found? Sixty-five percent of their managers' time had been spent going to meetings, another 25 percent *preparing* to go to the meetings, and the remaining 10 percent making notes/reports on the meetings (which no one ever read).

Many meetings are just an exercise in calling to order and dismissing. Doers spend their time doing, result-getters use time to get results.

Philosophizers, consensus-seekers, and the unconfident have to hold multiple meetings to give some appearance of activity. Meetings create the unfortunate illusion that because you've *talked* about it, you've done something about it. Then everyone goes, satisfied, back to their desks—until the next meeting to *talk* about the problem. At many a meeting people simply hem and haw, show off and stall, trying to come up with something worthy to be noted, when a good leader could have made a decision and everybody stayed home. We're too often afraid to stand up and say, "This meeting is unnecessary every week," because the word "meeting" is hallowed. *Don't you believe it!* I operate five different businesses and have served on numerous boards; I've discovered that my

happiness, energy, creative ability, and net worth all grew as my attendance at meetings decreased. I have about three meetings a week now instead of over twenty-five as I once had. (We do need a few meetings to communicate important information.) Too many people think "committee" means "meeting." If everyone fulfills his or her assignment, a couple of meetings a year to report and evaluate is plenty.

Unclutter your life of junk meetings (you've known all along what they are), and use the time to get the work done instead of "aying" and "naying" over it. Democracy should be a meeting of the *minds*, not the bodies.

If All Else Fails, Move

It has been given to us to love all man- and womankind, but sometimes we need to love at a distance for awhile.

There is a difference to learn here between helping and doing. If you are always around and easily accessible, people (even your close family) will grow to depend on your strength (help, credit, transportation, etc.). This can be bad in the sense that they may never develop their own strengths. In your deliberate absence, they often find out they can make things happen on their own and finally begin to build lives of accomplishment.

One Last Thought: Maybe Someone Is Trying to De-Junk You

Is it always the other guy? Could *you* be a junker? It *is* possible, you know, that you've cluttered your habits, and yourself, with so much junk that nobody wants you. Have you had some difficulty being wanted or needed, have you had to fight to maintain a relationship, job, assignment, or position? Maybe someone is trying to de-junk you (a much scarier thought than how you're going to de-junk someone else).

Did it ever occur to you the reason people avoid you, don't employ you, don't choose you for the team, leave you behind, forget to pick you up, never ask you out or over—is that maybe—just maybe—*you* are a junk friend or relative or teammate?

Junk kills the appeal of the finest things, even a human being. Maybe the TV that says gargling gives you lustier breath and hotbutt jeans make you irresistible is wrong, and your junk habits of constant undependability, bad debts, foul language, criticism, crudeness, rudeness, or sloppiness of appearance have turned you into a personal piece of junk. It takes more than one person to create a junk relationship.

Could Man's Best Friend Be Clutter?

Sometimes clutter does creep in *literally* on the hoof, or, more frequently, on paws.

Don't get me wrong—I love animals. I grew up around corrals with snorting horses, rooting pigs, pecking chickens, lovable lambs and others. I cried for weeks when my old dog Lucky was struck down by a car. Even cats, who do little but crawl on the back of snagged chairs and look surly, I can respect. I saw to it that my kids had chicks, pups, goldfish, hamsters, gerbils, turtles, and lizards. I've even read the statistics that not one of the ten most wanted criminals ever owned a dog—but with pets, as with anything, when you overdo it the benefits are reversed. The junk of pets can destroy the value of their ownership—or, in a pet phrase, "the tail wags the dog."

Have you ever put your "pet junk" to the test?

Pet cages
Pet snacks
Pet reducing diets
Pet exercisers
Pet portholes
Pet dinnerware
Pet piddle grit
Pet perfumes
Pet tags
Pet pills and powders
Pet toys
Pet ponchos
Pet footwear
Pet whiteners
Pet restraining devices
Pet training devices
Pet portraits
Pet family planning
Pet pedigrees (genealogy)
Pet patios
Pet swimming pools
Pet pets

What happened to the old pets that just curled up at the foot of the master's bed? Now we have to order a cedar-stuffed rollaway for them!

There are even junk breeds of animals—carefully bred to be so decorative that they're useless for anything, even pets. Nature produces excellent animals if we leave her alone—the Heinz 57 mongrel and the striped alley cat are first-class mousers or all-around pets. But that isn't good enough for some junk breeders. They have to do their genetic meddling and come up with a hybrid hound that looks good with the mistress posed in a sleek slit dress—but the poor dog has no strength, no stamina, no nerve, and can't even reproduce without human help. It's too delicate to take on a hike or even to play with the kids, but that pedigree makes us keep it—for what?

The funny part about pets is, the person who buys them is often not the person who really has to put up with them (change that litter, trot out in the rain for those walks, clean the tack and muck out the stall).

Remember, when you consider the value of a pet, that you want to be sure who has the leash on who. Plain old flea collars kill fleas; diamond-studded collars draw thieves. Somewhere in between you can have a pet lead you to a better life.

Geranium Junk

There is no doubt that plants give a dwelling warmth, beauty, style, and the message that nature still is the greatest designer and decorator of all. Anyone who doesn't harbor a plant or two might well be suspected of a cold streak—but it *is* possible to own so many that you can't see life through the leaves.

It was a cruelly chilly winter day when a pickup, apparently moving a family, pulled into the station for fuel. The driver was barely able to see through the clump of foliage in the seat next to him. Suddenly the foliage moved—and a woman crawled out from under the plants. Some chattering from the back let us know that under a burrow of old blankets and quilts there were three kids riding in the cold air in the open truck bed. The service-station attendant, a father of nine, suggested to the woman that perhaps it would be more humane to put the plants in the back of the truck and let the kids up in the cab. In total sincerity she said, "Oh, my plants would freeze if I put them back there."

The insidious thing about greenery junk is that you start out innocently with a small pot of forget-me-nots and they sprout into so many growths that indeed you *can't* forget them. (The general principle of plant propagation is: if you don't really care for it, it'll survive—and thrive—and multiply.) I've been in homes where the host did nothing for the three days of my visit but water and mist and clip vegetation; she couldn't go anywhere or do anything because her plants took so much care. Plants were made to enjoy, not necessarily to employ us full-time.

Most houses don't really have the right conditions for the plants we fancy—they never look anywhere near as good as they did when we brought them home crisp and sassy from the greenhouse. Soon all those brown tips and shedding leaves more depress than uplift us. And then, of course, we have to amass a plethora of preparations to treat their ailments and help them survive our basically inhospitable home environment.

Clip back some of that growth and watch the growth of human communication around you. You don't need a rain forest in your foyer to get atmosphere, a plantation of pygmy palms to convince people you're a sensitive son-of-a-gun—a few nice plants can do it.

Pitch all those spindly, sickly-looking specimens that make you feel guilty, or give them to a green-thumbed friend who thinks there's hope. Sure, they're alive—but barely—and you can bet that whatever they feel, it's not good.

Plant lovers, yes, your darkest suspicions are correct—I'm low enough to sneak in a silk or plastic plant or two, if it might save time and trouble.

Nothing on this earth influences the quality of our life, positively or negatively, as do our relationships. Surround yourself with de-junked or sincerely de-junking people; get the junk cleaned out and your life will glow with health and love. Maintaining constructive, inspiring relationships will keep a sparkle in your eye and goose bumps on your neck.

CHAPTER 19

Clutter's Last Stand

The *real* fate worse than death is the probability that **what we are now, we'll remain the rest of our lives.**

We can change our looks, location, age, job, and economic position, but what we are as people, we'll remain if the things, places, people that made us that way stay with us. The anxieties, unhappiness, discomfort, and disgust we're struggling with now might shift position but will remain with us, keeping us the same.

It's discouraging to think that a bunch of clutter could cheat us out of our future—a vibrant, zestful, rapture-filled life. It can! It *is!*

But we can have it all back, revive, restore, re-experience those fine fun feelings and love if we allow some room for them. Right now that room in our homes and hearts is piled with clutter—some we loaded in, some we absorbed, some that was dumped on or given to us. But how it got there doesn't matter nearly as much as now, the time to get it out.

Life doesn't begin at forty, sixty-five, twenty, thirty, when you get married, when you get promoted, or when you have grandkids—life truly begins when you discover how flexible and free you are without clutter.

Remember, any junk or clutter (house clutter, car clutter, mind clutter) can and will sprout into more of the same. We humans wrinkle and wither fast, mentally and physically, from the burden of worthless cargo.

Determining what is clutter may be our own opinion, but whether or not we keep it in our lives may not be strictly our own business. Because we can be sure that some way, someday, somehow, even right now, our clutter will not only hurt us, but drastically affect the lives of others.

Clutter is simply undealt-with junk. Usable things are used, valuable things contribute value, you'll seldom find good things cluttering life—it's the junk, the non- or little-needed that is hung onto for the sheer sake of owning and having. How long it stands and mows you down is only up to you. Clutter's last stand will free the years, the months, the weeks, the days and the hours you've spent hauling, digging, thrashing, sorting, hunting, protecting in the past. With the clutter will go the messes you've battled all your life—and defeating clutter will cost you nothing but a decision.

Remember, everything has a cost to acquire and to maintain. The majority of this cost you pay with your time and energy. To lead the life you really want to lead, you must eliminate the clutter and excess from your mind, home, and habits. It's simple, and one of the easiest ways to be "born again."

De-junking is the cheapest, fastest, and most effective way to become physically and financially sound, emotionally and intellectually happy.

Oh yes—before we close this book and let you get on with it (de-junking), let's clear up this business about our "high standard of living." Our American standard of living isn't so high—it's our degree of luxury and convenience that's high.

Take a hard look today at those you know who "have everything"—automatic back scratchers, rotating tie racks, computerized cars, instant food, world tours, better girdles, fancier foods, unlimited money, lofty positions. Honestly, in the things by which we should measure a life, how do they rate? The chance of unlimited comfort and luxury making you an unhappy, dissatisfied, restless human being would seem to be great.

A true *standard* of living is physical and emotional health, harmony, loving and being loved, sharing, serving, being satisfied, motivated, inspired, joyful, and in control. Our standards for these things can never be too high.

De-junking will truly raise your standard of living, give life back to you from the clutter that stole it from you.

I've tried to give you physical, financial, emotional, and aesthetic reasons to de-junk your life.

If I haven't convinced you yet, I'll back my message with the greatest book of all:

the Good Book (the Bible)

What is the complete, condensed message of the Scriptures? Isn't it totally

De-Junk Thy Life

of greed, envy, covetousness, lust, bad language, pride, cowardice, wasteful living, overdressing, underloving? Because these things crowd out joy, love, fulfillment. It was eloquently said:

"Therefore I say unto you, take no thought for your life, what ye shall eat, or what ye shall drink; nor yet for your body, what ye shall put on. Is not the life more than meat, and the body than raiment?"
"And why take ye thought for raiment? Consider the lilies of the field, how they grow; they toil not, neither do they spin:
"And yet I say unto you, That even Solomon in all his glory was not arrayed like one of these."
(Matthew 6:25, 28-29)

"He that loveth silver shall not be satisfied with silver; nor he that loveth abundance with increase: this is also vanity." (Ecclesiastes 5:9)

There is a time on earth for everything, so says Ecclesiastes (3:1-6)

1: To every thing there is a season, and a time to every purpose under the heaven: 2: A time to be born, and a time to die; a time to plant, and a time to pluck up that which is planted: 3: A time to kill, and a time to heal; a time to break down, and a time to build up; . . . 6: A time to get, and a time to lose; a time to keep, and a time to cast away. . . .

When the Lord commands it, how can we resist?

Like Moses, start kicking junk out of your life.

It will be a resurrection for you, your loved ones, and associates. I think we all agree now that de-junking is absolutely necessary for a high-quality life, so no matter how it hurts—become dedicated and aggressive, decide to cut your way out of the bag of junk and get out.

I'm hoping I've managed to give you a few strong hints of how, where, and when to begin de-junking. There is a time to stop war-dancing and circling around our junk and charge! A time to make our junk tremble in the trenches instead of us cowering from its clutter. Losing a few old habits and heirlooms might leave a tiny wound or two, but *you'll win! You'll*

conquer! You'll be free! No blood will spill from your defeated junk—but blood will again begin to flow for life instead of for objects.

Attack with the strength of a lion: start grabbing those junk items that have been smothering you, competing for your time and affection, costing you money and concern, and throw them out, give them away, donate them, sell them, burn them—anything—but get them out of your sight and mind. Ignore the outcries of onlookers who have to crawl out from under their own junk to give you reasons to cling on forever.

As the clutter goes, light will penetrate to you and then you can de-junk in a big way—ten times faster than you accumulated it. The fresh air of relief, of living will begin to envelop you, the exhilaration of true power and control will permeate your being.

Once you've de-junked you won't accumulate again as fast; you'll automatically have a built-in new sense of value that will inspire you to spot clutter and avoid it. The junk will seem to disintegrate by itself—people will give you less (if any), you won't buy any—you won't believe how naturally it works!

Start now—the older you are, the more you have to de-junk. And the longer you've been junked, the happier you'll be de-junked!

Thanks for buying and reading this book—I appreciate it. And thanks to all the people who contributed gems of junk wisdom to these pages. Especially my editor (and Head Pack Rat), Carol Cartaino, and Judith Holmes Clarke, who held a very large family at bay for six breathless weeks to finish illustrating these pages.

Learn more about how to save housecleaning time and money with these other bestselling books and video by Don Aslett:

Is There Life After Housework? Shows you step by step how to clean like the professionals do. 192 pages/ $8.95

Don Aslett's Video Seminar: Is There Life After Housework? 95 minutes of action-packed cleaning instruction. $29.95 (VHS)

Do I Dust or Vacuum First? Answers the 100 most-often-asked housecleaning questions. 183 pages/$7.95

Make Your House Do the Housework Hundreds of exciting ways to redecorate or design cleaning and maintenance out of your home. 202 pages/ $9.95

Pet Clean-Up Made Easy How to clean up every imaginable pet mess, plus prevent odor, stains, and maintenance problems. 144 pages/$8.95

Who Says It's a Woman's Job to Clean? Aslett gets men to start doing their share of the housework! 122 pages/$5.95

These books make great gifts for weddings, showers, or any special occasion, so use this coupon to order your copies today!

Order Form

Yes! Please rush me:

____ (1455) Is There Life After Housework?, $8.95

____ (1216) Don Aslett's Video Seminar, $29.95

____ (1214) Do I Dust or Vacuum First?, $7.95

____ (1122) Clutter's Last Stand, $9.95

____ (1668) Make Your House Do the Housework, $9.95

____ (10051) Pet Clean-Up Made Easy, $8.95

____ (2444) Who Says It's a Woman's Job to Clean, $5.95

(Please add $2.50 postage & handling for one book, 50¢ for each additional book. Ohio residents add 5 1/2% sales tax.)

☐ Payment enclosed ☐ Please charge my: ☐ Visa ☐ Mastercard

Acct. #_____ Exp. Date_____

Signature_____

Name_____

Address_____

City_____ State_____ Zip_____

Send to: **Writer's Digest Books** Writer's Digest Books
1507 Dana Avenue
Cincinnati, OH 45207

Credit card orders call
TOLL-FREE 1-800-543-4644
In Ohio 1-800-551-0884

For FREE information on:
☐ How to order professional cleaning supplies
☐ How to sponsor a Don Aslett Housecleaning Seminar/Workshop or speaking engagement in your area
☐ Don Aslett's schedule of appearances

Contact:
Don Aslett
P.O. Box 39
Pocatello, ID 83204

1384

Extra order forms to share with friends!

For FREE information on:
- How to order professional cleaning supplies
- How to sponsor a Don Aslett Housecleaning Seminar/Workshop or speaking engagement in your area
- Don Aslett's schedule of appearances

Contact:
Don Aslett
P.O. Box 39
Pocatello, ID 83204

Order Form

Yes! Please rush me:

____ (1455) Is There Life After Housework?, $8.95

____ (1216) Don Aslett's Video Seminar, $29.95

____ (1214) Do I Dust or Vacuum First?, $7.95

____ (1122) Clutter's Last Stand, $9.95

____ (1668) Make Your House Do the Housework, $9.95

____ (10051) Pet Clean-Up Made Easy, $8.95

____ (2444) Who Says It's a Woman's Job to Clean, $5.95

(Please add $2.50 postage & handling for one book, 50¢ for each additional book. Ohio residents add 5 1/2% sales tax.)

☐ Payment enclosed ☐ Please charge my: ☐ Visa ☐ Mastercard

Acct. #_____ Exp. Date_____

Signature_____

Name_____

Address_____

City_____ State_____ Zip_____

Send to: **Writer's Digest Books** Writer's Digest Books / 1507 Dana Avenue / Cincinnati, OH 45207

Credit card orders call
TOLL-FREE 1-800-543-4644
In Ohio 1-800-551-0884

1384

For FREE information on:
- ☐ How to order professional cleaning supplies
- ☐ How to sponsor a Don Aslett Housecleaning Seminar/Workshop or speaking engagement in your area
- ☐ Don Aslett's schedule of appearances

Contact:
Don Aslett
P.O. Box 39
Pocatello, ID 83204

Order Form

Yes! Please rush me:

____ (1455) Is There Life After Housework?, $8.95

____ (1216) Don Aslett's Video Seminar, $29.95

____ (1214) Do I Dust or Vacuum First?, $7.95

____ (1122) Clutter's Last Stand, $9.95

____ (1668) Make Your House Do the Housework, $9.95

____ (10051) Pet Clean-Up Made Easy, $8.95

____ (2444) Who Says It's a Woman's Job to Clean, $5.95

(Please add $2.50 postage & handling for one book, 50¢ for each additional book. Ohio residents add 5 1/2% sales tax.)

☐ Payment enclosed ☐ Please charge my: ☐ Visa ☐ Mastercard

Acct. #_____ Exp. Date_____

Signature_____

Name_____

Address_____

City_____ State_____ Zip_____

Send to: **Writer's Digest Books** Writer's Digest Books / 1507 Dana Avenue / Cincinnati, OH 45207

Credit card orders call
TOLL-FREE 1-800-543-4644
In Ohio 1-800-551-0884

1384